Oliver Optic

Shamrock and thistle: Young America in Ireland and Scotland

A story of travel and adventure

Oliver Optic

Shamrock and thistle: Young America in Ireland and Scotland
A story of travel and adventure

ISBN/EAN: 9783337210854

Printed in Europe, USA, Canada, Australia, Japan

Cover: Foto ©Andreas Hilbeck / pixelio.de

More available books at **www.hansebooks.com**

SHAMROCK AND THISTLE;

OR,

YOUNG AMERICA IN IRELAND AND SCOTLAND.

A STORY OF TRAVEL AND ADVENTURE.

BY

OLIVER OPTIC.

BOSTON:
LEE AND SHEPARD, PUBLISHERS.
NEW YORK:
LEE, SHEPARD AND DILLINGHAM.
1873.

To My Young Friend

ROBINSON LOCKE

This Volume

IS

AFFECTIONATELY DEDICATED

YOUNG AMERICA ABROAD

BY OLIVER OPTIC.

A Library of Travel and Adventure in Foreign Lands. First and Second Series; six volumes in each Series. 16mo. Illustrated.

First Series.

I. *OUTWARD BOUND;* or, Young America Afloat.
II. *SHAMROCK AND THISTLE;* or, Young America in Ireland and Scotland.
III. *RED CROSS;* or, Young America in England and Wales.
IV. *DIKES AND DITCHES;* or, Young America in Holland and Belgium.
V. *PALACE AND COTTAGE;* or, Young America in France and Switzerland.
VI. *DOWN THE RHINE;* or, Young America in Germany.

Second Series.

I. *UP THE BALTIC;* or, Young America in Denmark and Sweden.
II. *NORTHERN LANDS;* or, Young America in Prussia and Russia.
III. *VINE AND OLIVE;* or, Young America in Spain and Portugal.
IV. *SUNNY SHORES;* or, Young America in Italy and Austria.
V. *CROSS AND CRESCENT;* or, Young America in Greece and Turkey.
VI. *ISLES OF THE SEA;* or, Young America Homeward Bound.

PREFACE.

SHAMROCK AND THISTLE, the second of the "YOUNG AMERICA ABROAD" series, contains the history of the Academy Ship, and the students who sailed in her on the coasts of Ireland and Scotland, with their excursions into the interior. Whatever the volume contains of a descriptive character was derived from the note-book of the author, written in the midst of the scenes it describes, and from an extensive collection of works gathered in England and the United States. But the book hardly aspires to the dignity of a history, or even of a book of travels, though the writer has been careful correctly to set down all that would be presumed to lie within the limit of fact.

As a story, the volume contains, besides a variety of minor incidents, the history of certain runaways, who, disaffected under the salutary discipline of the ship, deserted from her, and travelled in strange lands under their own guidance, and on their own resources; but only to be captured, returned, and punished for their transgressions. It is not believed that any young reader will be fascinated by their experience in the path of error; but, on the contrary, that a strict devotion to duty, a cheerful submission to the requirements of wholesome discipline, and a faithful adherence to moral and religious principle, will be deemed the safest, because they are the truest incentives which can influence the youthful mind.

It is not so easy to convey useful and valuable information, even in regard to foreign lands, as it is to tell an interesting or an exciting story. The plan of this and the subsequent volumes of the series includes a certain amount of geographical and historical matter, which may not be as acceptable to the young reader as exciting incidents of personal adventure; but it is hoped there will be enough of the latter to season the former, and render the useful and valuable palatable to the reader.

With more of fear and trembling, therefore, than usual, the author presents SHAMROCK AND THISTLE to his friends, hoping that its story will please, while its historical and descriptive pages will instruct and benefit them.

HARRISON SQUARE, MASS.
September 30, 1867.

CONTENTS.

CHAPTER		PAGE
I.	GEOGRAPHY AND HISTORY.	11
II.	QUEENSTOWN TO CORK.	28
III.	BLARNEY CASTLE.	44
IV.	A QUESTION OF FINANCE.	59
V.	THE LAKES OF KILLARNEY.	75
VI.	THE GAP OF DUNLOE.	91
VII.	THE BOATMEN OF KILLARNEY.	107
VIII.	THE KEY OF THE SAFE.	123
IX.	SIXTY POUNDS IN GOLD.	139
X.	THE VOYAGE TO DUBLIN.	154
XI.	THE FAIR ARCHERS OF BELFAST.	169
XII.	THE JOURNEY OF THE RUNAWAYS.	185
XIII.	SOMETHING ABOUT SCOTLAND.	202
XIV.	THE DESERTERS IN GLASGOW.	217
XV.	THE LAND OF BURNS.	235

CHAPTER		PAGE
XVI.	Pelham's Adventure.	250
XVII.	Loch Lomond.	261
XVIII.	The Misfortune of the Runaways.	284
XIX.	Stirling Castle.	303
XX.	Paul Kendall in Edinburgh.	321
XXI.	Conclusion.	335

SHAMROCK AND THISTLE.

SHAMROCK AND THISTLE;

OR,

YOUNG AMERICA IN IRELAND AND SCOTLAND.

CHAPTER I.

GEOGRAPHY AND HISTORY.

THE Young America lay at anchor in the harbor of Queenstown. She had made her passage across the Atlantic in twenty-six days, during which time the regular studies of the scholastic branches of the Academy had been pursued with only an occasional interruption by bad weather. Her officers and crew had performed their sea duty to the satisfaction of the principal. There had been no serious accidents and no sickness on board during the voyage. Dr. Winstock could not command a patient for more than a single day; but his position was by no means an ornamental one, for there was hardly a busier person in the ship. It was doubtless owing, in a large measure, to his watchfulness and his valuable sanitary regulations, that the health of the students was so effectually secured.

Mr. Lowington, the principal, who had devised and inaugurated the system of instruction and discipline carried out in the Academy Ship, was entirely satisfied with the experiment. During the preceding year he had devoted his whole time and attention to the management of the institution, and being a gentleman of abundant wealth, this was no small sacrifice. He had devoted himself to his idea as a philanthropist, rather than as a speculator. The ship had crossed the ocean, not only to give the students a needed variety in their academic life, but to afford them an opportunity to see the wonders of the Old World, and thus to cultivate the taste, enlarge the understanding, and give them broader views of nature and humanity.

During the season before them, the ship's company were to be tourists as well as seamen and students. It was the intention of Mr. Lowington to adapt the course of study in geography and history to the localities to be visited by the pupils. The geography and history of Ireland were to be the prominent topics while the Young America was in the waters of that country, and while the students were visiting the scenes of great historic events. The revolution of 1688, in its relation to Irish affairs, could nowhere be so interesting and impressive as at Drogheda and on the banks of the Boyne, where the battle in which James II. was overwhelmed and the power of William III. established.

The principal anticipated great results from the summer cruise of the ship. Though a firm disciplinarian, he was not an austere man. While he was unwilling to give up the occasion entirely to frolic and intemperate sight-seeing, he intended that his pupils should enjoy themselves. The regular routine of study was to be pursued with as little interruption as possible, though it was not expected that the purely intellectual results would compare favorably with those of the preceding year.

As soon as the ship came to anchor in Queenstown harbor, boats from the shore began to surround her; but no visitors were allowed on board. The adult forward officers were placed at the gangways, and no amount of persuasive Irish blarney could induce them to allow any of the hotel runners, pedlers, or beggars, to place a foot on board. After dinner, the first business was to put the ship in order; but the boys were impatient to go on shore. There was a world of new sights and sounds on the land near them, and they were naturally very eager to mingle at once with them.

As soon as the decks were "swept and garnished," all hands were piped to muster, and the students sprang to their stations, hoping to obtain some idea of the programme for the future, and especially to learn when they were to be permitted to go on shore.

"Young gentlemen," said Mr. Lowington, "our voyage across the Atlantic is happily finished; and in our hearts let us thank God for his mercy in conducting us safely through the perils of the mighty deep. I have made many voyages, and this sentiment has been uppermost in my thoughts at the end of all of them.

"My young friends, you are naturally impatient to visit the shore. I sympathize with you in this feeling, and I shall not unnecessarily delay the privilege; but I wish to ask you what this ship is."

"The Academy Ship, 'Young America,'" replied several.

"Precisely so — the Academy Ship. Our first business, you are all aware, is not with the objects of interest on shore. This is an academy. You have certain duties to perform on board; certain lessons to learn and recite. This must be your first care."

"I don't know how we are to see anything of the country if we have to study and recite every day," said one of the crew.

"The routine will be entirely different in port from that followed at sea," replied Mr. Lowington. "You will turn out at six o'clock in the morning, wash down the decks, and put the ship in order. At eight the studies will be commenced, and continued, with a recess of half an hour for dinner, until half past one. The rest of the day will be occupied in visiting the shore. The lessons must be attended to for five hours a day; but the time will be varied as occasion may require.

"Young gentlemen, I propose, in the course of a week or ten days, to give you a brief vacation; and I have already planned an excursion to the Lakes of Killarney. We will take with us the gig and the four cutters. When we have visited Cork, Glengariff, and the Lakes, you will have seen all there is of special interest in the south of Ireland. In the course of two or three days we will go up to Cork. Now, my young friends, I wish you to curb this useless impatience, attend to your regular duties faithfully, and remember that the more progress you make in your studies, the greater will be your opportunities for visiting places of importance on shore. When you are dismissed from muster, you will pipe to the steerage, where Professor Mapps will give you his first lecture on the geography of Ireland."

The boys were dismissed, and they exhibited a commendable disposition to regard the good advice of the principal. Books relating to the geography and history of Ireland were straightway in great demand. There was an extensive library of books of reference on board, and before the professor commenced his lecture, many important facts had been collected by the zealous pupils.

"I beg your pardon, Mr. Lowington," said Dr. Winstock, as the principal stepped down from the hatch, "if I may seem to interfere with the discipline of the ship; but I wish to ask a favor. I desire to visit Cork this afternoon, and to take the second lieutenant with me, upon a matter of some importance connected with the ship, but which you must excuse me for not mentioning."

"Certainly, doctor," replied the principal, who appeared to be puzzled that there should be anything relating to the ship which needed to be concealed from him.

"There is no treason in my purpose," laughed the surgeon. "Mr. Kendall will make up his lessons in his own time."

"But he will lose the professor's lecture."

"We will not leave till that is finished."

Dr. Winstock had forty-three pounds ten shillings

in drafts on the principal for the purchase of the silver plate to be presented to Mr. Lowington, and he wished to visit Cork to obtain the gift. Unwilling to confide wholly in his own taste, he desired the assistance of Paul Kendall in making the selection.

After being dismissed from muster, the students collected in the steerage, which was the school-room of the ship, to hear the lecture of Professor Mapps. They seated themselves on the stools as near the foremast as they could gather. On the mast hung a large map of Ireland, in front of which stood the instructor.

Though the exercise in which the students were now to engage was called a lecture, it was more properly a conversation party, in which the pupils were expected to ask questions, and comment on the subject.

"Young gentlemen, where are we?" asked the professor.

"In the steerage," replied a wag near the professor.

"Excellent!" laughed Mr. Mapps. "Your wisdom surpasseth that of the foolish. Where is the ship?"

"In Queenstown Harbor."

"Where is Queenstown?"

"In Ireland."

"Good! We have reached the point. What is the area of the State of Massachusetts?"

"Eight thousand seven hundred square miles."

"Of New York?"

"Forty-seven thousand square miles."

"Of Maine?"

"Thirty-one thousand seven hundred and sixty-six square miles."

"Of Texas, the largest of the United States?"

"Two hundred and thirty-seven thousand five hundred and four square miles," replied one of the boys who remembered the figures, while all wondered what this had to do with the geography of Ireland.

"Very well. Now, what is the area of Ireland?"

"Thirty-two thousand five hundred and thirteen square miles," answered twenty of the boys, who had just obtained the information from the books.

"Ireland, then, is more than three times as large as Massachusetts; two thirds as large as New York, and one eighth the size of Texas, and of about the same area as the State of Maine. The longest straight line that could be drawn through the island would be from north-east to south-west, three hundred and four miles in length; and its greatest width is one hundred and ninety-four miles. Can any of you tell me the proper name, given as a whole, to England, Scotland, Wales, and Ireland!"

"Great Britain," replied a forward young man.

"No; Great Britain is the island which includes England, Scotland, and Wales. After the Irish revolution of 1798, the British government took advantage of the conquest it had just achieved to unite the two countries more effectually than they had before been united. The purpose was carried out in 1801, and the first article of the compact was to the effect that the two islands should henceforward be called The United Kingdom of Great Britain and Ireland."

"That is a pretty long name," suggested a student.

"The United Kingdom is sufficient for ordinary purposes," added Professor Mapps. "Can you mention any appellations given to Ireland?"

"The Emerald Isle," said one.

"The Green Isle," replied another.

"Both on account of the rich green of the island. The grass is the finest and best for cattle."

"The Gim of the Say," laughed another.

"A pet name derived from the emerald, which is green. But what is the favorite poetical name?"

"Hibernia," answered Goodwin.

"Erin," replied Paul Kendall.

"Erin go bragh!" added Pelham.

"Erin," said the instructor. "'Erin go bragh!' means 'Hurrah for Ireland,' or 'Ireland forever.' Eri, or Erin, is the name by which the island was called by the natives. It means 'western.' By the ancients it was known as Ierna, Iouerna, Iuverna; and from these it has been corrupted into Hibernia. The people of ancient Britain called it Iverdon, and the Saxons who conquered them, Ierland, which became Ireland, its present name, by one of the changes of spelling common in our language.

"Now, young gentlemen, glance at the map," continued the professor, taking his pointer. "Ireland is bounded on three sides by the Atlantic Ocean; on the east by the North Channel, which is only fourteen miles wide between the Mull of Cantire, in Scotland, and Torr Point, the north-eastern headland of Ireland; by the Irish Sea, which is one hundred and thirty miles broad, and St. George's Channel, seventy miles wide.

"The surface of the country is undulating; and there is seldom an elevation which rises to the dignity of a mountain, though some of them are, by courtesy, called such. The slopes are generally gradual, and there are extensive plains occupied by moorlands and bogs, from the latter of which is taken the peat — or turf, as the people call it — used for fuel by all the poorer classes.

"In glancing at the physical geography of the island, you perceive that the hilly regions are near the coast. In the south-west are found the greatest elevations. The highest mountain is Carrantual, one of McGillicuddy's Reeks, in the county of Kerry; but it is only three thousand four hundred and fourteen feet high. What is the height of Mount Washington?"

"Six thousand four hundred and twenty-eight feet," replied several.

"Of Kunchinginga, the highest in the world?"

"Twenty-eight thousand one hundred and seventy-eight feet."

"The Irish mountains, then, are hardly worth mentioning. The highest in the United Kingdom is Ben Nevis, in Scotland, which is about the height of Mount Mansfield and Camel's Hump, in Vermont. What is the largest river of Ireland?"

"The Shannon."

"How long?"

"Two hundred and twenty-four miles."

"English authorities call it two hundred and forty miles. The Thames and the Severn, in England, are of about the same length. We do not regard the Connecticut, four hundred and fifty miles in length, as a large river in our own country, though it is nearly twice as long as the largest rivers of the United Kingdom. Our ship now floats in Queenstown Harbor, or the Cove of Cork, which is the estuary of the River

Lee. This stream has its source in Lake Gougane, Barra, and has a course of thirty-five miles. The other principal rivers are the Barrow, Suir, Slaney, Erne, Foyle, Bann, Blackwater, Boyne, and the Liffey. What are lakes called in Ireland?"

"Loughs."

"The same as Lochs in Scotland. The lakes of the United Kingdom, measured by the American standard, are small affairs. Lough Neagh, in the north of Ireland, the largest, is a little larger than Lake Winnipiseogee, in New Hampshire, and Cayuga Lake, in New York. What are the four provinces of Ireland, Mr. Goodwin?"

"Ulster, Munster, Leinster, and Connaught."

"How many counties are there?".

"Thirty-two."

"The government of the country is administered by a viceroy, or lord lieutenant, appointed by the queen, who resides at Dublin. He has a privy council to assist him, the members of which are also appointed by the crown. Ireland is now represented in the British Parliament — of which I shall have something to say in the future — by four spiritual and twenty-eight temporal peers, with one hundred and five commoners."

"What are spiritual peers, Mr. Mapps?" asked Paul Kendall.

"Archbishops or bishops of the established church, who occupy seats in the House of Lords. A peer is a member of the upper house of Parliament, corresponding to our Senate. The country is not represented wholly with regard to the number of the population. Members are elected for boroughs, or districts, for cities, and even for universities. Each county in Ireland is entitled to two members, making sixty-four; certain towns have thirty-nine; and the University of Dublin has two.

"Each county in Ireland is governed by a lieutenant, — who is generally a peer of the realm, — assisted by deputy lieutenants and magistrates, appointed by the crown.

"Young gentlemen, perhaps you have already noticed that the climate here is milder than our own, though we are now nearly ten degrees farther north than Brockway. The summers are not so warm, nor the winters so cold, as with us. If you glance at your nautical charts, you will observe that the warm waters of the Gulf Stream flow in this direction; and they have a very sensible effect in moderating and equalizing the temperature. Ireland has about the average climate of Virginia, though its extremes of heat and cold are not so great.

"The moisture of the atmosphere favors the growth of the grass, though it injures the wheat crop. Oats and barley are the principal grains; flax is extensively produced in the north, while potatoes are raised in every part of the island, and form the chief article of diet of the poorer classes. The agriculture of Ireland is inferior to that of Scotland and England.

"A few words in regard to the history of Ireland will complete what I have to say at present. Nothing authentic is known of the early history of Ireland, though a very remote antiquity is claimed by Irish writers for their country. The first event of present importance is the conversion of the natives to Christianity, a work which was commenced by St. Patrick."

"Long life to him!" said Lynch, who was of Irish descent; whereat everybody laughed, including the professor.

"St. Patrick was a Scotchman —"

"Not a bit of it — begging your pardon, Mr. Mapps," interrupted Lynch again.

"What was he?"

"An Irishman, to be sure. How could St. Patrick be a Scotchman?"

"There are grave doubts in regard to his birthplace, I acknowledge," replied the professor, with a smile. "Some say he was born in Scotland, others in England, and still others in France; but none claim that he was born in Ireland. It is said that he was taken prisoner in this country in his youth, and was employed as a swineherd for seven years, during which time he learned the Irish language. Having first studied with his uncle, the Bishop of Tours, St. Patrick went to Rome, and was sent to Ireland, with thirty-four assistants, to Christianize the people, by Pope Celestine. After ten years of labor and discouragement, he converted the king, Laera II., and then spent the rest of his life in travelling over the country, making converts, and founding churches and monasteries. He died at the age of one hundred and twenty.

"After the introduction of Christianity, civilization and learning made considerable advances. A school, founded at Armagh, was celebrated all over Europe; and for a time the island had so great a reputation for learned ecclesiastics that it was called the 'Island of Saints.'

"In the eleventh century, Brian Boroimhe, King of Munster, drove the Danes from his own kingdom, and was crowned King of Ireland, at Tara, the ancient capital of the island, where a magnificent royal palace is supposed to have been located. Moore, the Irish poet, sings the fallen fortunes of the place in the well-known lines: —

> 'The harp that once through Tara's halls
> The soul of music shed,
> Now hangs as mute on Tara's walls
> As if that soul were fled.'

Brian Boroimhe, when Ireland was again invaded by the Danes, instigated by the King of Leinster, fought the great battle of Clontarf, in which he was slain. His body was conveyed to Armagh in solemn procession, placed in the cathedral, and for twelve days and nights the clergy continued their prayers and devotions over the corpse. Moore chants his praises in a poem: —

> 'Remember the glories of Brian the brave,
> Though the days of the hero are o'er;
> Though lost to Mononia, and cold in the grave,
> He returns to Kinkora no more.
> That star of the field, which so often hath poured
> Its beam on the battle, is set;
> But enough of its glory remains in each sword
> To light us to victory yet.'

"After the death of the powerful Brian, internal discord pervaded the island. It was the scene of various strifes, until the sovereignty of the country was given to Henry II., in 1174, by the pope; but it was not finally subdued till 1210, when a charter of liberties was granted to the people by King John. The obstinate Irish barons continued to resist the government of England, and rebellions have been as fashionable in Ireland as pipes are in Holland, the most noted of which were those of 1641, 1689, and 1798.

"Ireland has been grievously oppressed by England. Henry VIII. took the title of King of Ireland, though only a small portion of the country was really subject to the English laws. He introduced the Protestant reformation into the country; and the province of Ulster, in the north, was settled by Scotch and English people of this faith. During the civil wars in England, the Irish Catholics attempted to overthrow the new religion, and an insurrection broke out in Ulster, which extended through all parts of the island. Ireland was in a state of anarchy till 1649, when Cromwell came with his army and suppressed the rebellion.

"In 1688, after James II. had abandoned the English throne, and William and Mary had been proclaimed joint sovereigns, the self-exiled monarch, with the assistance of the French, rallied the Irish Catholics under his banner, established his court at Dublin, and held the country until his disastrous defeat in the battle of the Boyne. His power was completely overthrown in 1791. The Catholics were fiercely persecuted after the conquest; their estates were confiscated, and for the succeeding hundred years they were relentlessly oppressed. Catholics were not eligible to offices of trust, were excluded from the army and navy, not allowed to keep or to bear arms, and were otherwise deprived of their rights.

"The people were uneasy and discontented; they demanded equal privileges; and towards the close of the eighteenth century, as they again became restless under certain commercial restraints and the influence of the French revolution, the British government increased its severity, suspended the *habeas corpus*, dispersed meetings of the people with military and police forces, and quartered troops upon the inhabitants. The Catholic Irish formed secret societies, and invoked the aid of France, which furnished only assistance enough to encourage another outbreak — the rebellion of 1798. It was suppressed by Lord Cornwallis, — the one who surrendered his army at Yorktown, — lord lieutenant of Ireland, by the employment of conciliatory measures. In 1801 a more complete political union was effected between Ireland and her oppressor; but the rights of the people were not recognized in the compact, and they were far from satisfied. In 1803 another outbreak occurred at Dublin, under the leadership of Robert Emmet, an enthusiastic young man, who, at the suppression of the rebellion, perished on the scaffold; but his name and memory are still affectionately cherished by the Irish people.

"Catholic emancipation, which meant equality of rights to both the prevailing sects, was the great question agitated by the Irish for many years. Daniel O'Connell was the leading spirit in these agitations; and in 1829 an act embodying Catholic emancipation received the assent of the crown. The two sects were now equal before the law; but O'Connell and others continued to labor for the independence of the country, which, in spite of many rights and privileges granted to the people, was still grievously oppressed.

"Only one tenth of the population of Ireland belonged to the established church; yet tithes, or taxes for its support, were levied upon all alike. In our land this iniquitous law would breed a revolution in twenty-four hours; and we need not wonder that the Irish have been impatient, especially when this was only one of their grievances. In 1838 the manner of collecting tithes was modified, a fixed sum being levied upon the landholders; but, of course, it was ultimately paid by the tenants, and the tithes were concealed rather than removed.

"The separation of the two countries, as the only means of obtaining justice, has been the object of the Irish leaders; and in 1846 a new party, called the Irish Confederation, was formed; and in 1848, under the stimulus of the events in France which resulted in the flight of Louis Philippe, a revolt was attempted; but it was a signal failure. Several of the leaders were arrested, and some of them were sentenced to death for treason; but the penalty was commuted to transportation. Most of them were subsequently pardoned. Thomas F. Meagher, one of them, went to the United States, and distinguished himself in the Union army. John Mitchell, who fled from the storm in his own country, was unworthy of the cause in which he had been engaged. In conclusion, young gentlemen, Ireland has always been an oppressed land. Her history is a continuous storm of battle and insurrection. Though her condition has been greatly improved, her people are still deprived of 'equal rights.'

"I have taken this early opportunity to give you a very meagre outline of the geography and history of Ireland, that you may view with more interest and pleasure the historic spots you may visit."

The professor retired; the boys were dismissed, and hastened on deck, to gaze at the shores of the country whose history had just been related to them.

CHAPTER II.

QUEENSTOWN TO CORK.

"CLEAR away the professors' barge," said the officer of the deck, shortly after Mr. Mapps had finished his lecture.

The boat was lowered into the water, the crew piped over the side, and the third master detailed to take charge of it. The officer and crew were regarded as very fortunate in having an opportunity even to go as far as the shore, for all were burning with impatience to see something more of the Green Isle.

Paul Kendall came out of the cabin dressed in full uniform, with the anchor and three stars on his shoulder-straps, and the three gold bands on his sleeves. He had put on a new suit for the occasion, and being a well-formed young man, and graceful in his movements, he was not likely to bring any discredit upon American boys by his personal appearance. Dr. Winstock went down the accommodation ladder, followed by Paul, who was just then the envy of every student in the ship. The crew sat with their oars up, and when the passengers were seated in the stern sheets, they "let fall," and "gave way," at the orders of the coxswain.

"This is a beautiful harbor, Dr. Winstock," said Paul, gazing at the surrounding shores.

"It is one of the best harbors in the world," replied the doctor; "it is large enough to shelter the whole British navy. You see it is fortified in every direction; for if an enemy gained a foothold here, they could inflict immense damage upon the commerce and the power of England. The land on the port side is Spike Island; the buildings belong to the convict depot, and will accommodate two thousand men, who are employed in digging and building for fortifications, and on other work. The next is Rocky Island, which contains a powder magazine, occupying six chambers dug out of the solid rock. The third island is Hawlbowline, and the buildings upon it are storehouses for cannon and small arms."

"You have been here before, doctor," said Paul.

"Yes — a few years ago."

"What odd little steamers these are!" added the young officer, as one of them started from the wharf before them.

"They are certainly different from ours; but we shall have occasion to use one of them in going up to Cork, and you will have an opportunity to examine the structure more closely."

As the boat approached the landing steps, a crowd of people began to gather on the pier to witness the arrival of the boat, for the pilot had probably already proclaimed the character of the Young America to the people. The professors' barge went up to the wharf in man-of-war style, and landed her passengers. A couple of the oarsmen carried the valise and bag belonging to them up the steps. As they did so, about two dozen porters, each with a large metallic badge, on which was his number, strapped around his left arm, between the shoulder and the elbow, rushed forward, and seized the baggage — we should say "luggage," for the American word is not used in the United Kingdom.

"Long life to your ahnor" (honor), gasped one of them, in the midst of his struggles to obtain the coveted prize; "ye gave it me — number twinty-wan."

"I didn't give it to any of you yet," said Dr. Winstock.

"Number siventeen, your ahnor," shouted another.

"Whisht now! go way wid ye, you blackguards!" said a man dressed in blue, his head covered by a black hat trimmed with patent leather, who was evidently a policeman.

The officer cleared a place around the strangers, and Dr. Winstock inquired of him at what hour the next steamer left for Cork.

"Indade, sir, you are too late for the boat that goes up to Patrick's bridge, but ye can take the railroad boat in about an hour."

"I think we had better take some supper here then, Paul," added the doctor.

"As you think best, sir."

"Number nineteen," continued Dr. Winstock, selecting one of the porters who had been less forward than the others, "you can take the luggage to the Queen's Hotel."

"Thank your ahnor," replied the grateful fellow.

"Ye gave it to me, sir," growled number seventeen.

"Indade, thin, ye gave it to me," interposed number twenty-one.

"I gave it to none of you. Number nineteen has it now."

"I beg your pardon, your honor," said another man, in uniform, as he touched his hat to the doctor. "The custom-house officer, sir."

"You wish to examine the luggage."

"If ye plase, your honor. Give me the kay."

"Here is the key," replied Dr. Winstock, slipping a shilling into his hand.

"Thank your honor," replied the man, slyly.

The doctor unlocked the valise.

"Just rise the lid. That'll do, sir," replied the officer of her majesty's customs, as he closed the valise.

A half crown, or even a shilling, to the custom-house officer at Queenstown, if not expected, is gratefully received, and may save the traveller much annoyance; it is quite probable that some small parcels and "pirated books" escape confiscation by the process.

The porter, with the assistance of the policeman, obtained possession of the valise and bag, and the strangers followed him towards the hotel, which was situated but a short distance from the quay.

"God bless your honor!" said a ragged woman, stepping up to the travellers, with a low courtesy; "I'm a poor crayter, wid siven shmall childer, and I haven't a bit t' ate for thim."

"Go way wid yous, and don't be bodthering the gintlemin," interposed the porter.

"Would your honor joost give me the shmallest

bit of silver you have in your pocket?" persisted the beggar.

"I have no small change," replied the doctor.

"A pinny to buy bread, your honor," said a dirty boy on the other side.

"A pinny, or a ha'pinny for me fadther, who got sick, and didn't do a shtroke o' work for two moonths," pleaded another boy in tattered garments.

"One pinny, only a pinny for me," chimed in a girl.

"Paul, we shall have the whole town upon us, at this rate," laughed the doctor.

"I have a couple of sixpences," whispered Paul; "shall I give them to them?"

"No! That would be madness. You would sow to the wind and reap the whirlwind. They would persecute us to the death if you gave them a penny."

The beggars, reënforced by others, persisted in their demands, and the only safety of the travellers was in immediate flight. They pushed forward, heedless of the din of women and children who sued for pennies, and "shmall bits of silver," until they reached Queen's Hotel, into which the beggars dared not follow them. The porter was paid and discharged, and the visitors entered the coffee-room; for, unlike American hotels, those of the United Kingdom seldom contain public parlors, reading-rooms, or any similar apartment, for general use.

The coffee-room, in first-class hotels, is usually an elegant apartment, with carpeted floor and draperied windows. It is commonly furnished with small tables for little parties or single individuals. In some of the larger provincial towns there are commercial rooms, for the exclusive use of "commercial travellers," who are agents or "runners" for mercantile establishments in the large cities.

Dr. Winstock and Paul entered the coffee-room of the Queen's. It was about five o'clock in the afternoon, and a few of the tables were occupied by parties at dinner. They seated themselves, and began to examine the newspapers with which the room was supplied.

"What will you please to order?"

The question was addressed to Paul, who was just then absorbed in the "latest from America."

"I beg your pardon, sir. Did you speak to me?" replied Paul, glancing at the person who addressed him.

He was clothed in black pants and black dress coat, with a white cravat.

"What will you please to order?" repeated the individual in black.

"Order?" asked Paul, confused by the question.

"He is the waiter," said Dr. Winstock, laughing.

"The waiter! I thought he must be a doctor of divinity," replied Paul, measuring the servant from head to foot with his eye.

"I shall have a mutton chop," said the doctor.

"I will have the same," added Paul, turning to his paper again.

In due time the mutton chops appeared, and called forth the unqualified approbation of the travellers. They were rich, tender, and delicate; far superior to American mutton.

"These come of the rich grass of Ireland," said

the doctor; "though there is something in the breed of sheep. When I was in Ireland before, I lived on mutton, which is extra nice throughout the United Kingdom."

"How is it about the roast beef of old England?" asked Paul.

"The beef isn't any better than ours, Paul. I have eaten poorer beef in England than I ever did in America, while the best I have seen there does not surpass our own. I don't think you will like the style of living in this part of the world as well as that at home."

"I don't know; I think I shall get along very well," laughed Paul, as he buttered a slice of bread, and tasted it.

It did not suit him, and he added more butter from one of the little "pats" before him.

"What sort of butter do you call this?" demanded he, as he tried it again.

"Irish butter," replied Dr. Winstock, laughing.

"There is no taste to it."

"Yet it is nice, fresh butter."

"I don't think so; it tastes more like tallow, than butter."

"There is no salt in it, Paul; that is all. I assure you no better butter ever was made; but you have stumbled upon a custom which does not conform to your experience. In England, Ireland, and Scotland, as well as on the continent, they put little or no salt in the butter. You can either get used to it, or supply the deficiency; there is salt on the table."

Paul supplied the deficiency, and the supper was

finished to the satisfaction of both. The waiter brought the bill when requested to do so. It amounted to five shillings; and when he brought the change for a sovereign, he contrived to have some small coin included. He handed it to the doctor piece by piece, the sixpences last. He looked so wistful that it was impossible for an American to refuse his unuttered petition, and he was permitted to retain the last sixpence; whereat he seemed to be very grateful. The young officer was rather surprised to see the man whom he had mistaken for a doctor of divinity stoop to a sixpence; but he was destined to see bigger men than waiters "cotton" to small coins.

The coinage of the United Kingdom in common use is in gold, silver, and copper. The gold coins are the sovereign and half sovereign. The silver coins are the crown (five shillings), the half crown (two and sixpence), the florin, or two-shilling piece, the shilling, the sixpence, and the threepence. The copper coins are the penny and the half penny. The two-penny copper coin is now rarely seen.

The paper money consists principally of the notes issued by the Bank of England. The smallest bill is for five pounds. The notes are about three times the size of an American bank bill, are printed on white paper, made exclusively for the purpose, and are never issued a second time.

"Now, Paul, we have a few minutes to spare, and if we are not overwhelmed by the beggars, we will take a little walk," said Dr. Winstock, when he had paid the bill.

"The beggars are a nuisance," replied Paul.

"We shall be troubled with them in all the southern part of Ireland; after that we shall see but few of them till we reach Italy, which is the paradise of beggars."

There was nothing of special interest to be seen in the town. This part of the island is a favorite resort for invalids, on account of the mildness and salubrity of the climate. The American steamers land their mails here, and such passengers as wish to make the tour of Ireland, or to reach Liverpool in advance of the ship. A small tug usually meets the steamer off Roches Point, and takes the mail and passengers ashore. It requires about twenty-four hours for the steamship to run from Queenstown to Liverpool, while the trip is made by railway and steamer, by the way of Dublin and Holyhead, in about ten or eleven hours.

The Cunard steamers leave Liverpool on Saturday. If one sailed at ten in the forenoon, a passenger could start from London at five in the afternoon by the express mail train and overtake the ship at Queenstown, thus gaining eight hours, and avoid the rough sea of the channel.

Paul was rather surprised to find the streets and houses so much like those he had seen in America. There was hardly anything to remind him that he was in a foreign land, unless it was the beggars, who swarmed in the streets, and beset all persons that looked like strangers, and especially like Americans, for they have the reputation of being liberal donors. There was little to see, and but little time to see it, and the travellers hastened back to the hotel for their luggage.

"Paul, do you remember the lines, on the burial of Sir John Moore?" asked the doctor, on their return.

"I do.

> 'Not a drum was heard, not a funeral note,
> As his corse to the rampart we hurried.'"

"Do you know who wrote the poem?"

"I don't remember."

"It was the Rev. Charles Wolfe. He died at this place, in 1823, of consumption, and was buried here."

At the hotel, a little fellow, who acted as a porter and runner, offered to carry the valise and bag to the railroad boat. He was an odd youth, and one could not tell whether he was twelve or twenty. He was dressed in faded livery, and looked a little like the monkey in the circus. He shouldered the "bit of a box," — a trunk is a box in Ireland, — and led the way to the pier. He was full of mother wit, and amused the doctor so much that he gave him a shilling for his services.

The little steamer in which the travellers embarked for Passage, where they were to take the train for Cork, was as unlike the ordinary American steamer as anything could be. She was a side-wheeler, very long for her width, or very narrow for her length, as the reader pleases. There was no saloon on the deck, which had seats around it for the accommodation of passengers. The pilot stood on a raised platform at the stern, there being no wheel-house near the bow, as in our steamers. There was a small cabin aft, into which people might retreat in case of rain. But the little thing made good time, and for a short trip was comfortable enough.

The scenery on the shores of the River Lee, below Cork, is very attractive. The slope of Great Island, on which Queenstown is located, is covered with beautiful villas and other country residences. On the other side of the river the country is more irregular, with occasional exhibitions of rock, and picturesque steeps. The whole region is improved; there are no waste places; and the traveller obtains his first ideas of the dwellings of the wealthy class from the elegant mansions seen on the banks of the river.

"We are approaching Passage," said Dr. Winstock, as he pointed to the landing-pier. "It is somewhat noted as a watering-place; but in my mind it is associated only with Francis Mahony's Irish poem. Do you know it, Paul?"

"I never heard of it, sir."

"You will find it in Dana's House Book of Poetry, a copy of which is in the main cabin library of the ship. I remember a verse or two of it, for it is so mellifluously Irish, that I could hardly forget it.

> 'The town of Passage
> Is both large and spacious,
> And situated
> Upon the say;
> 'Tis nate and dacent,
> And quite adjacent
> To come from Cork
> On a summer's day.
>
> There you may slip in,
> And take a dip in

>   Forenent the shipping
>   That at anchor ride;
>   Or in a wherry,
>   Cross o'er the ferry,
>   To Carrigaloe,
>   On the other side.
>
>   Mud cabins swarm in
>   This place so charming,
>   With sailors' garments
>   Hung out to dry;' —

And that's all I remember of it. These poems, I think, add an interest to the places they relate to."

"They do, sir; and I shall certainly read that poem, when I return to the ship."

"You will find other Irish poems in the same volume."

The steamer hauled up at the pier; the travellers landed, and entered the railroad station. A porter took the valise, and placed it in the "van," which is the name applied to a baggage car. The fare from Queenstown to Cork was one shilling, first class. In Europe the railway carriages are divided into compartments, which are entered at the sides. Each division has seats for six or eight passengers, one half of whom sit facing the other half; those taking forward seats riding backwards.

Travellers are divided into three, and sometimes four, classes, depending upon the prices they pay. The different classes of fare from Edinburgh to London, for example, are as follows:—

First class, ...	£3 10s.
Second class, ...	£2 11s.
Third class, ...	£1 3s.

First class passengers are always provided with cushioned seats, stuffed arms and backs. In Ireland the only difference we noticed between second and third class accommodations was, that the seats were hollowed out a little like a kitchen chair in the former, while they were entirely flat in the latter; but in most parts of Europe second class compartments have seats with a leather cushion; in Germany and Switzerland they are about equal to our cars, but not in the United Kingdom.

The two vacant seats which Dr. Winstock found in the compartment were at the opposite ends, and they were separated for the time. The young officer was absorbed in viewing the country through which the train passed. He wished to ask some questions of the dignified gentleman who sat opposite to him; but he had learned to believe that the people with whom he was now brought into contact were haughty and reserved, and that he could not expect a civil answer from them. After proceeding a short distance, the train stopped.

"Is this Cork, sir?" asked Paul, forgetting for the instant his prejudices.

"No, sir; this is Blackrock. The next stopping-place will be Cork," replied the gentleman to whom the question had been addressed, in the kindest and blandest of tones.

"Thank you, sir," added Paul, astonished at the suavity of the native.

"You are a stranger, young gentleman," continued the person.

"Yes, sir; I belong to the Academy Ship, which arrived to-day."

"Ah, indeed!"

The gentleman wished to know something about the ship, and in return pointed out the objects of interest which could be seen from the window.

"This is Cork," added the native, as the train stopped. "Can I be of any service to you?"

"I am obliged to you, sir; but the gentleman with me has been here before," replied Paul, as they got out of the carriage. It is never called a car on the other side of the ocean.

"Now, Paul, you will have a chance to try a side-car, which is peculiarly an Irish institution. I never saw one anywhere except in this country."

A vehicle was engaged, and Paul realized that it was a queer establishment. There are seats for four passengers, who sit sidewise, facing *out*. Hanging over the two wheels are foot-boards, in front of the seats. The driver's box is on the forward part, but he does not sit there when he has but one passenger, occupying instead one of the side-seats. The vehicle has no top. Between the seats and behind the four passengers is a space for small pieces of luggage.

"Imperial Hotel," said Dr. Winstock, as he mounted the car with Paul.

"Impayrial Hotel, your honor," replied the carman, as he drove off, yelling at his horse like a wild Indian. "Does your honor shtop long in Cork?"

"Only till to-morrow."

"I'd like to dhrive your honor out to Blarney Castle in the marhning."

"I shall not be able to go. What street is this?"

"This is Albert Quay, your honor, and it's now we're comin' to Anglesea Bridge."

"Is this the River Lee?" asked Paul.

"No; this is the Sout' Branch; beyant you see the Lee," replied the driver, pointing down the stream to the junction of the two branches, a short distance below.

The principal part of Cork lies between these two branches, on an island.

"This is Sout' Mall, your honor, and beyant is the bank," added the talkative driver.

"You must not expect much of Cork, Paul," said the doctor. "St. Patrick's Church is the only building of any note."

"I don't care so much about the buildings as I do to see how the people live," replied Paul.

"You will not see much of them at the hotels."

"I have a commission to execute for the Irish girl who has lived in our family since I was a child. She was astonished when I told her I was going to Ireland, and I promised to call upon her brother-in-law."

"Do you know his address?"

"Yes, sir; No. 88 Patrick Street. He is a porter in an apothecary shop."

"Impayrial Hotel, your honor," said the driver, as he drew up in a narrow street before a plain edifice.

"How much is your fare?" demanded Dr. Winstock.

"Anything your honor plazes," replied the carman, touching his hat, and looking particularly amiable.

"How much is the fare? What is your price?"

"Whatever ye plaze, your honor."

"Name your price."

"Two shillings," replied the driver, in a low tone.

The doctor gave him his price, which was four times as much as he was entitled to receive.

"Thank your honor. If yous want a nice car, wid a fine harse, I'll call for your honor in the evening."

They entered the hotel, escorted by a porter in livery.

"What should I have paid that driver?" asked the doctor.

"Sixpence, sir, for the two."

The surgeon laughed, and so did Paul, at the deceit which was put upon them; but the fellow lost several good jobs by the swindle.

CHAPTER III.

BLARNEY CASTLE.

AFTER the rooms had been secured at the hotel, Dr. Winstock took a car to call upon a gentleman whose acquaintance he had made during his former visit, leaving Paul at liberty to walk about the city.

"Where is Patrick Street, sir?" asked Paul of a man who was standing on the sidewalk near the hotel.

"I'll show you, sur," replied the person addressed, leading the way through Pembroke Street.

Paul thought the man was even more obliging than he had found the people in the streets of New York and Boston, and he walked by the stranger's side with a feeling of gratitude and admiration towards his guide. "This is Patrick Street, sur," said the man, after they had gone through Winthrop Street, as he touched his hat.

"Thank you; I am greatly obliged to you," replied Paul.

"Patrick Street, sur; I'd showed you the way, do ye mind?" added the guide, touching his hat again.

"I know you did, and I'm very much obliged to you."

"Don't break your hand, sir," said the man, evidently dissatisfied with the simple thanks of the young officer.

"Don't break my hand!" exclaimed Paul, puzzled by the phrase. "I don't think I'm in any danger of breaking it."

"Faix, ye are not, sur, for the weight of a three-pence would break it."

Paul took a sixpence from his pocket, the smallest coin he had, and gave it to the man.

"Thank your honor," replied the guide, his face suddenly brightening up as he glanced at the coin in his hand. "Long life to your honor; and if you want e'er a b'y to show you any place, I'm idle just now, and I'll do me besht for your honor."

Paul did not think he should be likely to need his services, for he was quite disgusted with the servility of the man. His gratitude and admiration were changed into contempt; but before he had been in Ireland three days, he could not help thinking that every person he met was studying out a plan to get a sixpence out of him.

The young officer walked down St. Patrick Street, looking at the people, and gazing in at the shop windows. To him the appearance of the city of Cork was disagreeably similar to that of Boston and New York. There was nothing of interest to be seen; but presently he became painfully conscious that he was himself an object of interest, especially to the dirty boys and girls whom he met.

"Do ye mind the young shwell beyant?" said a juvenile "Greek" to his companions.

The remark reminded Paul that he was in full uniform; and being a modest youth, he wished his dress consisted only of plain clothes. Other annoying expressions came to his ears, but he paid no attention to them, and seemed not to hear them.

St. Patrick Street is the principal one in Cork, and extends in the form of a crescent from the bridge, with the same revered name, to Grand Parade, which is also a street of great pretensions, adorned with an equestrian statue of George II. Both these streets are wide and imposing, but the buildings are of all styles and heights, and with no claims to architectural beauty.

Paul found the brother-in-law of the faithful domestic in his father's family, and was warmly greeted. The man was glad to see one " who had come all the way from America," and Paul gave him half a sovereign, as he had been requested to do by Hannah.

" How did ye come to Ireland, Mr. Kendall?" asked Michael Shea, the brother-in-law.

" I came in the Academy Ship."

" Is it possible! How is my sister?"

" She was quite well when I saw her last."

" Is it possible! Do you stop long in Cork, Mr. Kendall?"

" I shall return to the ship to-morrow. All the officers and crew are to visit Blarney and Killarney, and I shall be up again soon."

" Is it possible! Now, Mr. Kendall, I'd like to have you go out to my little place with me and see my woman."

" I should like to go very much," replied Paul, who desired to visit the houses of some of the common people.

"Thin I'll go wid you to-morrow morning. Where are you stopping?"

"At the Imperial Hotel."

"Is it possible! I will come for you at tin minutes before eight."

"Very well; I will be ready."

"Indade, thin, Mr. Kendall, you are a fine-looking young man. It's a fine dress you wear."

"It is the uniform of the Young America. I am second lieutenant of the ship."

"Is it possible!"

"Both possible and probable," laughed Paul, as he took his leave, and hastened back to the hotel.

He felt that he had nearly exhausted Cork, even in his short walk; but early in the morning he visited the market with Dr. Winstock. The display of meats and vegetables was similar to what would be seen in an American city. Punctually at the appointed time Michael Shea appeared at the hotel, and just as the travellers finished their breakfast. A car was called, in which they were driven to Blarney Row. This part of the city was certainly very unlike anything Paul had seen in America, for it was occupied by the poorer classes of the city. The houses were generally of stone, whitewashed, with very few windows. That in which Michael Shea lived was one story high, with attic chambers. Being a porter in a store, he had good wages, compared with the common laborers, — who received from five to eight shillings a week, from a dollar and a quarter to two dollars, — and therefore occupied a better dwelling than the poorest classes.

Paul was ushered into the house, and duly presented

to the "woman," in the principal room. Perhaps the visitor was more interested in the apartment than in the persons, and while he was giving Mrs. Shea "an account" of her sister, he busied himself in scrutinizing the style of living. The floor was of hardened cement, often called a "mud floor." The furniture was meagre, and of the coarsest kind. At one end was a fireplace, in which a grate was set, with high jambs, on which the tea kettle and other cooking utensils rested. The fire was of soft coal, and Paul could not help thinking what a luxury a Yankee cook stove would be to the family.

It was breakfast time, and the visitor soon realized that he was expected to partake with the family; and as extra preparations had been made for the occasion, he was not a little embarrassed to remember that he had just eaten a hearty breakfast at the hotel.

"Draw up, and take a bit t' ate wid us," said Michael, as he seated himself at the table.

"I thank you; I took my breakfast quite early this morning, in order to be ready for you."

"Is it possible!"

Paul saw that he was grievously offending Irish hospitality, and he was compelled to compromise.

"I supposed you took breakfast much earlier than this. In America our working people have breakfast at six or seven o'clock; and really I did not understand that I was invited to breakfast. But I will sit down with you, and take a cup of tea."

The meal consisted of tea — few in the United Kingdom take coffee in the morning; of slices cut from an enormous loaf of white bread in the hands of Mrs. Shea, who first buttered the surface, and then cut off the slice for the guest; of boiled eggs, which in Europe are invariably eaten from the shell, the whole being placed in an egg cup; and of fried bacon, which consisted of rib pieces cured and smoked. The butter was fresh, but the visitor observed that the members of the family put salt upon it. This was an extra occasion, and the fare was doubtless much better than usual. Paul partook of a compromise breakfast, and having given and received all the information the time permitted, he bade good by to the hospitable Irish woman, and mounted a car with Mr. Shea.

"Don't break your hand," said the carman when Michael gave him sixpence, at the end of the course; and no Irish driver was ever yet satisfied with a regular fare.

Paul found Dr. Winstock at the hotel, and they went together to a store in Patrick Street, to see the silver pitcher which the doctor and his friend had selected the preceding evening. The young officer was perfectly satisfied with the plate, and directions for the inscription to be engraved upon it were left with the silversmith.

"As I have to call upon his worship the mayor, I must find a barber's shop now; for I left my razors on board the ship," said the doctor, after they had returned to the hotel.

"I think I will go with you, sir," replied Paul.

"You! Do you shave, Paul?" laughed the doctor.

"Not much; but I would like to have my hair cut."

It was not an easy matter to find a barber's shop in Cork. They were directed to one in Old George

Street, and while they were looking for it, one of those officious idlers, who are constantly studying out the means of extracting sixpences from the pockets of strangers, offered his assistance, and conducted them to the shop.

"Don't break your hand," said the vagabond, when Dr. Winstock gave him two pennies; but no notice was taken of him, and the travellers entered the shop.

Both of them revolted at the idea of such a shaving saloon. It was a small, dirty apartment, opening into another, in which the operator's wife and children lived. On the fire was a skillet of hot water, and in the middle of the floor stood a common, straight-back kitchen chair, in which the doctor seated himself after preparing for the operation. The professor of the tonsorial art took an old wooden box, such as our grandfathers used, and made his lather.

There was no proper barber's chair, such as we see in America, with a rest for the head; but the barber held the head with one hand, and used his brush or razor with the other.

"Will I shorten the hair?" asked the barber, when he had finished the face of his customer.

"No; I haven't much hair, and I can't afford to lose any of it," replied the doctor.

"Troth, ye haven't much, thin; but I have a nice grase made from the feet of goats, that would bring it out moighty foine," said the barber.

Paul consented to have his hair "shortened," though he couldn't help thinking of the elegant saloons and the elegant operators in his own country, as he sat down in the kitchen chair. The price, at least, corresponded with the meagre outfit of the shop, for it was only one penny for the shave, and two for "shortening" the hair. In Europe, those who are regarded as genteel people shave themselves; and even in London and Paris it is impossible to find a decent barber's shop.

After Dr. Winstock had been presented to the mayor by his Corkonian friend, the travellers took the steamer for Queenstown, at Patrick's Bridge. While they were riding down in the car, Paul wished to pay his share of the hotel bill, but the doctor was obstinate.

"I would like to see the bill, at any rate, sir," laughed Paul. "I want to learn something about the customs at the hotels."

"They are quite different from those in the United States," replied Dr. Winstock, as he handed the bill to Paul.

"I see they are; and I don't think the hotels compare with our own."

"You are right in the main, though in some respects they are superior. Even in some of the celebrated hotels of New York, it is almost impossible to get a civil answer from a clerk in the office; while in this country you will invariably be treated with respect, and every attention will be paid to you."

"Beds, 5s.," said Paul, reading from the bill; "two and sixpence each."

"They charge for each item separately; not so much a day, as at our hotels."

"Breakfasts, 5s. Attendance, 2s. What's that for?"

"It used to be the custom here for servants to

collect their own wages of the guests; now their fees, called 'attendance,' are charged in the bills; but they still have the habit of hanging around departing visitors, and most of them give sixpence, though there is no obligation to do so."

"I think almost every common sort of person that looks at you, expects you to give him sixpence," added Paul.

"That is true; Americans have the reputation of being free givers, and these plunderers make the best of their opportunities. They hardly expect an Englishman to give them anything for civilities thrust upon him."

At the bridge Dr. Winstock gave the carman a shilling; and though it was double the legal fare, the fellow grumbled, and begged for more; but the doctor was firm — and the American who travels in Europe with limited means must cultivate this virtue, or he will be robbed at every street corner.

The passage down the river was delightful, and was fully enjoyed by the travellers. At Queenstown, they employed a shore boat to convey them to the ship. The regular fare for a two-oar boat was sixpence; but the boatmen had the impudence to demand two shillings, which, however, they did not get.

Paul was a lion on board, and he had an interested audience while he "spun his yarn." In the afternoon, one half of the ship's company were permitted to go on shore and explore Queenstown.

"Did you have any money, Paul?" asked Pelham, the fourth lieutenant, who had been so rebellious at the time when the students had been compelled to deliver their money to the principal.

"Certainly I did. I drew on Mr. Lowington for thirty shillings," replied Paul.

"The fellows begin to feel bad about their money again," added Pelham. "We are going to have a chance to go on shore now, and if one of us is hungry, we haven't a penny to buy a biscuit."

"Mr. Lowington will do what is right about it, you may be sure."

"Well, I hope he will. I have always had a little money in my pocket, and I don't like to feel like a beggar."

"He gave small sums to those who went on shore this afternoon," added Paul.

"Well, I hope he won't be mean about it."

"He won't, you may depend upon it. And I hope all the fellows will use their money properly."

"Of course they will."

"I'm afraid some will not, which may stop their allowance."

"If the fellows don't get their money, there'll be another mutiny."

"Pooh!"

"You don't believe in the mutiny, Paul?"

"I'm sure I don't."

"I don't think much of it; but there will be trouble if the money is kept back."

Shortly after this conversation the boats came off with the boys who had visited the shore; and all hands were piped to muster, to enable the principal to inform them that the entire ship's company would visit Cork on the following day, and make an excursion to Blarney Castle. This intelligence was received with intense satisfaction by the boys. Dr. Winstock had brought an invitation from his worship the mayor for the whole ship's company to pay a visit to the city.

The next day, at ten o'clock in the forenoon, after two hours of study by the students, one of the little steamers, which had been engaged for the purpose, came alongside, and all the boys went on board, and also the occupants of the main cabin, the ship being left in charge of Peaks, the boatswain.

On their arrival in Cork, they were received and welcomed by his worship, who invited them to partake of a collation in the town hall at three o'clock. Mr. Lowington replied for the students; but in order to give the Irish magnate an opportunity to know what American boys are, Captain Gordon was called out, and made a very modest and pretty speech, thanking his worship for his kindness and hospitality, and promising ever to hold the pleasant city of Cork in grateful remembrance. Doubtless the mayor was surprised to hear a boy of seventeen make a speech, for it was more than H. R. H. the Prince of Wales could do at nineteen, when he was *fêted* and toasted in America.

After these ceremonies, the boys, who had been carefully charged, before they left the ship, to behave like gentlemen, were allowed to explore the city at their own pleasure, with positive injunctions to be at the town hall by three o'clock.

A little liberty was coveted by the boys. Two and

sixpence, in small coin, had been paid to each student, and all of them were in condition to enjoy themselves. It is probable that some of them drank more than one glass of ale, which is almost as plenty as water all over the United Kingdom ; and it is known that there were some excesses, though none of a serious nature. For instance, when a rude fellow in Great George Street ventured to say something about "a bit of a shwell," as Pelham passed, he was knocked over for his pains. This was more than any Irishman, or any Irish boy, could stand, and a mild type of "Donnybrook Fair" was actually in progress, when a couple of the city police stepped up, and drove off the vagabonds.

At the appointed hour, the boys, too much interested in the excursion to Blarney Castle to be tardy, were all on hand at the town hall. The collation was disposed of with excellent relish after the exercise of the morning, and with all the more relish because it was so different from the food to which they had been accustomed during the voyage. Fowl and ham is a favorite combination in the United Kingdom ; and this was the staple of the feast. Cold roast beef and cold mutton were also plentifully supplied, with crackers and Stilton cheese.

While the guests were occupied with the collation, twenty-four jaunting cars had been collected at Mr. Lowington's request, upon which the whole party mounted, and started for Blarney. The drive along the north bank of the river was exceedingly pleasant, and the excursionists obtained their first view of the "rural districts." The country was certainly very beautiful, but like most Americans who travel in the United Kingdom, our tourists were greatly disappointed because they could see so little of it. There were fine gardens and magnificent estates, but hardly a sight of them could be obtained, for they were all surrounded by high stone walls, sometimes ten feet in height, and the tops covered with sharp stones, and in some instances with broken bottles, to prevent the ingress of interlopers.

Farther from Cork, they came to open places, and obtained a more extended view of the country, and after gazing so long upon the waste of waters on their passage across the ocean, the fine, but not picturesque, scenery was fully appreciated by them.

After a ride of less than an hour, — for the distance is only five miles, and the carmen drove at a furious rate, — the procession reached the gates of the estate on which the castle is situated. As no vehicles were allowed upon the premises, the boys got down, and walked a short distance over the lawn, till they reached the ruin. Mr. Lowington gave the old woman ten shillings in full for the whole party.

"Go in there, and kiss the Blarney shtone," said the portress, as she pointed to a ruined apartment, on a level with the ground.

The boys rushed in, and vied with each other for the first chance to become eloquent so cheaply. The Blarney stone is a small stone, square in form, fixed into a larger one of irregular shape. The tradition is, that whoever kisses it becomes endowed with the sweet, persuasive, wheedling eloquence which is noticeable in the speech of the Corkonians.

> "There is a stone there
> That whoever kisses,
> O, he never misses
> To grow eloquent."

Blarney Castle, built in the fifteenth century, was the residence of the M'Carthys, Lords of Muskerry, Barons of Blarney, and Earls of Glencarty. It consists at present of a massive donjon tower, one hundred and twenty feet high, to which is attached the minor ruins. The boys went up the circular staircase, from which opened vaults, rooms, recesses, and loopholes. The walls were very thick, and conveyed an idea of the immense strength of ancient castles. Half way up, they passed out upon a portion of the ruin like a platform, overgrown with ivy, and walked round upon the crumbling walls, which were from three to six feet thick. From the summit of the tower they obtained a fine view of the surrounding country.

"Do you see that sheet of water?" said Professor Mapps, pointing to a small lake, about a quarter of a mile distant.

"Yes, sir! Blarney Lake!" shouted the boys.

"It is said that the Earl of Glencarty, who forfeited his castle in the revolution of 1641, threw all his plate into a certain part of that lake. Three of the M'Carthys inherit the secret of the spot where it is deposited, and any one of them, when he dies, must communicate his knowledge to another member of the family; for you know, in Irish parlance, if one can't keep a secret, three can; and it is never to be revealed until a M'Carthy is again Lord of Blarney, which may come to pass when the Fenians have fought their last battle in Canada."

Descending from the tower, the party were shown to the cave by a boy, who declared that it was three hundred yards deep; but the hole was so wet, dark, and "pokerish," that no one was disposed to test the truth of the statement. Fragments of the limestone which formed the cave were obtained, and then the dungeons where "the M'Carthy kept his prisoners" were exhibited. They were dark and horrible dens, and seemed to make real the romantic stories of such places which most of the students had read.

On their way from the castle to the Groves of Blarney, a few rods distant, Paul Kendall, who was interested in manners and customs even more than scenery and buildings, had an opportunity to inspect what was called a barn. It was a long, low brick building, used merely to shelter sheep and cattle in the winter, for all hay and straw is stacked out doors.

The Groves were the pleasure gardens of the castle, and were formerly filled with statues, grottos, alcoves, bridges, and other rustic ornaments. They are still very beautiful. The party were admitted by an old gardener, who was so fat and lame that he could hardly walk.

CHAPTER IV.

A QUESTION OF FINANCE.

THE Groves of Blarney were certainly very interesting and very beautiful, though it was too early in the season to see them to the greatest advantage.

> "The Groves of Blarney,
> They look so charming
> Down by the purling
> Of sweet silent streams,
> Being banked with posies,
> That spontaneous grow there,
> Planted in order
> By the sweet Rock Close."

The popular song describing the garden is peculiarly Irish, even to the "bulls" it contains, and has done more for the reputation of Blarney than its glories will warrant.

To Paul Kendall, old Tom Field, the gardener, was quite as interesting as the grounds. He pointed out the transcendent beauties of the spot with genuine Irish enthusiasm. The region was rocky in places, and the rocks had been turned to good account in increasing the picturesqueness of the gardens. From a ledge a flight of steps had been hewn out, which from some tradition had received the name of the "Witches' Stairs," and a grotto, partly natural and partly artificial, was called the "Witches' Kitchen." On the bank of a small stream, within the pleasure grounds, there is a very fine cromlech, which Professor Mapps explained. It was a kind of monument, consisting of a large flat stone, placed upon other upright stones as supports. These remains of the past are supposed to have been altars on which sacrifices were offered to heroes buried beneath them.

The rocks in the garden presented a curious appearance, being reduced to the most fanciful shapes by the action of time and the elements. Some of them had irregular apertures quite through them, large enough to admit the hand. Those of this kind, which had been partially covered with earth, had trees growing on their tops, the roots intertwined through the holes. There were English oaks, laurel and yew trees, in the garden.

After an hour had been spent on the grounds, and Tom Field had received ten shillings for his services, the boys were called together by the boatswain's whistle, and directed to return to the gate where the cars had been left. The ride back was by a different road from that taken in going, and the students were enabled to see more of the country. At seven o'clock they arrived at Patrick's Bridge, where they were to embark for the cove. Mr. Lowington had bargained with a stable-keeper for the cars, and he paid the regular fare to Blarney, which is two and sixpence, with sixpence "bonus" to each driver; but every one of them beset the occupants of his car, using the "blarney" of the region to extort something more from them. In some cases they succeeded; in others they failed.

At eight o'clock the steamer was alongside the ship, and the students were tired enough to sleep after the fatigues of the day; for after being confined so long to the uneasy decks of the vessel, it was hard work to travel much on the solid ground. For a week the boys were closely confined to their studies, though a portion of them made excursions, each pleasant afternoon to Hawlbowline, the fortifications, to Cloyne, and to Rostellan Castle. At the latter they saw an ancient sword, said to have belonged to the great Brian Boroimhe, and more cromlechs in the vicinity. But the great event to which they were looking forward was the visit to Killarney. The weather had been rather unsettled, and the grand excursion had been postponed to Wednesday, on the morning of which the skies were clear, with every indication of good weather, and it was announced that the boats would start at nine o'clock.

The financial relations between the principal and the students began to look a little stormy on the present occasion. Mr. Lowington had noticed, in the visit to Cork, that some of the boys had been drinking beer, and he had lectured them severely for it. He had strictly forbidden any such indulgence, and was disposed to stop their allowances of money if the offence was repeated.

The students had been supplied with money, to the extent of from ten to thirty pounds each, by their parents. The principal, to prevent gambling and other excesses, had taken possession of their funds, giving each a receipt for the amount received. But he intended to allow them small sums for pocket money when they went on shore, and he had exchanged a large quantity of the sovereigns for half crowns, shillings, and sixpences. If a boy wanted any of his money, he presented a written order to the principal, which, if approved, was paid by the pursers and indorsed on the original receipt in the hands of the drawer.

Before the ship's company went to Cork, it was understood that drafts to the amount of two and sixpence would be honored, and all the students had drawn for this sum. The money was kept in a small iron safe, set under the after companion way, for Mr. Lowington was obliged to keep large sums on hand for the current expenses of the ship. The principal kept the key in his state-room, and when drafts were to be paid, a box of silver was placed on the table, the steerage doors opened, the boys passing in at one and out at the other. The two pursers had charge of this business; and while one handed out the money, the other charged the amount on the book, and indorsed it on the receipt. An account was kept with each student; a page was headed with his name, and he was credited for the amount of money received from him, and debited for the sums paid to him. The pursers also recorded, on the same page, all clothing served out to the students.

It had already been given out that drafts for the excursion to Killarney for three shillings would be paid. Many of the boys thought this was a very small sum, when it was considered that the visit would occupy three days; but all the railway and hotel expenses were to be defrayed by the principal from his own funds, and the allowance to the boys was only to enable them to purchase slight refreshments, and to reward any servant or other person who might assist them as guides or servants.

"Three shillings!" growled Wilton; "when I have fifteen pounds in Lowington's hands. I never was mean yet, and I don't want to begin now."

"Isn't it enough?" asked Shuffles, now the reformed mischief-maker, and disposed to obey all orders and submit to all regulations without complaint.

"No, it isn't! and for one, I won't stand it," replied Wilton.

"What are you going to do?"

"I'm going to draw my order for ten shillings, at least. My father is rich, and don't want me to travel about with only three shillings in my pocket. I shall have to give more than that to the beggars."

"You needn't; a penny is enough to give to a beggar at any time; and they will know you are 'green' if you give them any more," replied Shuffles.

"Ten shillings is little enough, any how."

"I wouldn't grumble, Wilton," added Shuffles, quietly. "You will not need more than three shillings."

"I want more than that in my pocket. I should feel like a beggar myself with no more than three shillings. I'm going to do something, any how. What do you say, Monroe?"

"I say it is downright tyranny and meanness," answered Monroe, who had just paused before the other two boys. "What's three shillings? I spent all I had in Cork, the other day, before we went out to Blarney; and then I felt like one of the ragged urchins that asked me for a 'pinny.'"

As Shuffles was not a hopeful person with whom to talk of any insubordination, the two young gentlemen, who had been prominent members of the Chain League during the voyage, walked forward to consider what could be done to improve their financial prospects.

"I don't think Lowington has any right to keep my money when I want it," said Wilton, as they halted on the forecastle.

"That's plain enough; but if we spend all our money now, we shall have none later in the season; and we haven't begun to see anything yet."

"We can get more. Every fellow on board has written to his folks since we arrived. My father will send me a bill of exchange any time I want more money. I know he would be mad if he knew I was to be put off with three shillings!" replied Wilton, much excited by his grievances.

"If Lowington would give us a pound, or even ten shillings, we could get along very well."

"Do you know why he will give us only sixpence more for three days than he did for one?" asked Wilton.

"Because some of the fellows spent their money for beer in Cork," sneered Monroe.

"Well, if he don't give me more than three shillings, I will spend every penny of it for beer, or wine."

"That would punish you more than him. It gave you the headache before."

"I don't care for that."

"But what are you going to do? It's no use to talk about it."

"I'll tell you what I would do if I only had money enough."

"If!"

"Perhaps I'll have it yet," replied Wilton, suggestively.

"What would you do?"

"I would quit the ship, and travel on my own hook," answered Wilton, in a whisper. "I say, Monroe, wouldn't it be tip-top, if we had the funds, to cruise about without being tied to Lowington's coat tails! We could have a splendid time — couldn't we?"

"I believe you," said Monroe, delighted with the idea. "But what's the use of talking about it? We haven't the money; and if we had, we are tied to the ship."

"How easy it would be for us to slip off when we get to Cork, take the train for Dublin, and hurry up to London!"

"You would certainly be caught. Do you know why Lowington is so particular about our wearing our uniform on shore?"

"So that we may be recognized if we run away?" laughed Wilton. "But couldn't we buy some clothes?"

"Your fifteen pounds wouldn't last long if you had

to purchase a new suit of clothes. Besides, Lowington would telegraph, and send police officers after you."

"I could manage all that if I only had the money; and I mean to have it too," added Wilton, dropping his voice again to a confidential whisper.

"How will you get it?"

"Don't say any more about it now. We will talk the matter over when we are out of hearing. I'm going to give Lowington a chance to do the handsome thing first; if he don't do it, the consequences lie on himself, not on me."

The principal just then appeared to be in danger of something terrible.

"What will you do? Do you mean to get up another Chain?"

"Not I!" exclaimed Wilton, earnestly. "When I am going to do anything, I shall not tell every fellow in the ship, including the flunkies in the after cabin. Let us draw an order on Lowington for ten shillings each."

"You might as well draw it for a hundred pounds. He would pay one as readily as the other," said Monroe.

"Perhaps he would; that's nothing to do with it. If he won't pay it, I shall do the next thing."

"What's that?"

"I shall not mention it at present; but if you want to go up to London with me in a few days, on our own account, I'll help you through."

"To London!"

"Shut up — will you? Do you want to tell every

booby in the ship what we are about? I have given you a hint, and I shall say no more now."

"Are you going to draw the order for ten shillings?" asked Monroe.

"I am; and I would like to have half a dozen fellows do the same."

"I will, for one; and Sanborn and Adler will."

They went down into the steerage, and wrote the orders at one of the tables. Sanborn and Adler were induced, without much persuasion, to join them. Half past seven on Wednesday morning had been appointed for the payment of the orders. Mr. Lowington sat at a small table in the main cabin, and wrote his initials on each draft, before it was presented to the pursers. Wilton was near the head of the column, and behind him were his dissatisfied companions. When he reached the principal's table, he handed in his order.

"Ten shillings!" exclaimed Mr. Lowington.

"If you please, sir," added Wilton, with politic politeness.

"I cannot approve this order. Three shillings was the amount for which you were authorized to draw," said the principal.

"I don't think three shillings is enough, sir."

"Were you one of those who drank beer in Cork the other day?"

"I was, sir."

"If the offence is repeated, your drafts will not be honored again," added Mr. Lowington, as he altered the "ten" in the order to "three."

"I couldn't help it, sir," growled Wilton.

"You couldn't help drinking beer!" exclaimed the principal, looking sternly at the culprit.

"No, sir; I was thirsty, and I couldn't get any water."

"Couldn't you have asked for water instead of beer, in the shop you entered?"

"I didn't like to do that; it looks mean to go into a man's shop and buy nothing."

"You could pay for the trouble you caused, if you are so sensitive. Be that as it may, don't let me hear of your drinking beer again."

Wilton took his order, and passed on to the pursers, from whom he received his three shillings. He was angry, but not much disappointed, for he had hardly expected to have his order for ten shillings paid. The drafts of those who followed him were altered in the same manner. Even the officers in the after cabin were not allowed to draw for more than the stated sum.

"I wish I had the ten shillings I subscribed for that confounded silver pitcher," said Wilton, when he met Monroe after drawing their money.

"So do I. We were fools to make him a present for treating us in this mean and tyrannical manner. A shilling a day for the extra expenses of a gentleman's son!" exclaimed Monroe. "I wish there was some way to get up a breeze."

"There will be a way," added Wilton, mysteriously. "I'm not going to stand this sort of thing. It was well enough when we were at sea, and had no chance to spend money; but the shoe pinches here."

"We paid the ten shillings to get out of the Chain scrape. I suppose we ought not to complain of that," said Monroe.

"But the whole thing came out. Shuffles told the parson all about it."

"He didn't call any names."

"I don't care anything about that now. It is done, and can't be undone. If I can raise the wind, I will take care of myself."

"But you can't," said Monroe.

"But I can," replied Wilton, positively. "There are heaps of money in the main cabin."

"If there are, the fact doesn't concern you."

"Yes, it does; for some of my money is there, and I'm bound to have it, by hook or by crook. How much has Lowington got of yours, Monroe?"

"Fifteen pounds, less what I have drawn — fifteen and sixpence."

"You and I together have enough for a first-rate time," added Wilton.

"How can you get it?"

"Come up on the top-gallant forecastle," said Wilton, leading the way.

"I see you mean to get into some scrape, Wilton," continued Monroe, as they sat down on the bowsprit.

"You needn't get into it, if you don't want to do so. I'm going to make a sure thing of it, this time. Do you know where Lowington keeps the money?"

"In that iron safe, which is set in under the after companion way."

"That's so."

"You don't mean to say you intend to take the money out of the safe?" demanded Monroe, who was not prepared for so bold an expedient.

"What's the reason I don't mean it?"

"You wouldn't do such a thing."

"Yes, I would. Why not? The money is mine I didn't give it up of my own accord. It was taken from me — *stolen* from me!" added Wilton, with emphasis.

"Not stolen; he will give it back to you."

"He had no right to take it; no more right than I have to take his money. It is mine, and if I can get my fingers upon it, I shall take it."

"But you can't get at it."

"Yes, I can."

"It is locked up in the safe."

"I don't care for that. I can get the key. It is in Lowington's state-room; and I think I know just where he keeps it."

"Even if you had the key, you couldn't find a chance to open the safe. There is some one in the cabin all the time."

"How easy it would be for me to hide till they are all gone to-day!"

"You would be missed."

"Well, I could pretend to be sick, or 'cut up,' so that I should be punished by being left on board. As soon as they were all gone, I could get the key, open the safe, take my money, call a shore boat, and be off for Dublin and London."

"Old Peaks is ship-keeper, and he wouldn't let you leave."

"I could manage it somehow, I know. I could get up in the night, and open the safe then. Of course I have got to find out exactly where the key is first."

"I think it is rather risky business."

"Perhaps it is; but when we once get the money and leave the ship, we are all right. It would be easy enough to keep out of the way then."

"I don't know about that; but I don't think your chance of getting off is first-rate. It looks a little like the mutiny."

"Not a bit like it, let me tell you. I believe I can get the money just as easy as I can eat my breakfast when it is ready. Will you go in with me, Monroe?"

"I don't know."

"You don't."

"I shouldn't like to get into any scrape. I don't want to stay in the brig while the fellows are having a good time on shore."

"But just consider what a time we shall have when we get up to London. We can go over to Paris, too."

"I haven't any doubt that we should have a good time, but I don't exactly see how the thing is to be managed."

"I'll find a way to manage it. You leave all that to me, and do just what I tell you, and we shall come out all right, you may depend upon it."

"Lowington can't call it stealing, if we take only our own money," mused Monroe, biting his finger nails.

"Of course he can't. If he does, it don't make any difference — it won't be stealing."

Monroe was tempted by the unlimited freedom which the proposed runaway excursion would afford him; but though not what would be called a conscientious young man, he had some scruples about opening the safe, and he was determined that Wilton should do this part of the business himself. He had already reasoned himself into the belief that it would not be stealing to take his own money, even from the safe of the principal, and after this point had been reached, it was not so difficult for him to agree to the rest of the programme.

"Shall we try it on now?" said Wilton.

"To-day?"

"Yes; we can contrive to be left on board, somehow or other."

"But I want to go up to the Lakes of Killarney. They say the scenery is very fine."

"I don't care anything about the scenery. I've been to the White Mountains, and Lake George. There's nothing in Ireland to be compared with them. There's nothing at Killarney but a one-horse lake," said Wilton, contemptuously.

"The boats are going to be taken up there, and the fellows will have a first-rate time. I want to go."

"What's the use? Here's a capital chance to —"

"There goes the boatswain's whistle piping to muster."

"What do you say?" demanded Wilton, with much excitement. "To-day, or not?"

"Some other time," replied Monroe, as he hastened down the ladder, followed by his companion, who was decidedly in favor of carrying out his rebellious project at once.

He did not wish to go alone, and he was forced to abandon his scheme till another time, for Monroe was fully resolved to make one of the party to the lakes. While all hands were on deck preparing for the departure, he took occasion to visit the steerage, and examine the ground. He opened the door of the main cabin. No person was there, and he ventured to explore the premises. The door of Mr. Lowington's state-room was not locked; he opened it, and took a hasty glance within, but he did not see the key of the safe.

He then passed round to the after end of the cabin to survey the safe itself. To his astonishment, the key was in the door. At that instant he heard a step on the companion ladder. Here was an opportunity which might never occur again. Taking the key from the safe, he fled from the cabin, and succeeded in effecting his retreat before the entrance of the person whose footsteps had alarmed him.

"Wilton! Wilton!" shouted one of the boatswain's mates, at the head of the main scuttle.

"Here!" replied the truant from duty.

"On deck here! We are waiting for you," added the mate.

Wilton rushed into his room for his pea-jacket, and hastened on deck. He had not time to conceal the key, and he put it into his pocket.

"We are waiting for you to take your place in the boat," said Mr. Haven, the first lieutenant, as Wilton appeared in the waist.

"I forgot my pea-jacket, sir, and went down for it," answered the absentee.

"Take your place in the gig. You have kept us all waiting for you."

Wilton went down the accommodation ladder, and took his place at the stroke oar of the gig, which, with the four cutters, was to form the expedition. The gig pulled eight oars; each of the cutters six; and it required thirty-seven boys, including the coxswains, to man the five boats. Each of them carried three officers, and two of the faculty, besides seven or eight of the crew. Mr. Peaks was to go with the party, in order to take charge of the boats, the ship being left in the care of Mr. Bitts, the carpenter.

"Doctor, did you see the key of the safe?" asked Mr. Lowington, as he took his place in the stern sheets of the gig.

"I did not," replied Dr. Winstock.

"I thought I left it in the safe. I opened it to take out some money, and was called away. I suppose I put it away somewhere."

"Doubtless you will find it again," added the doctor.

Wilton did not believe he would find it.

CHAPTER V.

THE LAKES OF KILLARNEY.

WHEN the gig had received her crew and passengers, she pulled away from the ship, and waited till the other boats were ready, for they were to proceed in order as a squadron. The gig was to lead, and the four cutters were to follow, in couples, abreast of each other. New uniforms had been served out to all the boys after the arrival of the ship at Queenstown, and nothing could be neater and nicer than the appearance of the officers and crew in their new clothes.

"All ready in the fourth cutter, sir," reported Johnson, the coxswain of that boat; and she pulled out to her position in the line.

"Give way!" said Captain Gordon, in the gig, when all the boats had reported themselves ready.

The coxswains repeated the order, and the little squadron commenced its voyage up the river. It presented quite an imposing aspect, and attracted the attention of the people on shore and in other boats. Just above the Young America's berth lay two English ships of war, one of them a line-of-battle ship, called the Hastings. As the boat squadron approached her, a barge pulled by fourteen oars, with several officers in her stern sheets, put off from the accommodation ladder. From the flag in her bow it was evident that one of the officers was a rear-admiral — a fact of which Mr. Lowington informed Captain Gordon, that he might order the proper salute.

"Stand by to toss!" said the captain.

"All ready," reported the officers of the boats, passing the word in low tones from one boat to another.

"Toss!" added the captain; and as the order was repeated by the coxswains of the several boats, all the oars were raised to a perpendicular position, with the handles resting on the bottom of the boat, and the blades athwartships. As the admiral's barge passed the squadron, all the officers touched their caps and bowed, and the salute was duly acknowledged by the English officers.

"Let fall!" said the coxswain of the gig, when the barge had passed; and the oars were dropped into the water.

"Give way!" and the crew commenced pulling again.

Half way up to Cork, the oarsmen were relieved, and the other half of the crew pulled the remainder of the distance. The station of "The Great Southern and Western Railway" was near the bank of the river. Arrangements had been made for the transportation of the ship's company and the boats, the latter of which were taken out of the water by an army of porters, and carried to the platform cars, on which they were to be conveyed to Killarney. The boys were locked up in the first and second class compartments, and the train started immediately.

Dr. Winstock, with Paul Kendall and others, was in the coupé of one carriage, the front of which consisted of windows, that enabled them to obtain a fine view of the country through which they passed. Leaving the city, the train entered a very long tunnel cut through the solid rock, and the travellers were involved in darkness, which was only partially relieved by the lamps in the top of the compartments, which were lighted for this emergency. The air in the tunnel was cold and damp, and there was a general closing of the windows to exclude it.

"I don't think these cars are any better than ours," said Paul, as the car emerged from the tunnel. "I have heard a great deal about first class carriages on this side of the water, and that only dukes and lords ever thought of going first class."

"These carriages are rather inferior to those you will see in England, but they are very comfortable."

"They are comfortable enough, but they don't ride so easy as our cars."

"I don't think they do. There is no spring to them. They rest on six wheels, and there is an uncomfortable jar which we don't feel on our cars. But the principal idea is to keep 'first class' people by themselves. With us a millionnaire and a common laborer may sit side by side in a car; here you may be pretty sure of your companions, so far as social position is concerned. There is Blarney Castle, Paul," added the doctor, pointing to the left through the front windows of the coupé.

"I see it, sir; and there is an Irish cabin," added Paul, pointing to a one-story stone house with a thatched roof.

"That is a palace, compared with some you will see on the way to Killarney."

"I should like to go into one."

"Very likely you will have an opportunity before we return."

Paul was much interested in the view from the window, though he did not think Ireland was so fine a country as it had been represented to him by Bridget, and Hannah, and Mike, and Dan, who had lived with his father; but an Irishman may be pardoned for believing that his native land is the finest region in the world, especially if he has seen but a small portion of his adopted country.

"This is the Blackwater," said Dr. Winstock, as the train passed over a stone bridge.

"I've often heard of it; our Mike used to sing, 'Down by Blackwater's side.' It isn't much of a river."

"Here it is not; you must remember that Ireland is but a small country compared with your own, and you must not expect to find very large rivers; but it is quite a stream, and during my former visit to this country, I spent a week upon its bank. I went up in a steamer from Youghal, at its mouth, to Lismore, and I assure you it is a very beautiful river. There are plenty of old castles and ruined abbeys there, each of which has its legends. Strancally Castle, for instance, is a ruin among the rocks, directly over the river. The channel of the river at this place is said to have a fabulous depth, and the water to be reached by a subterranean passage, called 'Murdering Hole,' through which some cruel Irish baron conveyed the bodies of his victims. I didn't see the passage, and I don't believe the story."

"The man that drove our car when we went to Blarney, last week, told me some monstrous stories. If you were to tell them to a dead horse, he would kick your brains out," laughed Paul.

"At Killarney you will hear plenty of 'layginds,' but you can use your own discretion in believing them. During my trip up the Blackwater, I visited Mount Mellary Abbey, which is inhabited by a community of monks, whose austerities of life are hardly equalled in the annals of monastic rule. They subsist exclusively upon a vegetable diet, use no stimulants, not even tea, sleep but five or six hours, work very hard, and maintain perpetual silence."

"Don't they talk at all?"

"Not among themselves. A few, who teach their schools, do the business of the abbey, and receive visitors, must speak, of course. They have reclaimed a vast tract of land near Cappoquin by their labor. Here is Mallow Junction. We change carriages here, I believe."

As the train stopped a short time at this station, most of the boys got out to survey the premises. The railway buildings were plain, but very substantial. There were first class waiting-rooms, and second and third class waiting-rooms, and refreshment saloons, for passengers with the same distinctions of grade, for a first class traveller could not eat his luncheon and drink his coffee with a second class traveller; and when the boys saw the people who occupied the third class accommodations, they were rather grateful for the distinction.

All the waiting-rooms, and the "booking office," were on one side of the double track; but instead of compelling passengers to walk over the rails, to the imminent danger of being run over by an approaching train, there was an elevated bridge, under which the carriages passed, and travellers were forbidden to cross the track except by this bridge.

While they were waiting, the train from Dublin arrived, and the bells rang for the Killarney train to start. Paul and Dr. Winstock fortunately retained their places in the coupé by which they had come from Cork, for some of the carriages were to proceed in that direction.

"Why, this is a single track!" exclaimed Paul, after they had ridden a few miles.

"Yes — why not?" asked the doctor, amused at the earnestness of the young officer.

"Two or three years ago, an English gentleman stopped a few days at my father's. He was constantly running down our railroads, and complaining of single tracks. He said all the railways in the United Kingdom had two tracks."

"He was slightly mistaken, but he was right in the main. This railway is a small affair compared with the one from Dublin to Cork, and there is not much travel upon it. All the principal lines have double tracks in this country. You cannot deny, Paul, that some of our most important railroads have but single tracks, and that hundreds of people have been mercilessly slaughtered by collisions."

Paul could not and did not deny that this was true, and he was forced to confess that the arrangements for the protection of human life, even in what he had seen of Ireland, were vastly superior to those of the United States.

"Here is the bog, Paul," continued Dr. Winstock, as he pointed to the low lands on the right hand side of the road.

"That's the poor man's coal mine," laughed Paul.

"Yes; and outside of the cities it is the only fuel used. In some parts of the United States, peat is used as fuel. There they dig it out from ditches; here, you perceive, they take a slice off the top of the ground, so as to leave the land level behind them. You see the turf spread out to dry, and piled up in heaps."

"Yes, sir; and there are some more Irish cabins. They are mean houses."

"Very poor; you would find but one room in those houses, and in some of them you would see the pig and the cow sharing the quarters with the family; or, at least, all living under the same roof, and that a very small one."

"Isn't it strange they have no fences here?" added Paul, who was comparing the region with what he had seen in Ohio and New England.

"They do have them, but they call them ditches here."

"O, yes! I remember laughing at Mike when he

called a rail fence a ditch, out at my father's country place."

"Precisely so; and the fences here are ditches. There is one," said the doctor, pointing to a field. "They dig a trench, and throw all the earth on one side, rounding it into shape, as soldiers do when they construct earthworks. Sometimes they plant a hedge on the top of the embankment."

"I should think a cow would walk right over it."

"As a general thing, they form a sufficient barrier to prevent the passage of animals from one field to another; if not, the hedge is entirely effectual."

"How many times have I seen that sign since we left Cork!" said Paul, as they passed one of the frequent notices — "All persons trespassing on these grounds will be prosecuted to the extent of the law," or something of similar import.

"People here are not allowed to enter other people's estates without permission. Land owners or tenants are more exclusive in their ideas than in America. Shooting and fishing are not allowed, as they are with us. The privilege of hunting and catching the fish in the streams is bought and sold. In some places a license may be obtained for shooting or fishing upon payment of a fixed sum; in others, the right is held by noblemen and gentlemen exclusively for themselves and their guests."

"I read that there were plenty of salmon in the rivers in this part of Ireland," added Paul.

"They are taken in great abundance; but no one can catch a fish without a license."

"I think it is a hard case, if a fellow can't go a

fishing without asking some two-and-sixpenny lord or baron," said Paul, contemptuously.

"The custom is certainly very different from our own; but I can see no reason why the owner of a piece of land should be compelled to permit all the loafers and vagabonds of his neighborhood to hunt and fish upon his grounds."

"Kanturk!" said the guard — so the conductor of the train was called — as the carriage stopped.

"Kanturk — what a name!" exclaimed Paul.

"It was formerly spelled K-e-a-n-t-u-i-r-k, 'Keantuirk,' meaning a boar's head. I suppose some great Irish chieftain killed one of these animals here, some time or other, and the act gave a name to the place. The ruins of an unfinished castle may be seen about four miles off. It was commenced by M'Donough Carthy, in the time of Queen Elizabeth; but as the English oppressors of the country thought it might be dangerous to Albion's rule, the builder was forbidden to continue the work."

"Millstreet," said the guard, half an hour later.

"Milk Street!" exclaimed Paul.

"No; Millstreet. Near it is Drishane Castle, built by another of the McCarthys, and forfeited in one of the revolutions of which Professor Mapps told you."

"What a capital way they have to manage their passengers here!" said Paul. "They don't let people into the station unless they are going by the train."

"It is a good plan. The government manages the railroad companies better than it does the people."

"There are mountains," added Paul, after the train had started.

"Small ones; that pair nearest to us are called The Paps. Behind it, farther off, are the Muskerry Mountains, and those as far as you can see are McGillicuddy's Reeks, the highest in Ireland."

At three o'clock in the afternoon the train was approaching Killarney, and the boys were all on the lookout for the lakes; though nothing could be seen but the mountains in the distance.

"There are plenty of hotels in Killarney," said Paul. "Do you know at which one we stop, doctor?"

"At the Railway Hotel."

"That is not near the lake," said Mr. Fluxion, who was in the same compartment.

"No; it is about a mile and a half from the lower lake: but I think it is the best hotel."

"I stopped at the Royal Victoria when I was here," added Mr. Fluxion.

"Perhaps I should have gone there, if an incident had not occurred to prevent me from doing so."

"What was that?"

"I intended to stop at the Lake Hotel, which is the only one on the border of the lake. I was on the point of getting into the omnibus which runs to that hotel, when the driver told me the house was full. Just then a runner for the Royal Victoria hailed me; his manner did not suit me, and I told the porter to put my trunk in the car for the Railway. 'The Royal Victoria, patronized by the nobility and gentry, and the best in the place,' said the runner. 'Railway,' I answered, firmly. 'You are a fool!' added the bully runner. I looked at him sternly.

"'Pon my word, you are a fool; and you'll find it so,' repeated the ruffian. I couldn't go to a hotel where they employed such blackguards as he was; and I shall do my best to keep my friends from going there. I found the Railway Hotel to be an excellent establishment, and for that reason Mr. Lowington is going there."

"It's a very good reason," replied Mr. Fluxion.

"That was the only instance of incivility in an employee of a hotel in Europe that has come to my knowledge."

The train stopped, and the boys hastened to get out of the carriages.

"Lake Hotel," shouted a porter.

"Royal Victoria!" said a tall, dark-visaged fellow. "Royal Victoria, sir?" addressing Dr. Winstock.

"No; you gave me Royal Victoria enough the last time I was here," replied the doctor, curtly.

"I beg your pardon, sir; but what do ye mane be that?"

"You called me a fool the last time I was here; and for that reason this party, about a hundred in number, will stop at the Railway Hotel."

"'Pon me sowl, you were a fool, thin. I say it again; you are a fool!" added the runner, angrily.

"See here, my hearty," interposed Boatswain Peaks, as he took the ruffian by the collar. "I don't allow any man to speak like that to the doctor."

"Take your hand off," said the runner, his Irish blood stirred by the incident. "Take your hand off, or I'll black yer two eyes."

Peaks twirled the fellow round, and pitched him

towards the door of the station-house. He sprang forward, and if a couple of the constabulary had not interfered, there would doubtless have been a fight.

Mr. Lowington reproved the boatswain for touching the bully, whom the constables threatened to arrest if he did not instantly leave the station-house. There was no need of omnibuses for the party, for the Railway Hotel was but a few rods from the depot. Each student had a small bag, containing his night shirt, his comb and brushes, and other small articles; but the crew of the Young America carried but little luggage. As the boys approached the hotel, they were astonished at the elegant grounds, adorned with beautiful gardens around it, while the building itself was large and imposing. An arrangement had been made with the landlord by letter for the accommodation of the ship's company; and the large numbers, so early in the season, did not produce a panic. Extra beds had been put up for the boys.

Before entering the hotel, the boatswain's whistle piped the boys into line, and the beggars and tatterdemalions of Killarney began to gather to witness the unwonted sight; but they were driven from the yard by a small squad of the constabulary, who had been summoned to the premises for the protection of the party. The lines filed into the hotel, and up stairs, where the rooms where assigned to the students. A lunch was ready in the coffee-room for them, of which they partook, and then went out to see the town. It was a dirty place, filled with beggars, runners, — often called "touters" in the United Kingdom, — and vagabonds anxious to serve as guides.

The streets in the lower part of the town were densely packed with small Irish hovels, and the Celtic language was heard on every hand. It is said that a considerable portion of the people of the County of Kerry speak only the Irish language. The houses were dirty, and the men, women, and children were filthy, to a degree which the students had never seen even at the Five Points in New York. The men wore knee breeches and iron-bound brogans — just as they are sometimes seen emerging from emigrant ships in America. As the students walked through this part of the town, they were assailed by beggars on every side, and were compelled, in self-defence, to retreat. The business streets of the place were more respectable, but it was impossible to escape the mendicants.

Continuing the walk a little farther, they came to the grounds of the Kenmare estates, and from filth, poverty, and wretchedness they were transported by a vision of loveliness, for nothing could be more attractive than the domain of this nobleman. The earl has an income of seventy thousand pounds a year, or three hundred and fifty thousand dollars. His tenants and his laborers live in the most abject poverty, the latter receiving from five to seven shillings a week for their services. Truly the contrasts of wealth and poverty are tremendous in this nobility-ridden land. More than one of the students, as they gazed upon the miserable Irish hovel, and then at the magnificent grounds around Kenmare House, thanked God that they were not born in Ireland.

"It's a fine country to emigrate from," said Pelham, as his party returned to the hotel.

"What are those large buildings, doctor?" asked Paul, as they stood on the front steps of the Railway.

"One is a poorhouse, and the other an Insane Asylum. That large establishment," continued Dr. Winstock, "is called the Union Workhouse, and contains about four hundred paupers. Such establishments are styled simply 'Unions.'"

"When shall we go to the lakes? We haven't even seen them yet."

"To-morrow morning. It is dinner-time now," replied the doctor.

Many of the hotels at watering-places, like Killarney, have a *table d'hôte*, though such an institution is almost unknown in the cities of the United Kingdom. At the Railway, the hour was half past six; and though Dr. Winstock objected to a hearty dinner at this time in the day, he was obliged to submit. "Mine host" followed the French fashion. He not only called his soup "potage," his fish "poisson," and his salmon "saumon," but every guest was obliged to eat by programme. After soup and fish, every dish on the bill of fare was passed to each diner, and it was half past seven before the boys could "see the thing through." They were tolerably patient, however, for the food was a change from that to which they had been accustomed on board of the ship. At an early hour the party retired, sleeping on shore for the first time since they left their native land.

They were tired enough to sleep without rocking. The boys were permitted to turn out in the morning at their own pleasure, and before sunrise some of them were exploring the neighborhood, while others slept till seven o'clock, wearing away the fatigues of the preceding day. Breakfast at an English or Irish hotel is a very different affair from the same meal in the United States. Hot biscuit, buckwheat cakes, corn bread, and the varieties of fish, flesh, and fowl, cooked in every conceivable style, as in the large hotels of our own country, are not known. A plain breakfast consists of tea, or coffee, and bread and butter, to which the guest may add a chop, steak, or eggs, by paying an extra price. On a side-table in the coffee-room are usually arranged a few cold dishes — a boiled ham, a leg of mutton, a fowl, and pasties. The visitor generally goes to this table himself, and cuts out such as he wants.

Mr. Lowington, feeling that the students needed something more substantial than bread and butter, had made a special arrangement with the landlord, and the party were supplied with chops, steaks, and boiled eggs without limit, to fit them for the heavy work of the day.

At eight o'clock the crew were piped in front of the hotel, and the plans for the day were announced. The excursion was to include a trip through the three lakes in the boats, and a walk of four Irish miles through the Gap of Dunloe. There were ninety-six persons in the party, besides Boatswain Peaks, and they were divided into two equal companies, one of which was to proceed in cars to the Gap, and the other in the boats to the vicinity of Lord Brandon's cottage, at the head of the upper lake, where the two parties were to meet and have a lunch at about twelve o'clock. At this point, those who had come round through the Gap were to take the boats, and return by the lakes, while the others were to proceed through the Gap by the same route the first had taken, riding home in the cars, which were to wait for them at Kate Kearney's Cottage.

By this plan both parties would have an opportunity to explore the three lakes, and observe all the objects of interest in the Gap. The day was bright and clear, and the boys anticipated a splendid time; for not a few of them had consulted the guide-books, and obtained some idea of the scenes they were to visit.

Dr. Winstock and Mr. Fluxion had both been the round of the Gap and the Lakes, and knew the place and the people. The surgeon suggested to Mr. Lowington that, as the boatmen on the lakes were deprived of a job by the bringing of the gig and cutters, they might make trouble. The principal consulted the landlord on this subject, and paid him a handsome fee for the boatmen of the Railway Hotel, who alone had any claim upon the party; and "mine host" promised that his employees should not disturb him, either by threats or solicitations. Doubtless he kept his word, but the trouble came from another quarter.

CHAPTER VI.

THE GAP OF DUNLOE.

TWELVE cars were drawn up near the hotel for the use of the shore party, and the young tars, in the highest of spirits, leaped into their places. The principal and the surgeon had seats in the cars, while Mr. Fluxion and several of the professors went with the lake company. Dr. Winstock contrived to have Paul Kendall, who was a prime favorite with him, at his side in the forward car, while Mr. Lowington, the better to overlook his charge, occupied a place in the rear vehicle.

The procession passed through the principal street of the town, in which its appearance excited the curiosity of the people, and roused the beggars from their transient lethargy. But no notice was taken of the vagrants, and passing the magnificent Catholic Cathedral, and the spacious workhouse, or Union, the tourists obtained their first view of the lower lake, which is called Lough Leane. There was certainly nothing very remarkable about it, though it was a very pretty sheet of water.

" I don't think that is much," said Paul.

" It is all low land down here, and you see none of the beauties of the lakes. Wait till you reach the upper lake, and I am sure you will be satisfied," replied the doctor.

"I am quite interested in the sights on shore. It seems to me, Dr. Winstock, that the Unions in Ireland are bigger than the palaces."

"The mystery to me is, that they are no larger; for I should think all the laboring people would sooner or later need a home in the almshouse. Most of these people work for about five shillings, or a dollar and a quarter a week — men with families; and though the pig may pay the "rint," and the cow feed the babies, there seems to be but little left to pay the other expenses of the family. If they can get a poor piece of meat on Sunday, they are lucky. There are the ruins of Aghadoe Church, Paul," continued the doctor, pointing to the top of a hill.

The party stopped for a few minutes to explore the ruins of the church and castle, which had probably been the residence of a bishop, though nothing authentic was known in regard to them. The boys were not much interested in the ruins or the antiquities of the place; and though Professor Mapps gave a learned disquisition on history, his hearers were rather impatient under it.

The ride of eight miles, however, through the country was full of interest. They had an opportunity to see the country residences of some of the gentry, as well as the hovels of the poor. Occasionally, as they passed one of the latter, a woman, or a squad of boys and girls, would start out from their dens, and charge upon the cars, begging for a "pinny," with the usual tale of a sick father, a dead mother, or starving children. In one instance a woman ran after the cars for more than half a mile, trying to present to any of the party a bunch of heather flowers. At last Mr. Lowington gave her a couple of pennies, which she picked up, but still pursued the car, insisting that he should take the bouquet, which he did, and she returned panting to her cabin.

When the procession reached a cross-road within a mile or two of the Gap, a small regiment of guides, mounted on ponies, as they called them, — though most of the animals were full-sized horses, — besieged the party.

"Have a pony, your honor, to ride through the Gap," said one to the doctor.

"We shall walk through," replied the surgeon.

"Bedad, your honor, it is foor Irish miles through the Gap, and your honor could niver shtand it. Ye shall have the harse, and meself will go wid yees, and pint out all saynery, for six shillings."

"No; we prefer to walk."

"It's a lahng walk; and your honor could niver shtand it."

"I'll try."

"Take the harse for five shillings, your honor."

"I don't want him."

"Sure, the young gintlemin will faint wid the walk."

"They can stand it, I think," laughed the doctor.

"Bedad, your honor shall take the harse for foor shillings," added the persistent fellow, in a confidential whisper.

"No; I don't want him at any price. Go on, driver; don't stop here any longer," said the doctor to his Jehu, who was disposed to favor the applicants.

While this "solitary horseman" blarneyed on one side of the car there were two more on the opposite side, and each of the vehicles was beset by from two to four of the guides. They were all alike unsuccessful, for Mr. Lowington's plan did not admit of their being employed, as he was unwilling to trust the boys on horseback. The line went forward again, but the importunate guides were not to be got rid of so easily. They pursued the cars, galloping their horses from one to another, so eager that they seemed to be in great danger of overriding each other. Prices went down to two shillings, without any effect, and the assailants were not shaken off till they were very near the Gap.

"God bless your honor, but I'm a poor widdy woman, with siven shmall childrin, and niver a bit for 'em t' ate," shouted a ragged woman, as she rushed up to the car in which Dr. Winstock was seated. "Give me a pinny, your honor, for I live in the Irish Castle, — there it is beyant;" and she pointed to a miserable, dilapidated shanty, not more than four feet high, and hardly more in length or breadth, and looking like a very mean pig-sty.

"The Irish Castle!" replied the doctor. "That's a very good joke, and the laborer is worthy of her hire."

He gave her a penny, and Paul gave her another.

"Thank yer honor," cried she, picking up the money. "Take me posy," she added, presenting a bunch of heather flowers to Paul, "to remimber the lady of the Irish Castle by."

At the side of the car was a boy of fifteen, who had run there for the preceding mile, begging a job to guide the gentlemen through the Gap, to point out the "saynery," and tell all the "layginds." His perseverance at last won the doctor, and he was engaged. His name was Dan Hartnett; he was barefoot, and his clothes hardly covered his body; but he was full of Irish wit and vivacity.

"Beyant ye see Kate Kearney's Cottage," said the driver, pointing to a one-story house, much superior to the ordinary buildings of the poor. At this place the boys all got out, and were presently assailed by dealers in bog wood and arbutus ornaments, combs, paper-cutters, and similar articles, and by women with merchandise of more doubtful utility.

"Have a shmall sup of mountain dew wid goatsh milkye?" said a woman to Paul Kendall, as he jumped down from his seat.

This woman, Dan told him, was the granddaughter of the veritable Kate Kearney, the heroine of the Irish song: —

> "Did you ever hear of Kate Kearney,
> Who lives by the Lakes of Killarney?"

Probably the original Kate was a myth, and her pretended descendant used the name as an inducement for people to trade with her.

"Mountain dew!" replied Paul. "What's that?"

"The poteen, to be sure," added the representative of Kate Kearney.

"What's poteen?" asked Paul.

"Sure, don't you know what poteen is!" laughed the woman. "Isn't it whishkey?"

"Then I don't want any," answered Paul, decidedly.

"Whishkey and goatsh milkye is an iligant dhrinkye for a young gentleman wid such foine clothes," she continued, glancing at Paul's brilliant uniform.

"No whiskey for me."

"It's very loight and noice," interposed Dan, who evidently wanted a sup himself.

"I don't want any."

Mr. Lowington soon found out what the suspicious bottles contained, even without any information from the surgeon, though it is quite possible that a few of the boys tasted the intoxicating beverage. The principal directed Dr. Winstock to proceed, and sternly ordered the students to take their places in the cars. After riding about half a mile more, the procession halted, for vehicles could go no farther. At this point the scenery was becoming wild and picturesque. It was now about ten o'clock in the forenoon, and the carmen were directed to wait at this point for the other party. The students in the cars had endeavored to obtain some information from these men in regard to objects of interest on the route, but it was impossible to understand half they said on account of the "rich brogue" they used.

The driver of Paul's car was full of fun, and anxious to tell all he knew, which was not much. Like all his class, he seemed to be studying out some way to make an extra sixpence or shilling. When another car approached, the driver invariably hailed him in a loud tone.

"How are you, Patsey? I see you are in for a grah-too-ity!" was the usual cry; at any rate, the "gratuity" was always rung in, apparently for the purpose of reminding his passengers that an extra shilling was expected of them.

In the passage through the Gap it was arranged that Dr. Winstock should lead the way, and the principal bring up the rear. The boys were not to be confined to any particular order of march, and the line was to move very slowly and rest frequently. Before the party started, Professor Mapps collected them under the shadow of an overhanging rock, and proceeded to give them a lesson in physical geography, which included a description of the Gap of Dunloe.

It is a wild and narrow mountain pass, between McGillicuddy's Reeks on the one side, and Tomies and Purple Mountains on the other. It is about four miles in length, and bounded on each hand by the high mountain sides, which in some parts are perpendicular steeps. Through the Gap runs the River Loe, a small but rapid stream, which in different places expands into five sheets of water, called together the *Cummeen Thomeen* lakes, each of which has its individual name.

"Before us is the Cosaun Lough," said the professor, as the procession moved up the Gap.

"It's nothing but a puddle," laughed Paul.

"Lakes are on a small scale in Ireland," replied the doctor.

"A shilling for the poother, your honor, and we'll fire two shots till ye hear the aycho," shouted a man, rushing excitedly up to the surgeon, who was in the van.

"Fire away!" replied Dr. Winstock.

The man, with another, had a couple of small iron cannons, about a foot in length, which they discharged when their fee was insured. The effect was really sublime, and from the lofty crags came back the echoes of the gun, repeated several times. The boys were delighted with this exhibition of the reverberating peculiarity of the pass and two more shots were fired to satisfy them.

At Kate Kearney's Cottage a bugler had been engaged to enable the party to listen to the echoes of his strains. Several musicians of this kind find employment in awaking the echoes of this wild region for the gratification of tourists. He blew a long blast on his instrument, which was five or six times repeated by reverberation in different places, the first time nearly as loud and clear as the original sound; then less distinctly, till the last, which was very faint.

As Paul and Dr. Winstock tramped cheerfully along the path at the head of the line, Dan told them the "layginds," and pointed out the famous places. Now he called their attention to the Eagle's Nest, a high cliff, at the top of which lived the majestic bird; and then he pointed down into the lake, where some saint had imprisoned some demon. He was full of improbable stories.

Beyond the first lake they crossed a stone bridge, beneath which the waters of the stream madly dashed, and came in sight of Black Lake.

"Forninst that lake, your honor, St. Patrick put down the lasht shnake in Ireland," said Dan.

"Is the snake there now?" asked Paul.

"Av coorse he is."

From the bridge they saw a couple of the constabulary on the path at the side of the lake. Just ahead of the party were two girls, who had kept near the tourists since they left the cars. Each of them had a bottle of "mountain dew," and another of goat's milk. Dan claimed that one of them, a pretty, brisk, and witty girl, full of fun and nonsense, was the "colleen bawn;" but doubtless a dozen of them took the same name for interested purposes. She made a great many vain efforts to sell her "poteen," but without success. Then she proposed to give a sixpence for a shilling, and finally offered her photograph, labelled "Black-eyed Bridget," for sale. Paul bought one, and still keeps it in remembrance of the Gap of Dunloe.

"Whisht now, Bridget," said Dan to the wild girl. "Beyant is the conshtables."

She gave a timid glance in the direction of the lake, and seeing that the officers were approaching, she and her companion fled up the steep mountain side, and disappeared among the rocks and shrubs.

"What does that mean?" asked Paul.

"The conshtables beyant are lookin for the gurdls that sills the poteen. It is agin the law to sill widout a license, and sorra bit of a license these gurdls has."

As the party paused on the bridge, the officers joined them. They were very civil men, intelligent, and dignified in their bearing. Dr. Winstock said something about the excise law, and one of them explained the nature of their duties in the pass, and some of the tricks to which the girls resort to escape detection.

He thought Dan could give them valuable information, if he was so disposed; but the guide stoutly protested that he knew nothing about their business.

On the bank of the Black Lake was a blind fiddler, who, at the approach of the party, struck up " Yankee Doodle." He was attended by his wife, who gave him his clew to the nationality of the tourists; and the peasantry are remarkably shrewd in detecting an American, wherever they find him. The blind man played and sang, and the echoes of his song were clearly returned from the cliffs on the other side of the water. The bugler played Kate Kearney, and it seemed as though his double was on the other side of the lake playing the same air. Then Dan Hartnett did something to bring out the echoes.

"How are you, Paddy?" shouted he.

"— are you, Paddy?" responded the echo.

"You ould rogue!"

"— ould rogue!"

"You're a dirty blackguard!"

"— dirty blackguard!"

"You always will have the lasht wurrud."

"— the lasht wurrud."

"That's a very fine echo, but not so wonderful as one I have heard of somewhere in Ireland," said Dr. Winstock.

"What was that, sir?" asked Paul.

"'How are ye, Misther Echo?' calls Paddy."

"'Moighty well, I thank ye: how are ye yourself, Paddy?' replies the echo."

"That was certainly a very wonderful one, and there seem to be none of that kind in the Gap of Dunloe," laughed Paul.

Having passed the constables, the party were again joined by the girls with the whiskey and goat's milk. They seemed to be so much pleased with the appearance of the young gentlemen in their fine uniforms, that they were unwilling to leave them, and they hovered on the flanks of the line till they reached the upper lake; but they did not sell any " mountain dew," though they disposed of a few photographs, and perhaps received the free gift of a few pennies from some of the young tars, who from their small store of three shillings could not afford to buy the pictures.

The scenery of the Gap was sufficiently attractive to gain and keep the attention of the boys. At one place the bugler played a tune, and at another the cannon men fired their guns, and demanded payment for the " poother." From one end of the pass to the other, there were men, women, and children using their utmost efforts to obtain a penny, a sixpence, or a shilling, but only a few of them were successful. At the appointed time the procession halted at a romantic spot on the upper lake, where the boat party had already arrived. As the two divisions of the ship's company discovered each other, they gave three rousing cheers. The boys mingled together, and began to tell their adventures. Dan received two shillings from Dr. Winstock, and was cordially recommended to Mr. Agneau, the chaplain, who had come up in the gig.

The lunch which had been provided by the landlord of the hotel, and sent up by the fleet, was now served out to the boys; but Mr. Lowington found that some one had made a blunder, and sent ale for the party to drink. The principal would not permit it to be touched by the boys, and the bottles were given to guides, boatmen, and other natives who thronged the spot.

"I suppose we shall have a better time the rest of the way than we had coming up the lakes," said Wilton, as he seated himself on the grass with a sandwich in his hand.

"I had a good time in the pass," replied Pelham, the fourth lieutenant, who sat near him.

"You are an officer, and won't have to row," added Wilton: "a twelve mile pull is no joke."

"You took it easy all the way."

"I suppose we did."

"What's that?" suddenly demanded Pelham, as Wilton, while in the act of stretching himself on the grass, dropped the key of the safe from his pocket.

Wilton quickly picked it up, and thrust it back into his pocket, and was covered with confusion at the accident.

"What key is that?" demanded Pelham, in a low tone, so that none but Wilton could hear him.

"It's an old thing I had to make a cannon with. I am going to use it for a whistle in the Gap. They say the echoes there are a big thing. Do you know anything about them?" replied Wilton, as indifferently as he could.

"Where did you get that key?" repeated Pelham.

"O, it's an old thing I had. They say there's going to be a row down below, Mr. Pelham. Have you heard anything about it?"

"There's going to be a row on board the ship, when you return, about that key. Do you think I'm a baby, that you can cheat me like that? Why don't you tell me where you got that key?"

"I brought it with me from home."

"Perhaps you did — you can tell that to the marines."

"I did — honor bright."

"It's a safe key."

"I don't know — is it?"

"Let me see it."

"I don't want to show it here, where somebody will see it, and be suspicious, as you were. It's all right, but I don't like to be accused of anything I know nothing about."

"I suppose not," sneered Pelham. "If I mistake not, I heard Mr. Lowington asking the doctor if he had seen the safe key, just before we left the ship. I think you can give him some information, and perhaps you would like to have me introduce you to him."

"This key has nothing to do with him."

"Let me see it."

"Not here. I will show it to you when we are alone."

"Wilton, you are up to something," continued the fourth lieutenant, shutting one eye, and gazing at the culprit through one corner of the other.

"I've got an idea," added Wilton, laughing; for, finding the officer was not disposed to be severe, or virtuous, like Paul Kendall, he had by this time concluded that it would be best for him to take Pelham into his confidence.

The fourth lieutenant had been a prominent member of the Chain League, and Wilton knew that he was not satisfied with the result of that enterprise. Though

Pelham had barely escaped being drowned in the winding up of the conspiracy, that event seemed to have made no particular impression upon his mind. In a word, Wilton felt that the lieutenant was one of " our fellows," and if he did not conclude to join the new enterprise, he would not expose him.

" What's the idea?" demanded Pelham, curiously.

" Have you finished your lunch, sir? If you have, we will walk up here a little way, where others can't hear us, and I will tell you something about it."

" Come along," said Pelham, rising and walking away, with Wilton at his side. " Now, what's the idea — talk fast, for you will start soon on your tramp."

" I don't know what you think about it, Mr. Pelham, but some of the fellows believe we are not treated just right," Wilton began.

" What's the matter now?"

" About the money, I mean. You didn't think Lowington had any right to take our money away from us when we were on the passage; but it seems to me the shoe pinches worse now than it did then."

" Go on, go on!" interposed Pelham, impatiently. " Don't spin a yarn, but tell me squarely what you are up to."

" About the money, I mean; to give us three shillings to spend in three days! My father gave me fifteen pounds, and he didn't mean I should go about like a beggar."

" Well, officers are treated no better than seamen, so far as money is concerned."

" I'm going to have my money, and spend it as I

want it. When it is all gone, my father will give me as much more as I ask for."

"You mean that you have the key of Mr. Lowington's safe in your pocket, and you intend to help yourself," added Pelham.

"That's just what I mean. Of course I'm not going to take anything that don't belong to me, but I'm bound to have what does belong to me. If you would like your own money, you have only to tell me so, and you shall have it."

"The money will be missed, and the fellows will be searched."

"We are going in for a good time on our own account, when we get the funds."

"Who are 'we'?"

"Ike Monroe and I. You and he are the only fellows that know anything about it. You won't let on — will you?"

"Of course not," replied Pelham, promptly; and the answer was very encouraging to Wilton. "What are you going to do?"

"We are going to have a good time. We are going to leave the ship just as soon as we get the money, and before Lowington has a chance to look for it."

"What then?" asked Pelham, excitedly; for the scheme seemed to commend itself to him.

"We shall take the train for Dublin, and if we can't get off at Cork, we shall leave when the ship gets to Dublin, and then go to London. We shall have a jolly time, you had better believe. What do you say to it?"

"How many fellows know about it, did you say?"

"You are only the third one."

"Don't mention it to another one."

"You will be one of the party then?"

"I will, perhaps, if the thing is well managed. I don't mean to be caught and be brought back to the ship in disgrace. If I get away from her, I shall never come back. I agree with you, Wilton, about the money. I never felt so much like a beggar as I have since we came on this excursion. I have never been satisfied with the conduct of the principal in taking our funds from us. I think I will go with you, but I want to know more about it before I go in."

"Party for the Gap, form in the path," said Mr. Fluxion, and the conference for the present was ended; but Wilton felt that it was a lucky accident which had enabled the fourth lieutenant to discover the key of the safe.

CHAPTER VII.

THE BOATMEN OF KILLARNEY.

THOUGH it was early in the season when the ship's company of the Young America made the tour of the Gap and the lakes, there was a considerable number of tourists present. Each of the principal hotels has from six to twelve boats, and employs from twenty to thirty oarsmen for the accommodation of their guests. The boats are very good ones, built like a ship's long-boat. They are well painted, and kept neat and dry. In the bow each carries the British flag, with the name of the hotel to which the craft belongs upon it. The rowers, though they are of the lowest class of the Irish peasantry, are stalwart fellows, well trained at the oars, and are neatly dressed in white frocks, with hats bearing the name of the hotel in gilt upon them. Like all the common people, the study of their waking hours is to make an extra shilling or sixpence, and they do not let their passengers escape without many very broad hints, and often direct appeals for the " gratuity." They are paid by the hotels, whose proprietors discountenance any begging of this kind.

The landlords of the hotels usually make the arrangements for their own guests, providing the cars, boats, and lunches for the trip, and charging the items in the bill of the tourist. The rates are certainly reasonable, especially as a single car and a single boat accommodates three or four persons, among whom the expense is divided. It is usual for visitors to club together, not only to reduce the charges, but for the sake of each other's company.

One of three persons paid, in 1865, as his proportion of the expenses of the excursion we have described, for the car, three shillings and fourpence; for the boat, pulled by two men twenty-four miles, occupying the whole day, two shillings and sixpence; for the lunch, two shillings; and for fees to guides, &c., two shillings and sixpence; making the total expense to each person ten shillings and fourpence, or about two dollars and a half.

With these boats the Young America party had nothing to do; but they saw several of them at the head of the upper lake. There was one from the Royal Victoria, with a party of ladies and gentlemen. As the students embarked in the gig and cutters, the oarsmen of this boat made some remarks which evinced ill feeling, and which attracted the attention of Dr. Winstock. He knew that these men were very tenacious of their privileges as the boatmen of the lakes. He told Paul that when he was going down the lakes in his former visit, he had expressed his surprise that no steamer was employed. "Arrah, we'd breakye her," said one of his rowers.

The gig, with Dr. Winstock and Paul in the stern,

and a bugler and pilot in the fore sheets, was to lead in the passage down, and the cutters were to follow in single line. While the Royal Victoria boatmen were still growling, the gig put off from the shore, and the eight juvenile oarsmen, the regular crew of the boat, pulled the even man-of-war stroke, which called forth many expressions of admiration from the ladies and gentlemen on shore, who waved their handkerchiefs gayly to the young tars.

"This is magnificent!" exclaimed Paul, with enthusiasm, as the boat receded from the shore, and enabled him to obtain a full view of the beautiful lake.

"This is the finest scenery we shall see," replied the doctor.

The upper lake is about two and a half miles in length by three quarters of a mile in breadth. It contains twelve islands, varying in size from a square rod to an acre. From the shores of the lake, in many parts, the mountains rise abruptly from the water's edge, and the forest reaches to its very brink.

"Eagle Island on the right," said the pilot; and he began to repeat the legend of the place; for there is not a cliff nor a corner in the vicinity which has not its story.

"And this is Arbutus Island on the left;" and that had its story; but it derived its chief interest from the shrub which gave it a name.

The bugler blew a blast at the points which were noted for their echoes, and the effect was very pleasing. There seemed to be no opening at the lower end of the lake, and the tourists wondered where they were to find a passage for the boats.

"When the Marquis of Watherford was here, I wagered a bottle of whishkey with him that he could not tell where the opening was," said the pilot, who had now come aft and taken his place at the tiller ropes of the gig. "I won the wager, and his lordship paid it."

"I don't see any opening," said Paul.

"There it is beyant," added the pilot.

"I don't see it."

"That ye can't," laughed the pilot; "but its betune the rocks forninst the hill beyant. I'll wager your honor a bottle of whishkey ye can't till betune which rocks we go."

"I shall neither give nor take any whiskey," replied Paul. "But I think the passage is between the first and second rocks."

"You see."

The gig passed the place indicated, and then, turning half round, entered an opening some distance beyond the place Paul had indicated.

"Your honor has lost the wager!" exclaimed the pilot.

"I didn't make any wager. I never bet," said Paul, rather indignantly.

"Niver mind," added the man.

"We settle it now," interposed Dr. Winstock, who realized that the fellow meant to claim the wager when he had a better opportunity. "There used to be an association among the boatmen here for mutual assistance."

"There is now, your honor. We have a ball in the boat-house to-morrow night."

"Here is four shillings for the society funds," added the doctor, handing the pilot the money. "The young gentleman does not bet, and has nothing to do with whiskey."

"Thank your honor." But it was evident that the man was not satisfied with this settlement, especially as the surgeon said he should inform the other boatmen of his little gift, in order that the money might not be expended for whiskey.

The gig, followed by the cutters, each of which was provided with a guide, passed Colman's Eye, and entered the Long Range, which is a river, several miles in length, connecting the upper with the middle lake. The channel was narrow, and the view on each side was pleasant, and sometimes approached the sublime. There was a considerable current in the river, and the oarsmen were required to pull just enough to give the boats steerage way. It was evident that the rowers down the lakes had a much easier time than those who ascended the river.

"Man-of-war Rock," said the pilot, pointing to a mass of stone which bore a very remote resemblance to the object indicated by its name. "The Four Friends," he added, half an hour later, as the boats passed four small islands. "Beyant is the Eagle's Nest; we'll shtop here, and try the echoes."

The Eagle's Nest was a rugged and precipitous mass of rock, rising seven hundred feet above the river, full of crevices, in which the eagle builds his nest. The pilot told the story of a man who, in attempting to rob the nest of one of these majestic birds, fell from the cliff, and " broke every bone in his body." The bugler played a strain upon his instrument, and the echo was more remarkable than any the tourists had yet heard. The call was repeated at least a dozen times, reporting back from mountain to mountain, and from cliff to cliff, sometimes loud, next fainter and fainter, and then, after a pause, louder again, and finally dying away almost insensibly. At one time the return notes would come back considerably modified, and then the original strain would be exactly repeated. The experiment was continued until the boys were satisfied, and then the boats proceeded on their way, stopping at a point near Miss Plummer's Island, where the inevitable whiskey and goat's milk bottles were offered to the travellers.

"Now, we're comin to O'Sullivan's Punch Bowl, and here is the Meeting of the Wathers," added the pilot.

" The Meeting of the Waters!" shouted Paul, springing to his feet.

> "'There's not in the wide world a valley so sweet,
> As that vale in whose bosom the bright waters meet;
> O, the last rays of feeling'" —

" Hold on, Paul!" exclaimed Dr. Winstock, laughing. "This isn't the place, and you may spare your enthusiasm."

"Not the place! Isn't this the 'Meeting of the Waters' that Moore sang about?"

"No; that is in the County of Wicklow, on the

east coast, where the Avon and Avoca Rivers unite. I have been there; and though it is a very pretty spot, I don't think it compares with this."

"Now, my lads, mind your oars. The wather runs very shwift here. Let 'em hang and dhrag at the side of the boat," said the pilot, as the gig approached the Old Weir Bridge, under which, and for some distance beyond it, there was a pretty smart rapid.

"Stand by to trail!" shouted Raymond, the coxswain of the gig, who sat by the pilot's side; and the rowers lay upon their oars, ready for the expected order.

"Now, we're comin into it," said the pilot.

"Trail!" added the coxswain; and in obedience to the order, the oars were thrown out of the rowlocks, and dragged at the side of the boat.

The gig shot into the swift current. Her bow seemed to drop down, as she rushed at a furious pace through the rapid, emerging into the middle lake.

"Bedad! but that was foinely done!" said the pilot.

"We know how to handle a boat," replied Raymond; "and we don't mind a little sweep like that."

"Begorra! but it's no fool of a boatman that goes through that without getting broke."

"Pooh! we've been through places a hundred times worse than that. These lakes are nothing but puddles."

"Troth, thin, didn't the R'yal Victoria's min say ye'd all be broke whin ye come to O'Sullivan's Punch Bowl?"

"We are all right, and now the four cutters have slipped through," added Raymond.

The pilot was rather vexed that the perils of the Long Range, and of the lakes, were not appreciated. The gig passed through only a corner of Middle Lake, which is also called Torc and Mucross Lake. The character of its scenery is different from that of the upper lake, being tamer and less picturesque, but it is a lovely place, especially at the lower part, while the channels between Dinish and Brickeen Islands and the main land are pleasant, and even romantic. Through the passage between the two islands the boats passed into Glena Bay, which forms a part of Lough Leane, or Lower Lake, five miles long and three miles wide, extreme dimensions. It is enclosed by mountains on the south and west, and contains upwards of thirty islands, the largest of which has an area of twenty-one acres.

There are plenty of "layginds" about the great O'Donoghue and the McCarthys, lords of the manor. Of the former there were two; "O'Donoghue of the Glens," who was a very bad man, and "O'Donoghue of the Lakes," who was a very good man. The story-tellers say that once in seven years there appears, in the mists of the early morning, the form of O'Donoghue the good, mounted on a splendid white horse, with the fairies attending upon his state, and strewing his path with flowers. When he comes to his ruined residence everything is restored to its former magnificence, and his castle, with all its surroundings, is reproduced as it was in the ancient time. Those who dare to follow him over the lake may walk dry-shod through the deepest parts, and go with him into the mountains where his treasures are said to be concealed; and the visitor will receive a liberal gift for the boon of his company. Before sunrise the spectral form recrosses the lake, and disappears amid the ruins of his castle.

Glena Bay is the most beautiful portion of the lower lake, and the boat squadron of the Young America floated upon its waters, which were sheltered by dense foliage on three sides. On the shore opposite Brickeen Island there was a picturesque cottage, which immediately attracted the attention of the boys.

"Beyant," said the pilot, pointing to this cottage, "is where Her Majesty the Queen took a lunch whin she came to the lakes. Faix, thin, there was foine times on the lakes. There was three hunder and sixhty boatsh, brought up from Cork, and Tralee, and Valentia. Bedad! but it's bad weadther on the lake below, the day," he added, turning round and glancing at the body of the lake.

"What do we care for that?" said Paul, laughing at the idea of bad weather on a little fresh-water lake.

"Bad weadther! Sure no boat can go across. The say is very bad sometimes, and boatsh don't go over for two or tree days."

Paul laughed at the idea of being deterred from crossing the lake; nevertheless a strong north-west wind stirs up a sea which is trying to the nerves of fresh-water sailors. The pilot said ladies were often seasick on the passage from Glena Bay to Ross Island; but our young tars did not give his croakings a second thought. The rowers lay upon their oars for a time to permit the company to observe the scenery.

"Begorra! there comes the R'yal Victoria boatsh," exclaimed the pilot, suddenly. "Faix, they are all full of min."

There were five boats flying the flag of the hotel indicated, though there were not more than six or eight men in each, but in the foremost one Paul recognized the burly runner whom Boatswain Peaks had knocked down in the railroad station.

"I'm afraid we shall have some trouble," said Dr. Winstock, when Paul had called his attention to this bully.

"I hope not, sir."

"These boatmen are very jealous of their privileges; and you know an Irishman is always as ready to fight as he is to drink his whiskey."

The hotel boats were approaching the gig, which was at the head of the line, and it was evident that the boatmen had business with the visitors.

"Ye can't crass the lake beyant the day, sir," said a man in the bow of the foremost boat, when it came near the gig.

"Why not?" demanded Dr. Winstock.

"It's very bad, your honor, and the boatsh would be shwamped."

"We will risk that."

"Pon me sowl, ye can't thin! Don't ye see the white caps on the waves forninst the middle of the lake?"

"We don't mind them."

"Sure ye will moind them before ye go far."

"We are used to bigger waves than those," laughed the doctor.

"Pon me wurrud, you'll see," added the man, shaking his head. "Ye'll want boatmen that's used to the lake to take ye's over."

"I think we can get along very well."

"Sure, your honor had no right to come here wid yeer own boatsh to take the bread out of poor min's moudths," continued the fellow, waxing angry when his cautions were not heeded.

This remark clearly introduced the real business of the boatmen, and Dr. Winstock prudently made no reply.

"Begorra! they'll kill ye all!" said the pilot, in a low tone.

"Mr. Kendall, you are the ranking officer in this boat, and I leave you to manage this business," added the doctor, anxiously.

"As we can't fight, I suppose we must run," replied Paul, with a smile which showed that he did not regard the danger as very serious.

"Very loike your honor will do the right thing by us," added the spokesman of the boats. "Give me forty shillings, — that's eight shillings a boat for us, — and we'll drink your honor's health, and wish ye long life for your honor and the young gintlemin."

"If you want money, you must see the gentleman in the farther boat," replied the doctor, pointing to the fourth cutter, in which Mr. Lowington was a passenger.

"Beyant?"

"Yes."

"Don't let 'em go by ye's, b'ys, till I sphake to the gintleman," said the fellow, in a low tone, to his companions.

The boat containing the spokesman pulled to the rear of the line.

"I think we had better return where we can be within hail of Mr. Lowington," said Paul. "If there is to be any trouble, we should keep close together."

"Very well, Mr. Kendall, just as you think best," answered the doctor.

The gig came about and pulled to the position of the fourth cutter. The three cutters which had occupied the middle of the line also came about and followed the gig. By the time the boatmen had come within hail of the fourth cutter, her companions had ranged up near her.

The spokesman proceeded to inform Mr. Lowington, as he had Dr. Winstock, that he could not cross the lake while the waves ran so high, and came by the usual course of "blarney" to his impudent demand for forty shillings.

"What claim have you upon me for forty shillings?" asked the principal, mildly.

"Isn't your honor takin the bread out of our moudths by bringing yeer own boats here?" said the man, indignantly.

Mr. Lowington explained that only the boatmen of the Railroad Hotel had any just claim on him, and that he had paid them their full wages and perquisites. But they were not satisfied, and insisted that the forty shillings they demanded should be paid.

"I shall not pay you a penny," said Mr. Lowington, decidedly.

"'Pon me wurrud you will, or we'll break your boatsh," added the spokesman.

"Sure, his honor won't mind forty shillings," interposed the pilot in the gig. "They'll kill the whole of yes 'f ye don't give it to 'em."

"I wouldn't give them a farthing," said the doctor.

"Nor I," added Paul.

"Mr. Kendall," called the principal, "come alongside, if you please."

The gig was pulled up to the fourth cutter, and Boatswain Peaks, by Mr. Lowington's direction, stepped on board the gig.

"You will lead the way as before, with the pilot, Mr. Kendall," added the principal. "Let there be no quarrel, and let nothing be said or done to irritate these men."

"I will answer for the gig, sir," replied the second lieutenant, who at the same time could not help wondering why Peaks had been ordered into his boat.

The five hotel boats had pulled away a short distance from those of the Young America, apparently for consultation. On board of them there was a confused jabbering in a strange tongue; or at least it was so full of the rich brogue that nothing could be understood. The tall runner's voice was distinctly heard above the others, and it was evident that he, at least, had some other purpose than extortion. He kept looking at Peaks, as though he meant mischief.

"That man will kill you, boatswain, if he gets a chance," said Dr. Winstock.

"Then I hope he won't get any chance," laughed Peaks.

"He will lay you aboard."

"If he does, and there is any Davy Jones's locker at the bottom of this fresh-water puddle, he'll find his way there."

"Give way, Mr. Kendall," said the principal.

The order was repeated by the second lieutenant, and then by the coxswain, when the gig moved off down the lake, the cutters following her in their proper order. But the hotel boats had taken a position where they could intercept the little squadron, and when the line moved they pulled for the gig, apparently with the intention of running her down.

"Break her in bits!" shouted the burly runner, who had stationed himself in the bow of one of the boats, which was in advance of the others.

"Break up all!" shouted a dozen voices.

"This begins to look serious," said Dr. Winstock, anxiously.

"Pull steady, fellows!" added Paul, rising in the stern sheets, and surveying the situation. "Keep her as she is, coxswain."

The runner's boat was pulled by six oarsmen, and she quickly distanced her fellows, which now changed their course, and made for the three rear cutters.

"First cutters, stand by me!" cried Paul to Pelham, who was the officer of the boat next behind him, and which was in immediate peril.

"I will," replied the fourth lieutenant; and whatever else he was, he was prompt and courageous.

"Steady!" added Paul, coolly, when the runner's boat was within a few yards of the gig.

"There's the blackguard!" shouted the bully. "Give me a hoult of him, and I'll break his sconce!"

THE ENCOUNTER WITH THE BOATMEN OF KILLARNEY. Page 121.

"Hard a starboard!" said Paul, suddenly. "Toss — oars!"

Just as the heavy hotel boat was about to crush into the side of the gig, the latter turned short towards the shore, with her oars all up, so that her assailant could not foul them. At this moment Pelham was urging the crew of the first cutter to their utmost endeavors, for the fourth lieutenant was disposed to be belligerent under provocation, and he was determined to have "a hand in the fight," if there was one.

As the gig, obedient to her helm, came about, and forged ahead towards the shore, the bow of the runner's boat was brought up to her quarter, so that the big bully in the bow was close to the seat occupied by Peaks.

"Now, you dirty blackguard," roared the runner, reaching forward to get hold of the boatswain, "I'll teach you manners."

As the fellow reached forward, Peaks seized him with both hands, and dragged him over the bow, holding him between the two boats. The boatswain was almost as big as his antagonist, and his muscles were of iron.

"Haul him in, Peaks," said Dr. Winstock, fearful perhaps that the boatswain would carry out his threat to send the bully to "Davy Jones's locker.".

Before he had time to do that, or anything else, a tremendous crash attracted the attention of all in the gig. The first cutter, at the top of her speed, had struck her sharp stem into the broadside of the hotel boat. Her ribs and streaks snapped like pipestems; and in an instant she was full of water.

"Let fall! Give way!" shouted Kendall; and the gig, with Peaks still dragging the runner in the water, shot ahead towards the shore.

"Bowman, stand by with the boat-hook, and clear away the wreck!" cried Pelham in the first cutter, which had cut through and nearly run over the hotel boat.

CHAPTER VIII.

THE KEY OF THE SAFE.

"NOW stand out of the way, Mr. Kendall, and I'll snake this vagabond into the boat," said Peaks, when the gig was clear of the hotel craft; and with a vigorous effort he dragged his prisoner into the stern sheets.

The fellow was not a boatman, and it was plain by this time that he had a wholesome dread of the water. The pluck had all gone out of him; and though he looked ugly, the sharp discipline he had received at the hands of the stalwart boatswain had produced a salutary impression upon him.

"Now, my hearty, if you want to break my sconce, it's just the right time for you to begin," said Peaks, as he tossed his captive upon one of the thwarts.

"Don't provoke him, Mr. Peaks," interposed Dr. Winstock.

"It's him that's provoking me, sir. It's hard work for me to keep my hands off him; but I'll obey orders. What will I do with the baggage now?"

"Let him alone where he is. How is it with the men in the stove boat? Do they need any assistance?"

"They are doing well enough — holding on to the wreck," replied Peaks.

"I don't think it would be safe to take them into the gig," added Paul. "They are too quarrelsome to be in the same boat with us; besides, the rest of the boatmen had better look out for them in preference to injuring us."

"As long as they are not in peril of drowning, we will not meddle with them," continued the doctor. "The villains haven't stove any of our boats — have they?"

"No; our boys have pulled out of their way, and they can't get near enough to break our boats," answered Paul. "But I think we had better go back and report to Mr. Lowington. If this fellow should make any trouble — "

"If he does, I'll pitch him overboard," interrupted Peaks, glancing at his prisoner.

"I should like to have Mr. Lowington say what is to be done with him. Starboard, coxswain."

"Starboard, sir."

"The hotel boats have given up the chase," said Paul, glancing towards the head of the bay. "Now they are pulling back to the rescue of those on the wreck."

In a few moments more, the gig and the fourth cutter were within a few yards of each other, and the oarsmen of all the boats ceased rowing.

"What have you there?" asked Mr. Lowington, as he discovered the runner in the gig.

"This is the man that made all the trouble. He attempted to lay violent hands on Mr. Peaks, and Mr. Peaks dragged him out of his own boat into ours," replied Paul.

"What boat was stove?" asked Mr. Lowington, quietly.

"The six-oar hotel boat. She was trying to run us down, when the first cutter went into her and stove her side through."

"Give my regards to Mr. Pelham, and say that I am greatly obliged to him for his prompt action," added the principal, apparently unmoved by the exciting event which had just transpired.

The boys in the gig, who had feared Mr. Lowington would not approve the conduct of the fourth lieutenant in smashing the hotel boat, looked at each other and smiled significantly. It was a clear case to them, and they were rejoiced to have the act approved by the highest authority in the ship's company. Though Paul, by his good management, had saved the gig from destruction, the ruffians in the hotel boat were bent upon mischief, and in a fight they would have had the best of it. The smashing of their boat made them harmless.

"What shall we do with this man?" asked Paul.

"Run in at that point, by the island, and put him ashore."

"Put me ashoor — is it?" exclaimed the ruffian, jumping to his feet.

"Sit down, my hearty!" said Peaks, in such a tone that the fellow instantly obeyed.

"Sure that place is moiles from ony house or road," added the runner.

"It's just the spot then for one like you," replied Peaks, in the most consoling manner.

"You'll have to pay for the boat you broke," growled the ruffian.

"I think not," interposed Dr. Winstock. "It is plain to me that the landlord of the Royal Victoria does not countenance the conduct of his boatmen, and I hope he will make them pay for the damage done to his boat. So far as our party is concerned, Sir Phelim M'Guire, the magistrate, whom I know to be a gentleman and a scholar, will settle the difficulty; and if he doesn't send some of these vagabonds to the penitentiary for their pains, he is not the man I take him to be."

The runner, who had a proper respect for magistrates, did not say anything more. He was doubtless satisfied that he and his friends had "waked up the wrong passengers," when they attempted to impose upon a "Yankee ship and a Yankee crew." Americans in Ireland and elsewhere in Europe good naturedly submit to extortion and imposition; but any attempt to bully or intimidate them is usually resented with Brother Jonathan's characteristic promptness.

The gig made a landing at the point near an island called Darby's Garden, and the runner was invited to go on shore. Peaks wrestled with his inclination to lay violent hands upon him, out of respect to the principal and the faculty.

"Bad luck to ye!" exclaimed the ruffian, turning to gaze at the gig as it backed out from the shore. "I'll mate ye yit."

"When you *mate* me, I'll be there," replied Peaks.

The fellow, vexed and angry at his defeat, picked up a large stone, and hurled it at the boat; but fortunately it fell short of the mark, and dropped into the water.

"If you say the word, Mr. Kendall, I'll go ashore and larrup that Greek till he don't know his mother tongue," said the boatswain.

"No, Mr. Peaks; I think not."

"We will act only in self-defence," added Dr. Winstock.

The gig came about and resumed her position at the head of the line. The hotel boats had gone to the assistance of the stove barge, and were now engaged in pulling in the discomfited crew. Paul ordered the coxswain of the gig to give the ruffians a wide berth. The enemy showed no disposition to renew the battle. It had been shown that the cutters could pull two yards to their one, and it was useless for them to chase. The Young America's boats were so well handled that, even manned as they were by boys, they were more than a match for the hotel boats. The expedition therefore was permitted to proceed on its course without further interruption.

"Bedad! I was sure they'd kill ye's," said the pilot in the bow of the gig, when the squadron had fairly passed the enemy.

"We are not so easily killed," replied Peaks.

"But, sure, ye can't crass the lake the day. Don't ye moind how rough the weather is?"

Peaks laughed, and so did the boys, at the fears of the pilot, who had hardly spoken a word since the party entered Glena Bay.

"A tempest in a mud puddle!" chuckled the boatswain.

"O, well! you'll see," added the pilot, ominously. "Don't ye see the two hotel boats that came down wid us have put back?"

"Those are fresh-water boats," answered Peaks.

"Where is the cascade, pilot?" asked Paul.

"Beyant. opposite the island; but ye can't go there to-day. The wather would break the boats."

"We will try, it at any rate," replied the young officer, as he sat down in the stern sheets.

"I am afraid the pilot is more than half right," said Dr. Winstock. "The wind is fresh, and the waves break on the shore where we should land. The boats are liable to injury on the rocks."

"We will look at the place. What kind of a cascade is it?"

"O'Sullivan's Cascade. It is a pretty and romantic spot; but it does not compare with a dozen similar scenes among the White Mountains. Those who have visited Glen Ellis Falls and the Crystal Cascade would not be likely to linger long at O'Sullivan's Cascade. It is a series of three waterfalls, the highest having a descent of about twenty feet. The stream flows in a bed beneath overhanging rocks, the whole overarched with foliage so that the sun does not penetrate the recess. It is quite pretty, and if we can land, it would be well to visit it; but it would not be a great loss if we should fail to see it."

The gig had by this time got out where the wind had full sweep, and the lake was quite rough; but no one thought there was any danger, though the head sea occasionally threw a bucket of water into the boat. It gave the boys a hard pull, however; and as they had been taught to do when the work was trying, they cheered themselves with a song, very much to the astonishment of the pilot, who predicted that all the boats would certainly go to the bottom.

Before the gig reached the landing-place for the cascade, word was passed from boat to boat, from Mr. Lowington, to head the squadron for Innisfallen Island.

"Now, ye can see O'Donoghue's white harses," said the pilot, as the gig changed its course.

"I see no horses," replied Paul.

"The white waves is the harses, do ye's moind?"

The boatmen on the lake call them so; and it is a much more sensible idea than the popular superstition in regard to the animal.

"Have we seen any shamrock yet, Dr. Winstock," asked Paul, as the boat approached the island.

"Doubtless we have. It is a kind of wood sorrel, not clover, as some have supposed. It has three leaves; but there is some doubt about the true shamrock, — they don't know exactly what it is. The *oxalis acetosella* is believed to be the genuine plant."

"I don't see why the Irish people should have adopted it as their national emblem; and I don't believe they would if they had to call it by such a jaw-breaking name as that you just mentioned."

"Moore, the poet, in a note to one of his Irish melodies, 'O, the shamrock,' says that St. Patrick, when preaching about the Trinity to the heathen in Ireland, used to pick up a sprig of the shamrock to illustrate his meaning; and perhaps for this reason the plant was adopted by the Irish as their national emblem."

"Where can I find the poem about the shamrock?" asked the young officer.

"In Moore's works; they are in the ship's library. Look among the Irish melodies. I remember a verse or two: —

> 'Through Erin's Isle,
>   To sport a while,
> As Love and Valor wandered,
>   With Wit, the sprite,
>   Whose quiver bright
> A thousand arrows squandered,
>   Where'er they pass
>   A triple grass
> Shoots up with dew-drops streaming,
>   As softly green
>   As emeralds seen
> Through purest crystal gleaming.
> O, the shamrock, the green, immortal shamrock!
>   Chosen leaf
>   Of bard and chief,
> Old Erin's native Shamrock.'"

The story of the poem goes, that Valor claimed the shamrock, and Love put in a counter claim; but Wit declared that the three leaves in one plant typified the union of Love, Valor, and Wit."

The boats came up alongside a kind of stone pier on the island, and the crews all landed. The place is certainly very beautiful, and its lovely scenery fully justifies Moore in calling it "Sweet Innisfallen;" but its chief interest lies in its historic associations. It is covered with groves, lawns, and glens, with thickets of flowering shrubs and evergreens. The arbutus and holly flourish here, and the oaks are large and luxuriant in their growth.

On the island are the ruins of the Abbey of St.

Finian, in which an old historical record, now celebrated as the "Annals of Innisfallen," was found. It was written about five hundred years ago, and is carefully preserved in the Bodleian Library, connected with Oxford University. They afford much valuable information in regard to the kingdom of Munster.

The students wandered over the island, explored the ruins of the monastery and the cottage. The pilot pointed to a tree which he said was sixteen feet in girth, and to another which was over a tomb, the roots imbeded in the earth on each side of it.

After an hour spent on the island, the boatswain's whistle piped the several crews on board the boats, which were now headed towards Ross Island, the landing-place of excursionists down the lake.

"It's a beautiful island," said Dr. Winstock, gazing back at the wooded shore.

"'Sweet Innisfallen, fare thee well;
  May calm and sunshine long be thine;
How fair thou art let others tell,
  While but to *feel* how fair be mine.

'Sweet Innisfallen, long shall dwell
  In memory's dream that sunny smile
Which o'er thee on that evening fell
  When first I saw thy fairy isle!'

So sang Moore."

"It seems to me you know all Moore's poems, Dr. Winstock," said Paul, laughing.

"When I was in Ireland before, I read and re-read them in the midst of the scenes described. I remember only a passage here and there."

A pull of a mile brought the boats to the end of the

cruise, at the ruins of Ross Castle, which the boys visited. A tower is still standing, which the party ascended, and from the top obtained a delightful view of the lake and its shores. This castle was built by one of the O'Donoghues. It was the last stronghold in Munster to surrender to the English in 1652. Lord Muskerry, commanding the Irish forces, having been defeated in Cork, retreated to Ross Castle, where he held out against the repeated assaults of the English, until an attack by water was made upon his position. An ancient Irish proverb declared that Ross was invulnerable until it should be invested on the lake side. The English general, being unsuccessful in his efforts to capture the place with the means at his command, procured a number of boats. The Irish, satisfied that the prophecy had been accomplished when they saw the boats, which they called ships of war, surrendered at once, without another blow. Each of these boats held one hundred and twenty men, and the general ordered one of them to seek a convenient landing-place on the island. The garrison, supposing an attack was intended, immediately surrendered.

After what had transpired at Glena Bay, Mr. Lowington did not deem it prudent to leave the boats without protection, lest the belligerent boatmen should injure them; but Peaks soon raised a force of men, including a couple of the constabulary, to take them to a safe place. The cars ordered to convey the party back to the hotel were at Ross Castle. The students were glad enough to be relieved from the labor of pulling, and took their places in the vehicles. On the return, they passed through the demesne of the Earl of Kenmare, where they saw his lordship's pheasant grounds, his rabbits, groves, gardens, and finally Kenmare House. This nobleman kindly allows strangers to pass through his grounds, in various parts of which notices are posted forbidding any of his employees to *ask* money of visitors. This exhibits a proper spirit on his lordship's part; but though his employees do not ask money in words, they do by their wistful looks, and it is almost as hard to resist the one as the other.

The ship's company dined at the Railway Hotel, according to the French programme of mine host. The exciting events which had occurred on the lake were duly reported to him, and he promised to have the boatmen properly punished, which probably he never did. The next day the forenoon was spent in visiting Muckross Abbey, Torc Cascade, and other places of interest on the eastern shore of the lake. In the afternoon the boats were placed upon the train, and the party returned to Cork, where the gig and cutters were again put into the water, and the squadron pulled down to the ship. The first grand excursion was finished, and the boys were delighted with it.

On the day following the return of the ship's company from Killarney, Mr. Lowington was permitted to know the secret which Dr. Winstock had so zealously guarded when he visited Cork on the day the ship arrived. The silver plate came on board, and when the principal had mustered the crew for purposes of discipline, Paul Kendall stepped forward and presented it as the grateful offering of the students. Mr. Lowington was duly and properly surprised, and made a very eloquent speech on the memorable occasion.

So far as Ireland was concerned, the curiosity of the students was satisfied, and that troublesome impatience which had worried the boys on their arrival had worn away. They still had London, Paris, Edinburgh, and Switzerland to look forward to, but they were content, most of them, to take things as they came. They returned to their studies with renewed vigor, and for a week no interruption of the regular academy course was permitted by the principal, though in this time the ship went round to Bantry Bay, and the boys explored the wonders of Glengariff during three afternoons.

On her return from the Bantry cruise, the Young America anchored again at the cove, to obtain the mail for the officers and crew. There was a letter for nearly every person on board the ship; but happily there was no unpleasant news from home to darken the hearts of any. As a mail for the United States would close that night at Queenstown, all the boys were required to write to their friends at home. Mr. Lowington was particular in this respect, and a letter directed to his parent, guardian, or other friend, was required of each student, whether he wished to write or not. But most of them were glad of the opportunity to inform the loved ones on the other side of the ocean of the incidents of their travel on shore. While nearly all of them spoke in the highest terms of regard and respect of the principal, a few grumbled, and complained especially of his "tyranny" in doling out the pocket money to them in shillings and sixpences. But no questions were asked in regard to the contents of the letters: it was only necessary that a letter of some kind should be written.

Immediately after the return of the ship's company from Killarney, Mr. Lowington had renewed the search for the key of his safe. Though he had a couple of duplicate keys, for use in case of loss or accident, he was strenuous in his efforts to discover the missing one. It could not be found. No one had seen it; no one knew anything about it, for of course Wilton and those to whom he had intrusted his secret did not scruple to lie about it. Pelham, who had accidentally possessed himself of the fact, was not quite willing to embark in the enterprise proposed by Wilton. He had gained considerable credit for his prompt action in smashing the hotel boat on the lake, and being just then in high favor, he regarded the desertion rather coldly.

When the ship lay in Bantry Bay, and only one shilling was allowed to each student for an excursion to Glengariff, his indignation was again aroused, and he was prepared to listen to the proposal of Wilton. On the return passage to the cove of Cork he found an opportunity to question him more particularly in regard to his plans.

"What have you done with that key, Wilton?" he asked in a low tone, as they met in the waist.

"It is safe," replied Wilton, with a meaning smile.

"I'll bet Lowington will find it yet, if it is on board the ship."

"I'll bet he won't."

"Where do you keep it?"

"That's telling; you advised me to keep things to myself, and I intend to do so. Even Ike Monroe don't know where it is."

"Won't you trust your own friends?"

"O, yes; but, you see, I don't want to tempt them. I don't mind telling you, but I shouldn't care to have any fellow in the steerage know where it is."

"Of course I could have blowed on you when Lowington was making such a row about the key."

"I knew you could, but you wouldn't. When you want your money, you can have it, you know," added Wilton, with a smile, which seemed to be full of confidence in his after-cabin friend.

"Of course, when you take the money from the safe, there will be an awful row," said Pelham.

"To be sure there will; but I don't intend to be on board when that row comes off. I expect to be a hundred miles off by that time."

"When are you going, Wilt?" asked Pelham, with more familiarity than he was accustomed to use in his relations with the crew.

"Just as soon as you are ready. I have been waiting for you."

"I'm ready now. That last shilling at Glengariff broke my back."

"Are you ready, though?"

"I am, honor bright. But I don't see how we are to get off."

"That will be easy enough. Ike Monroe and I are in the second cutter, and you can easily get permission to go ashore in her when our boat is going."

"We shall be in Queenstown to-night, if the wind holds fresh. To-morrow will be mail-day, and as we sail for Dublin on Monday, the boats will be constantly going ashore," continued Pelham, musing.

"But the money?"

"Leave all that to me," replied Wilton, confidently.

"I would rather leave it to you than do the job myself," added Pelham, whose moral code was honor rather than principle. "I don't like that kind of operations."

"Why not? You don't call it stealing — do you?"

"Well, I don't know."

"If it is, the receiver is as bad as the thief," said Wilton, bluntly.

"I don't know that I should exactly call it stealing," added Pelham, wincing under the remark of his confederate.

"Of course it isn't stealing. That's taking what don't belong to you. I'm going to take what does belong to me. That money's mine, and I'm going to have it. I say Lowington had no more right to borrow my money in the way he did, than he had to borrow my head and give me a receipt for it. It's no use of talking. What's mine's mine, and it belongs to me."

"Don't talk so loud, you fool," said the fourth lieutenant, impatiently.

"It's a good deal safer to speak right out. If they see you whispering, they know something is wrong. Don't you suppose we can get ashore Monday morning before the ship sails?"

"I don't know — why?"

"I can get the money a good deal better on Sunday than I can to-morrow. Perhaps we can get off on Sunday afternoon or evening."

"I don't know. After we come to anchor, I may be able to find out something."

"Well, keep your eyes wide open, and let me know just as soon as you see an opening," said Wilton, as Pelham walked off, at the approach of another of the officers.

"What was the fourth luff saying to you, Wilt?" asked Monroe, a few moments later.

"He is to be one of our party."

"Pelham?"

"Yes; he's a regular nob, and we shan't lose anything by taking him with us."

"Are you going to tell all the fellows about the key?"

"No one else. We shall be off to-morrow or next day; so be sure you don't leave your jacket on board when the second cutters are called away."

"But what's the plan?" demanded Monroe, anxiously.

"Hang the plan! Never mind that. We can't tell anything about it till the time comes," replied Wilton, as he prudently left his friend, and mingled with the rest of the crew.

CHAPTER IX.

SIXTY POUNDS IN GOLD.

AT ten o'clock on Friday night the Irish pilot in charge of the Young America ordered the anchor to be let go off Queenstown, near the berth the ship had before occupied. After the recitations had been finished on the following day, the students were required to write their letters. While they were thus engaged, Mr. Lowington passed through the steerage, and informed the boys that a yacht race was about to take place, and the crew might leave their letters to witness the start.

Anything like a boat race was enough to excite the students to the highest pitch, especially as they were anxious to witness the working of these English cutters. All of them tumbled up the hatchway, leaving their writing materials on the mess-tables. Five yachts were in position, ready to slip their moorings at the signal; and as the wind was strong from the south-west, the race promised to be full of interest. The students hastened up the rigging, securing available places in the tops, on the yards and the rigging, to watch the aquatic contest.

Mr. Lowington and the professors had placed their chairs upon the top-gallant forecastle, for they were too dignified to mount the rigging, and the officers were on the rail. The cooks and stewards were in the fore rigging, and every person on board had obtained the best place he could find, and all eyes were directed towards the yachts. Wilton stood on the rail, leaning against the stretcher of the main shrouds; but he did not seem to be as much interested in the prospective race as his companions. He was thinking of something besides the graceful cutters; and when the signal for the start was given, he quietly slipped down from his position to the deck, while all eyes were strained to take in the movements of the several contestants. After a glance at the faculty and the officers to satisfy himself that he was not observed, he moved over to the steerage hatch, and went below.

Every soul on board was on the spar deck, eagerly watching the race, and no one was thinking of him. He could hear the cheers of the multitudes which crowded every boat and vessel near the ship. Hastening to his berth, which was close by the ladder, he removed the coverlet, and thrust his arm into the berth sack, which proved to be the hiding-place of the key. It was drawn from its resting-place, and after a furtive glance up the hatchway to satisfy himself that he was still unobserved, he entered the main cabin, and stood before the closet which contained the iron safe.

Here an unexpected difficulty occurred; the closet door was locked. But he had gone too far to retire without an effort to effect his purpose. He went into the principal's state-room, where he found several keys on a nail. With them he returned to the closet, and after trying several of them, he found one which fitted the lock. As he opened it, a rousing cheer from the ship's company above assured him that everybody was absorbed in the progress of the race. Inserting the large brass key in the key-hole of the safe, he opened the door.

In a couple of small drawers in the safe he found the money, one of them containing the gold and the other the silver, each done up in small rolls. Wilton had tried to persuade himself, while contemplating this act, that he was an honest boy; that he only intended to take what was his own: but now that the deed was to be consummated, he had not time to count the money, and take just the amount which belonged to him and to the friends he represented. He meant to take enough, and he did. He slipped three of the rolls of gold into his pockets without knowing how much they contained. Closing the drawers, and locking the safe and the closet, he returned the key of the latter to the nail in Mr. Lowington's state-room.

His heart beat violently, and his hands trembled as he closed the door of the main cabin, and hastened to his berth again. In spite of his philosophy, he was not satisfied with what he had done. He was fearful of consequences, and he could not help thinking how dismal it would be to spend a week in the " brig," instead of going to London " on his own hook." But the deed was done; he had the money, and he had the safe key, either of which being found upon him would expose his guilt. He had no further use for the key, and he decided to get rid of that at once. His quarters were on the starboard side, while the ship's company were all on the port side. The bull's eye in the passage was open, and reaching his arm through the aperture, he dropped the key into the deep waters of the bay. That was gone, and it could not rise up to condemn him.

He was almost tempted by the oppression of his guilt, and the fear of detection, to drop the three rolls of gold overboard; but another cheer from the rigging convinced him that all hands were still intent upon the race, and he began to reproach himself for being "chickenish." Then, as he thought of travelling unrestrained, with genial companions, to London and Paris, his evil purpose was confirmed.

What to do with the rolls of gold was a troublesome question to settle. But it was Saturday afternoon, and the mattresses would not be aired again for four days. If they were, each student conveyed his own on deck, and he could remove the gold for the occasion, as he had the key. The three rolls of gold were taken from his pocket. They were very heavy for their size, and he could not resist the temptation to open one of them and ascertain its contents. He was appalled to find that it contained twenty sovereigns. The whole amount abstracted from the safe was therefore sixty pounds. It was clear to him that, even by his own theory, he had stolen at least fifteen pounds, for neither he nor his companions for whom he acted had over twelve or fifteen pounds on deposit.

This reflection was not a pleasant one; but Wilton comforted himself by resolving not to spend any more than belonged to him. Whether his act was stealing or not, it was too late to restore the money or any part of it to the safe, for he had thrown the key overboard. Rolling up the package he had opened, he placed the three little bundles in the hair of the mattress, and with his needle and thread, took a few hasty stitches in the rent he had made to admit the key. He did not think it would be safe to go on deck again, and he took a position behind the main hatch ladder, ready to join the students when they came below.

Of course he could only think of the deed he had just done, and consider the probability of being discovered. It was not likely that Mr. Lowington would immediately ascertain that the gold had been taken from the safe, which might not be opened again before the ship arrived at Dublin. But he did not feel secure, and he determined to inform his companions of what he had done at once, and get off as soon as possible, — that very day if an opportunity was afforded them.

The yachts went out of the harbor, and disappeared beyond Roches Point. The boatswain's whistle piped the students below again to finish their letters. When the first squad of them came down, Wilton joined them, and no one observed that he had not come down with them. In an hour the letters were all sealed and stamped, and put into the ship's mail-bag, which had to be sent on shore before five o'clock.

"I've done it," said Wilton, when he met Pelham in the waist, after the letters had been collected.

"Done what?"

"Drawn our money," whispered the cunning operator.

"No — have you?"

"I tell you I have; don't you believe me?"

"I don't just see when you did it?"

"When all hands were looking at the race."

"How much?"

"O, never mind that now. I got all that belongs to you. We must get off at once — to-day, if we can."

"All right; I'm ready," replied Pelham, eagerly.

"Can't you get sent off with the mail in the second cutter?"

"I don't know."

"Ask permission."

"That will show me up just as soon as we are missed."

"No matter if it does. What do you care for that after you get clear of the ship? I will tell Monroe in a few minutes, and we will be ready when the second cutters are piped away," said Wilton, impatiently.

"But I don't know that I can get the command of the boat."

"Try it, at any rate. We must get ashore to-night, somehow or another."

"We needn't be in such a hurry."

"If you don't go to-night, I shall throw the gold overboard; for I'm not going to have it found upon me."

"Don't do that; if you can't keep it safe, give it to me; I have a good place in my state-room to keep it."

Wilton was suspicious, and did not like this idea. He insisted that the plan must be carried into execution that day, or it would be a failure.

"What are you going to do after you get on shore?

My uniform will tell everybody who I am," said the prudent Pelham.

"Bother your uniform! Let us get ashore, and then we'll look out for the rest. Go and ask the captain at once to let you take the mail ashore in the second cutter," replied Wilton, anxiously, as he abruptly left the lieutenant, and sought his other confederate.

Monroe was duly informed of the progress which had been made in the execution of the contemplated scheme. He had no doubts or scruples, and he was ready to leave the ship at a moment's notice. Pelham desired to perform his part in the enterprise to the satisfaction of Wilton; but it would look suspicious for him to ask permission to convey the mail on shore, and he did not like to do it.

"Whoever takes the mail ashore to-night will have a good time," said he carelessly to Paul Kendall, who was pacing the quarter deck.

"Why so?" asked the second lieutenant.

"Those yachts will be coming back about that time, and the officer will have a good chance to see them; and I think there will be some fun."

"I have just been detailed for that duty," added Paul; "but I don't care anything about it."

"You are lucky, as you always are, Kendall."

"Do you want to go, Pelham?"

"Well, I should like to; but if you are going, of course that is settled."

"I am not very desirous to go, and if you are, I will ask Captain Gordon to give you the order."

"O, no, Kendall! It is too bad to impose upon a

fellow because he is good-natured. I won't take the job away from you."

"I really don't care anything about it, and I should be glad to have you go, since you wish it," said Paul, warmly.

"Thank you, Kendall. When I can do as much for you, let me do it," added the fourth lieutenant, as politely as though he had not been meditating treason and desertion. "Which boat were you going to take?"

"The captain told me to take the one I preferred. He will do you the same favor."

"I prefer the second cutter."

Paul walked over to the starboard side of the ship, where the captain was "planking the deck" in his solitary and dignified state, and, touching his cap, preferred his request in favor of his fellow-officer. The answer was satisfactory, and half an hour later, when the occupants of the main cabin had finished their letters, the second cutters were piped away. Wilton's heart leaped as he heard the order, and he rushed into his mess-room to obtain the rolls of gold.

It was intensely provoking at that critical moment to find Morgan, one of "the chaplain's lambs," reclining in his berth, opposite the one occupied by Wilton. He could not remove the bed-clothes and cut the stitches he had put in a couple of hours before without being observed by his exemplary messmate. He had not a moment to spare. Pelham had not notified him that he had carried out his part of the programme, and the call for the second cutter's crew had sounded.

"Is that you, Morgan?" said he, hurriedly. "Mr. Lowington wants to see you at once."

"See me!" exclaimed the "lamb," springing out of the berth, fearful that he had done some awful thing.

"Yes, and be quick about it," replied Wilton, sharply.

"Where is he?"

"On the top-gallant forecastle: if he isn't there, wait till he comes;" and Morgan hastened to the principal, dreading a reprimand for some infraction of the ship's rules.

Wilton tore open the rent in the berth sack as soon as Morgan had departed, and transferred the three rolls of sovereigns to his pockets. Rushing up the hatch ladder, he reached the gangway only a few moments behind the rest of the crew.

"Who told you I wished to see you?" said Mr. Lowington, within a few feet of where the chief culprit stood; and the words sounded like the knell of doom to him.

"Wilton, sir," replied Morgan, who had gone to the top-gallant forecastle to report to the principal, but seeing him on the quarter deck, had concluded not to wait for him.

"Wilton," said Mr. Lowington.

The rogue turned and touched his hat, looking as innocent as his guilty fears would permit.

"Did you tell Morgan I wished to see him?"

"Yes, sir."

"Who told you to do so?"

"The word from you was passed below; I heard it, and took it up."

"From whom did you take it?" demanded Mr. Lowington, to whom the affair looked like one of the practical jokes which were constantly practised upon "the lambs," in spite of the prohibition of the principal.

Wilton looked, and happening to see Adler, whom he could trust, on the fore-top-gallant yard, took his cue from this circumstance.

"Adler, sir," replied he.

"Where is he?"

"On the fore-top-gallant yard, overhauling the bunt gasket, sir."

"He has gone aloft quick, then. Pass the word for him."

"Shall I pipe aboard, sir?" asked the fourth lieutenant, trembling for the safety of his confederate.

"You will wait a moment, Mr. Pelham."

The word was passed for Adler, and he came down the top-gallant back-stay with a celerity which seemed to rob the principal's remark about his speed in going aloft of its force.

"Here, sir," reported Adler, touching his cap to the principal.

"Did you pass the word to Morgan as coming from me?" asked Mr. Lowington, who had, since Adler came in sight, kept his sharp eye fixed on Wilton, so that he had no chance to wink or make any sign.

"Yes, sir; I did, sir;" replied Adler; and the two "sirs" he used were some evidence to the principal that he was lying.

"From whom did you take the word?"

"From McKeon, sir."

" Return to your duty. Pass the word for McKeon."

McKeon was out on the flying-jib-boom, hauling in a down-haul, whose end had fallen overboard. He came at the summons.

" Did you pass the word for Morgan?" demanded the principal, sternly, for by this time he comprehended the game of " our fellows ; " but he was determined to follow the clew till it ended somewhere.

" Yes, sir," replied McKeon, promptly.

" From whom did you receive it?"

" I don't exactly remember who it was, sir," replied he, looking about the deck.

" You don't!"

" I do not, sir ; but I think it was from Lynch. I am pretty sure it was he ; it sounded like his voice."

" Where is Lynch?"

" On the main royal yard, sir," replied McKeon.

" It seems to me that every one who passed this word has suddenly taken to going aloft," said Mr. Lowington, dryly. " Pass the word for Lynch."

" I beg your pardon, sir," said Pelham, showing his watch ; " but it is half past four now, and the mail closes at five."

" Pipe into your boat, then, Mr. Pelham. Wilton, you will report to me immediately on your return," replied Mr. Lowington.

" I will, sir," replied he, with a sly wink at Monroe.

The crew of the second cutter, followed by their officer, descended the accommodation ladder, and took their places in the boat. Wilton felt that he had escaped " by the skin of his teeth," and the gold in his pocket, which had seemed to weigh a ton as he stood at the gangway, now felt much lighter. He was prudent enough, however, to keep his own counsels, and not to look at Pelham. The cutter pulled away from the ship, leaving Mr. Lowington still engaged in the business of ferreting out the author of the practical joke, as he regarded it, which had been played off upon one of the "lambs," as "our fellows" called the "good little boys."

The principal was not a victim himself, however he may have seemed to be to some of the students. He had made a note in his memorandum book of each name which had been given to him, and was fully satisfied that the owner of it had told him a lie. He expected to find an end to the chain, and to be ready, by the time the second cutter returned, to bring up Wilton "with a round turn." Lynch came down from the royal yard.

"Did you pass the word for Morgan to report to me?" demanded Mr. Lowington, as the main royal boy reported to him.

"I think I did, sir."

"Don't you know?"

"We are so much in the habit of passing the word that we do it without minding much about it."

"I suppose so," replied the principal. "As this affair occurred within ten minutes, you will state distinctly whether you did or did not pass the word for Morgan."

"I did, sir. I thought you meant some time ago, sir."

"From whom did you receive the order?"

"From Sanborn, sir. I was standing by the combings of the main hatch, sir, just going aloft."

"Where is Sanborn?"

"He was just going forward when he gave me the word. There he is, sir, on the fore-cross-trees, looking out for the yachts."

"Pass the word for Sanborn," added Mr. Lowington, entering the name of Lynch on his book.

The star-gazer on the cross-trees came down, and the question was put to him as it had been to the others.

"I believe I did pass the word, sir," replied Sanborn.

"From whom did you receive it?"

"I think it was from Wilton, sir."

"Are you sure it was from him?"

At that moment McKeon, who had remained to watch the progress of the investigation, shook his head significantly.

"No, sir; it was not Wilton. It was Shuffles, now I think of it."

McKeon and Lynch were disgusted at the stupidity of Sanborn, who had only jumped "out of the frying-pan into the fire;" but Mr. Lowington had backed over against the rail, satisfied that the change in the reply had been made on account of some hint given by one of the others, so that he could see the faces of all.

"Shuffles — was it?" said the principal.

"Yes, sir," answered Sanborn, who did not dare to equivocate again.

"You are very sure?"

"Yes, sir."

"Where is Shuffles?"

He was in the fore-top with Mr. Agneau, the chaplain — an association which boded dismay to the rogues. He was sent for, and soon appeared with his clerical friend at his side. The question was put to him as to the others. Shuffles found himself in an awkward and unpleasant predicament. He saw that his shipmates had been "playing a game" upon the principal, and that he was expected to sustain them. Since the arrival of the ship from the United States, he had behaved himself in the most exemplary manner. Without "putting on airs," and without shunning his former companions, he had frequently proved the sincerity of his reformation. It was true he had not before been placed in a situation in which he was required to be loyal to the truth at the expense of his associates; and it is possible that, if the chaplain had not been at his side, thus reminding him of the solemn promises he had made, he might have been recreant to his new-found sense of duty. If he declined to answer the question, it would be rebellion, and it would be equivalent to exposing his friends. He could only save them by a lie. Mr. Agneau did not speak; but the influence of his presence was strong.

"I did not, sir," replied Shuffles, after some hesitation.

"You did not pass the word to Sanborn?" repeated Mr. Lowington.

"No, sir."

"What have you to say, Sanborn?"

"I say that he did."

"When was it?"

"About fifteen minutes ago," interposed McKeon,

fearful that Sanborn, not so well informed as himself, would make a blunder.

"You say that Shuffles is lying — do you?" demanded the principal, sternly.

"I suppose he is. I only know that he gave me the word about a quarter of an hour ago."

"Where was he when he gave it to you?"

"In the waist, sir," answered Sanborn, who was very indignant at what he regarded as the treason of Shuffles.

"I beg your pardon, Mr. Lowington, but which is the waist?" asked the chaplain, who was singularly ignorant of the nautical vocabulary, and hardly knew the waist from the quarter-deck.

"On deck, in the middle of the ship," replied Mr. Lowington, with a smile of pity for one who had been so long on board of the ship and did not know where the waist was.

"I wished to be quite sure in a matter of so much importance," replied Mr. Agneau. "Shuffles was not in the waist a quarter of an hour ago. He had been with me where we were found when you sent for him, over half an hour."

"Where was that?"

"In the fore-top," replied the chaplain, who was fortunately sure of this term, though he would not have ventured to mention it unless required to do so.

"That is sufficient," continued Mr. Lowington, as he turned on his heel and went aft, intending, when the second cutter returned, to summon all whose names he had taken, and punish them as they deserved.

CHAPTER X.

THE VOYAGE TO DUBLIN.

"THE yachts are coming!" shouted the young tars, in various parts of the Young America's rigging, as the leading vessel in the race appeared at the entrance of the harbor.

"All hands on deck, ahoy!" shouted the boatswain, after he had piped the call.

Mr. Lowington had directed Captain Gordon to pay the winning yacht the highest compliment known in the naval service; and he was all the more ready to do this when he discovered by the private signal, that the foremost yacht was owned by a gentleman who had extended many courtesies to the officers of the ship.

"Stand by to man the yards!" shouted the first lieutenant, when the crew were piped to muster; and the order was repeated by all the officers at their stations.

Life lines had been extended from the port to the starboard lift, about four feet above each yard; from the fore-top-gallant stay to the foot of the fore-mast, and from the mizzen-mast to the topping-lift over the spanker-boom. When the yards are manned, the sailors stand on these spars, and also on the bowsprit and spanker-boom, with their arms extended on the life-lines, by which they are supported in their lofty positions. .

The race was a very exciting one, and the leading craft was only a short distance ahead of two others; and all of them, under every stitch of canvas, though the wind was blowing fresh, were " roaring " through the water at a furious pace.

" Lay aloft — man the yards! " shouted the first lieutenant, when the winner of the race was within a quarter of a mile of the ship.

The crew sprang into the rigging, eager to see the yachts which had been concealed from their view by the high bulwarks, and anxious to make a good appearance in this manœuvre; for on account of the possibility of accidents, it was seldom performed. The lines of young seamen ascended the rigging, keeping equally distant from the deck till they reached the cross-trees, where they began to scatter, and run out on the yards. As the first yacht passed the bow of the Young America, every boy was in his place on the spars, and the appearance was very beautiful.

" Three cheers for the Calypso! " cried the first lieutenant, through his trumpet.

They were given by the prescribed formula, all as one voice, and with a hearty good will. The Calypso dipped her ensign three times, her officers acknowledged the compliment with frequent bows, and the crew returned the cheers.

" Lay down from aloft! " called the first lieutenant, when the yacht had passed the ship.

The boys were then permitted to watch the coming

in of the rest of the contestants in such positions as they chose. The race was finished, and the excitement on board subsided. At six o'clock, when all hands were piped to supper, according to the port routine, the second cutter had not returned, and Mr. Lowington began to be a little uneasy about her. It even occurred to him that Wilton, who had been implicated in the practical joke, had run away, and that the others were looking for him. He had not missed the money taken from the safe, and there had been no appearance of insubordination on board; so that he had no reason to suspect any serious violation of the rules.

At half past six he ordered the professor's barge to be manned, and with Mr. Fluxion, and the third lieutenant, as officer of the boat, went ashore to ascertain what had become of the absentees. The second cutter was found at the landing-place, in charge of Pierce, her coxswain, who was now impatiently awaiting the appearance of his officer. He reported the facts to Mr. Lowington.

"Who was the officer of this boat?" asked the principal.

"Mr. Pelham, sir," replied the coxswain.

"Where is he?"

"I don't know, sir. He ordered Wilton and Monroe to carry the mail-bag to the post office, and followed them himself. I haven't seen or heard from them since; and that was about two hours ago."

"Very well, coxswain, you will return to the ship," added Mr. Lowington, without betraying his anxiety to any of the crew.

The second cutter shoved off, and pulled for the Young-America. Leaving Goodwin, the third lieutenant, in charge of the barge, with strict orders to permit none of her crew to go on shore, Mr. Lowington, accompanied by Mr. Fluxion, walked up the pier. They visited the post-office, and found that the mail-bag had been left there.

"These fellows have gone on a lark, I suspect," said the professor of mathematics.

"Where do you suppose they have gone?" asked the principal, anxiously.

"Very likely up to Cork. They will be back soon; at least to-morrow, or next day."

"How could they go to Cork? I doubt whether all three of them have a shilling, all told."

"They will be back all the sooner."

"I think we have prevented some running away by not letting the students have much money. This is the first time any of the boys have attempted to get away, and it will be a bad example. I am sorry."

"So am I; but these fellows can't have gone far with empty pockets."

"We must follow them up promptly. Wilton was at the bottom of a trick played off upon Morgan, and I think he is keeping out of the way to avoid consequences."

"They run together."

Mr. Lowington inquired of all the policemen he met if they had seen the runaways, and finally traced them to the steamer which connected with the railroad for Cork. This boat had just returned from Passage, and the fare-taker informed him that three young gentlemen, one in uniform, had gone up in the steamer.

"Did they pay their fare?" asked Mr. Fluxion.

"They did, sir; one of them in a blue jacket gave me a sovereign, and paid for the three — first class."

"A sovereign!" exclaimed Mr. Fluxion, with a meaning glance at the principal.

"It was, sir; and he had more of them."

"When does this boat go to Cork?" asked Mr. Lowington.

"In tin minutes, sir."

After a brief consultation, it was decided that Mr. Fluxion should proceed to Cork by the steamer and railroad, and with the assistance of the police, arrest the runaways. Mr. Lowington returned to the barge, which pulled off to the ship. He said nothing, and no one ventured to ask him any questions. While the crew of the barge were wondering where Mr. Fluxion had gone, the principal was vexing his brain to ascertain where the runaways had obtained the sovereign, and "more of them," which the fare-taker had seen in their possession.

It was not till he had entered the main cabin that the missing safe key occurred to him. The thought threw a flood of light on the dark transaction. He opened the safe, examined his cash-book, and then counted the rolls of gold. Three of them were missing. Mr. Lowington was painfully agitated. The discovery of the crime was appalling to him. He had no idea when or in what manner the key had been purloined, or the safe opened. It was not the loss of the money which disturbed him, but the consequences which must result to the boys who had taken it. He trembled as he thought of the riot and debauchery into which they would probably plunge, with so much money in their possession.

Though he would hardly have expected better things of Wilton and Monroe, he was grieved and disappointed to think that Pelham, the fifth officer in rank in the ship, had forfeited his claim to the respect of his superiors. Mr. Fluxion was a shrewd and energetic man, and the principal hoped to hear on the following day that the runaways had been captured, and their career of dissipation arrested.

The next day was Sunday, and in the forenoon Mr. Fluxion appeared. His arrival created a decided sensation on board, for the students had thoroughly canvassed the desertion of their companions, and readily inferred that the professor had been in search of them. His return without them was an indication that the runaways had managed to escape his vigilance. None of the officers or crew, however, were the wiser for his coming. All that was said about the absentees was uttered in the main cabin, whose occupants kept their own counsels. Mr. Fluxion reported the result of his mission to the principal in the state-room of the latter. He had traced the deserters to the Royal Victoria Hotel in Cork, where they had dined in the coffee-room. They had paid the bill and left before seven o'clock. The police in St. Patrick Street had seen three young gentlemen, one in uniform, at a later hour; but nothing more definite than this could be ascertained. He had telegraphed to the police of Dublin to be on the lookout for them.

"Pelham is a smart fellow, and in my opinion, fearing we should be after them, they have taken a side-car, and gone to some hotel ten or a dozen miles from Cork, where they intend to stay over Sunday."

"Did you instruct the policemen at the railway stations?"

"I did; but there was a train left for Youghal at seven o'clock. No one had seen them, however; yet it is possible they went in that direction. I returned for further instructions."

Mr. Lowington imparted to him the astounding intelligence that the safe had been robbed of sixty sovereigns. The matter of finding the runaways was fully committed to the professor, and with his valise he returned to Cork before noon. As the ship was to sail for Dublin on Monday, he was instructed to join her there.

The Sunday services on board of the Young America were conducted as usual. The students were unable to obtain any information in regard to the absentees. Mr. Fluxion had gone on shore with his valise, which indicated an absence of several days at least. As the professor of mathematics was the principal's right-hand supporter, and the most active and energetic man in the ship, it was evident that the runaways were to be pursued with vigor and determination, and that Pelham and his companions would be brought back before many days elapsed. Of course the students knew nothing about the three rolls of gold, and were not aware that the absentees were so plentifully supplied with funds for their excursion.

At six o'clock, on Monday morning, the pilot who

was to take the ship out of the harbor came on board; but the students were still fearful that the departure would be postponed on account of the desertion of the fourth lieutenant and the two seamen. It was a fine morning, and the wind was fresh from the northwest, which made it fair for the first part of the voyage.

"All hands, up anchor, ahoy!" piped the boatswain soon after the arrival of the pilot.

The doubt was removed, and every officer and seaman sprang to his station with an alacrity which showed how strong was their desire to visit new scenes and witness new sights. The top-sails, top-gallant-sails, spanker, and head-sails were loosed ready to be set, the capstan was manned, and as soon as the anchor was a-weigh, the jib was hoisted. The ship began to swing round as soon as she was clear of the ground.

"Haul out the spanker!" shouted the first lieutenant; and when the order was executed, the ship swung round so that she headed to the opening of the harbor. "Lay aloft, sail loosers!" he continued; and the nimble tars sprang up the rigging like so many cats.

"Is it possible!" exclaimed Captain Carneybeg, the pilot, as he observed with what facility the ship was handled. "These b'ys are the smartest sailors I ever saw in all my life, and I've been to sea thirty years."

"Boys are smarter as sailors than men. What they lack in muscle they make up in agility," replied Mr. Lowington.

"And you haven't spoken a word yet, sir," added the pilot.

"Not a word."

"All done by these bits of b'ys."

"Everything. I have no doubt they will take the ship to Dublin without a hint from me. Of course I watch them very closely; but it isn't often that I am called upon to interfere."

"Lay out and loose top-sails and top-gallant-sails!" continued the first lieutenant.

In a few moments the ship was going at a lively pace down the harbor. Several yachts and other vessels complimented her by dipping their colors, and by cheers, and these courtesies were appropriately answered. When the ship was clear of the land outside of Roches Point, the pilot went over the side into his canoe, and the Young America was again in charge of her own officers. The sea routine was now in operation, as it had been during the passage across the Atlantic. The starboard watch came on duty as soon as all hands were dismissed.

"Keep her E. $\frac{1}{2}$ S.," said the second master to the quartermaster conning the wheel.

"E. $\frac{1}{2}$ S.," repeated the quarter-master.

The ship was to run for the Saltee Light-Ship, about ninety nautical miles distant. The course on the chart appeared to be N. by E. $\frac{1}{2}$ N., but the variation of the compass is about twenty-four degrees west. All sail was set, and the usual sea order of the ship prevailed. The port watch came on duty at eight o'clock, and the starboard watch attended to their studies till twelve.

At three o'clock the calculations of the masters were proved to be correct, and the Saltee Light-Ship was discovered just where it ought to be.

"Keep her E. $\frac{1}{2}$ N.," said Joseph Leavett, the fourth master, when the ship was off the light-vessel.

"E. ½ N.," replied the quarter-master.

The sails were trimmed, and the Young America took her new course, which being continued for eighteen miles would bring her up with Tuskar Light, a little north of Cansore Point, the south-eastern extremity of Ireland.

At half past five the ship was off the Tuskar, which is a remarkable rock, that looks, when the beholder is several miles distant, like a vessel bottom upwards. It rises fifteen feet above high-water mark, and has on it a light-house, similar to the Eddystone, one hundred and one feet high. Many of the students had heard of this celebrated rock and light, and were anxious to see them.

The wind hauled to the westward at dark, and continued to blow a six-knot breeze during the night. The ship's course was N. E. by N., and at eight bells she was off Arklow Light-Ship. At four bells in the mid watch the second master was observed to be quite nervous. He examined the compasses very carefully, and went up into the foretop to observe the contour of the hills. Mr. Lowington, knowing the difficulties of the navigation, had come on deck about one o'clock. He asked some questions, looked at the compasses, noted the bearings of the lights, and examined the outline of the shore, but he offered no hints or suggestions.

"All right!" exclaimed Martyn, the master on duty. "Keep her N. W. by W. ¾ W."

"Do you know where you are, Mr. Martyn?" asked the principal.

"I do, sir. Those two lights are Wicklow Head.

I have brought the Great Sugar Loaf to bear through the Gap," replied Martyn, with enthusiasm.

"But where is Arklow Bank?" asked Mr. Lowington.

"When Arklow Head lights bear north-west, we are clear of the Arklow Banks," replied the master, who had learned his lesson by heart.

"You have done well," added the principal.

"Thank you, sir. It is my watch below now."

Martyn explained to the master who took his place, the situation of the ship, and went below. On the cabin table was spread out a large chart of St. George's Channel, which all the masters had carefully studied, and each one had written out the bearings and sailing directions. Their experience enabled them now to work with accuracy, and those who had been on duty were delighted that everything had come out as it should, and that they had found everything where it ought to be. Careful allowances were made for the tides, and it was a joy to the young navigators to find their calculations were correct.

At four o'clock, when the ship was within a couple of miles of the shore, off Wicklow Head, her course was changed to N. by E. $\frac{1}{4}$ E., which would carry her through a channel from five to eight miles wide, between the main shore and a series of sand banks, the most southern of which is India Bank. Perhaps some of our readers will wonder, while there were several lights to be seen, how the masters could tell one from another. Besides the chart, they were provided with a book containing the sailing directions for the channel. By the descriptions in this work, they identified each light.

On Wicklow Head there are two light-houses, one hundred and eighty yards apart, each having a *fixed* light. One is two hundred and fifty, and the other one hundred and twenty-one feet above high-water mark. The next light to the south of it is Arklow Light-Ship, which shows a single light, thirty-nine feet high, *revolving* once every minute. Wicklow Light-Ship shows a *red* light. These three lights, which are all in sight at the same time, can be known by these descriptions.

Light-houses are not, as some shore people suppose, to give light to those who sail on the sea, but for the mariner to take his bearings from. If he can see the light, and identify it by its description in his sailing directions, he knows where he is. For example, a ship bound from Liverpool to Portland, if she approaches the coast in the night, would first discover the lights on Cape Elizabeth. They are two in number, three hundred yards apart, and one hundred and forty feet above the level of the sea, one being about south-west of the other. The eastern is fixed, and the western revolves once in a minute and a half. From the relation of these lights to each other, those in the ship can tell where she is. If she approaches them from the north-east, the two will be in range, and the revolving light behind the fixed light; if from the east, they will be close together, the revolving light being behind the other; if from the south-east, they will be full distance apart, and equally distant from the ship. To a vessel approaching from the south-west, the two lights would be in range, and the revolving light in front of the other.

At eight o'clock the ship took a pilot off Dublin Bay, and at eight bells the anchor was let go off Kingstown. Not a single recitation had been lost on the passage, though it was rather trying for the watch below to study while the ship was going up Dublin Bay; but Mr. Lowington, who was acting as professor of mathematics in the absence of Mr. Fluxion, was inflexible, while he was kind, and assured the boys they would have an opportunity to see every object of interest before they left the port.

Dublin contains about two hundred and fifty thousand inhabitants, and is situated on both sides of the River Liffey, which divides it into nearly equal portions. The river below the town widens so as to form Dublin Bay, on which is situated Kingstown, the deep-water port of the Irish metropolis. It was formerly the little fishing village of Dunleary; but being visited by George IV., who bestowed upon it the royal patronage, its name was changed, and it became a fashionable watering-place. It is connected with the city by railroad, and the Dublin and Holyhead steamers — part of the great mail line between London and Queenstown — start from here, though the steamers direct from Liverpool and Glasgow go up to the city.

As soon as the anchor of the Young America was let go, the port routine of the ship was restored. In the afternoon all the boats made an excursion to Howth, on the north shore of the bay. Howth Castle was visited, whose history Professor Mapps related. It was the residence of an ancient family, which has furnished many warriors and noted men. Grace O'Malley, a chieftainess of the western part of Ireland, after a visit to Queen Elizabeth in London, landed at Howth, and claimed the hospitality of the lord of the castle, who refused even to furnish her any refreshment. The western lady was spiteful, and to revenge herself kidnapped the heir of the proud noble, and kept him a close prisoner until his father promised that on no pretence whatever should the gates of Howth Castle be shut at the dinner hour. Up to a recent date this promise has been kept.

The party next ascended the Hill of Howth, a rugged steep, five hundred and sixty-three feet above the level of the sea. From this point they had a fine view of the surrounding scenery, including Ireland's Eye, a picturesque island, on which are some ruins. There were plenty of cromlechs, cairns, and ruins, of which the guides had strange "layginds" to tell about the blessed saints who lived there and were pestered with evil spirits. The good St. Nessan, who lived on Ireland's Eye, being visited by a fiendish enemy while he was reading the sacred book of Howth, hit him with the holy volume, and knocked him across the bay with such force that the steep rock was split into a yawning chasm.

"Don't ye belave it?" demanded the Irish guide, when some of the boys looked incredulous.

"That's a whopper," answered one of them.

"A hopper — was it? To be sure it was. Didn't the faynd hop acrass the wather whin the blissed saint shtruck him? But it's thrue, ivery word of it. Don't I show ye the place where he shtruck? and isn't that the hole in the rock he made whin he hit it?"

It was useless to deny the truth of the story in the face of this confirmation, and the party passed on to other scenes. At dark the boys returned to the ship, tired out after the hard pull and the long walk they had taken, and all hands turned in at an early hour.

CHAPTER XI.

THE FAIR ARCHERS OF BELFAST.

AFTER study hours the next day, the entire ship's company took the train at Kingstown for Dublin. Leaving the station in Great Brunswick Street in side cars, four and twenty of which were readily procured, the party proceeded to Dublin Castle. In passing through College Street, the procession of cars encountered the carriage of the lord mayor of the city, which produced a sensation among the republican young gentlemen. The principal vehicle occupied by his worship was drawn by four horses, driven by a fat, measly-looking coachman, with a jolly red face, dressed in extravagant livery. Two footmen also, bedizened with finery, stood upon the back rack. Behind this carriage was another, containing the lord mayor's officers. From a side window of one of them was projected the huge mace, which is the emblem of his lordship's authority. The two vehicles were flanked by mounted policemen, belonging to the Irish constabulary. The boys were rather amused than impressed by the pageant, which was more befitting a travelling circus company than the chief magistrate of a great city.

Dublin Castle was originally built for the defence

of the people from the wild inhabitants which once infested Ireland. It has been repeatedly altered and improved till but little of the former structure remains. In the language of the Young America's company, " it isn't much." The cars were driven into the courtyard, and the party were conducted through the state apartments by a female servant. They were miserable rooms for so " big a gun " as the Lord Lieutenant of Ireland, whose official residence the castle is. The boys passed through the viceregal apartments, the reception, breakfast, sitting, and ball rooms. The ceilings were high, and some of them were adorned with valuable paintings; otherwise they were not much different from, or better than, the rooms in an American country tavern.

From the castle, the procession of cars went to St. Patrick's Cathedral, the most elegant and interesting church in Dublin. It has been recently repaired and rebuilt at the sole expense of an Irish brewer, at a cost of one hundred thousand pounds. St. Patrick built a place of worship near the fountain, where he baptized his converts, which was the site of the present cathedral. It is not, as might be supposed, a Catholic, but a Protestant church. It contains a tablet to the memory of Schomberg, who was killed at the battle of the Boyne; and within its vaults repose the remains of Dean Swift, and " Stella," the heroine of his poetry.

Passing Christ Church, the party crossed Richmond Bridge, over the Liffey, which, at this point, the tide being out, was an unsightly bed of soft mud, and arrived at " Dublin Four Courts," an extensive and imposing pile of buildings on King's Inn Quay. It takes its name from the four courts of Queen's Bench, Chancery, Exchequer, and Common Pleas, which hold their sessions within its walls. The procession paused only long enough to view the exterior of the building, and then proceeded to Sackville Street, in the centre of which is the Nelson monument, a fluted column one hundred and twenty-one feet high, surmounted by a colossal statue of the hero of Trafalgar. Stone steps in the centre of the pillar lead to the base of the statue, where a platform, guarded by an iron railing, affords those who take the trouble to climb up, a fine view of the city and the surrounding country.

Sackville Street is the principal one of the city. It is very broad, but there is nothing grand or imposing in the buildings. The procession passed down this street, crossed Carlisle Bridge, which is the head of navigation on the Liffey, and returned to the railway station.

"Well, Paul, what do you think of Dublin?" asked Dr. Winstock, when the party returned to the ship.

"I don't think very much of it," replied the second lieutenant. "I expected, from what I had heard Irishmen say of it, to find a magnificent city."

"You are disappointed."

"I am; but I was much interested in the sights I saw. It don't compare with New York or Philadelphia."

"We remain here but a few days."

"I am glad of it, for I have seen about enough of Dublin."

But the next day, when the party visited the suburbs of the city, Paul was better pleased. The ship's company went out to Rathmines, Rathgar, and other places in the vicinity. Though they saw no elegant residences, the region around the city was very pleasant. Most of the cottages and tenements, occupied by the middling class of people, in humble imitation of the more wealthy and titled "nobs," had their distinctive names, as "Victoria Terrace," "Redan Lodge," "Rathgar Ville."

The next day was wholly given up to an excursion by railway to Drogheda, Kells, and the battle-field of the Boyne, in which Professor Mapps was the central figure. He pointed out the spot where King William stood when he was wounded, and the bridge on which Schomberg was killed. An obelisk, one hundred and fifty feet high, indicates the spot where the king commanded the battle, and where Schomberg died.

On the return of the party to the ship, Mr. Fluxion was on board. His appearance created a great deal of excitement, especially as he came without the runaways. Mr. Lowington greeted him cordially; but there was a deeper shade of sadness on his face than was usually seen there. They retired to the principal's state-room, where the professor of mathematics made his report in full. He had traced the deserters to Youghal, then to Waterford, where they had taken a steamer for Liverpool.

"When did she sail?" asked Mr. Lowington, anxiously.

"Last night; but I telegraphed immediately to a friend of mine there, instructing him to cause the three boys to be arrested for stealing."

"For stealing!" exclaimed the principal.

"Isn't that what you call it when they take what does not belong to them?"

"Yes; but I do not care to hand them over to the law."

"The police will do nothing but detain them, until some one appears against them."

"Then you must go to Liverpool at once, and see them."

"I shall be there very early to-morrow morning."

Mr. Fluxion immediately went on shore, and embarked in the steamer for Holyhead, whence he was to go by railway to his destination. Mr. Lowington still kept his own counsels in regard to the runaways. The professor had gone again, and this fact indicated to the crew that the search had not been given up.

On Friday morning the ship sailed for Belfast, and on Saturday morning came to anchor in the Lough, about a mile from the shore. In the afternoon, the ship's company embarked in the boats, and went up to the city, landing at the foot of the principal street. Dr. Winstock was acquainted with an Irish gentleman who was a large linen manufacturer, and to him the party were indebted for kindly showing them, not only the public buildings, gardens, and college, but his linen factories.

Belfast is more like an American city than anything the voyagers had seen in Ireland. Since 1821 its population has increased from thirty-seven thousand to one hundred and twenty thousand. The whole city stands upon the territory of the Marquis of Donegal, to whom the whole town belongs, and to whom the citizens pay rent. Belfast is a neat and thriving place, and owes its commercial importance to the linen trade. The whole of the north of Ireland is engaged in the production of flax, which is manufactured into linen, Belfast being the centre of that trade.

About eighty per cent. of the people of Belfast are Protestants, and beggars are rarely met with, as in Dublin and Cork. The boys visited the Botanical Gardens, a large tract of land, laid out in lawns, flower-beds, and walks, and containing a conservatory well stocked with tropical plants. In this garden they witnessed an archery match between two clubs of young ladies. The affair was an event of considerable importance, and the band attached to the barracks was in attendance. The young ladies were dressed in archery costume, and handled their bows exceedingly well. At the conclusion of the trial of skill, the ship's company cheered the victors. As they were about to depart, the young ladies expressed a desire to see more of the visitors, and Mr. Kennedy, the doctor's friend, introduced the parties. The band played for half an hour longer, and the officers and crew made themselves as agreeable as possible.

The young Americans were as gay and gallant as the occasion required, and Mr. Lowington soon found that the discipline of his party was becoming impaired. The young ladies, their fathers and mothers, were inviting the officers and seamen to dinner, until there was hardly one of them who had not asked the captain's permission to accept. Captain Gordon applied to the principal for advice. Mr. Lowington was in doubt; but it was so long since any of the ship's company had entered a dwelling-house, or mingled with the society of ladies, that he was unwilling to deny the requests. He thought that the visits would do them good, and afford them an opportunity to observe the society of the better class of people.

These courtesies required something at the hands of the representatives of the school, and Mr. Lowington immediately arranged an excursion in the ship for Monday. The boatswain, at the captain's order, piped the crew together, and they were instructed to accept the invitations. The excursion for Monday was announced, and they were directed to invite the whole family where they were entertained to participate. The boats would take off the guests at Queen's Bridge at eight in the morning.

The students were delighted; and just then all of them believed Mr. Lowington was the best man in the world. They divided into little parties, and went to the houses of their new-found friends. They were very generously entertained, and we doubt not their accounts of their native land, their descriptions of the ship, the voyage, and their travels in Ireland, were as interesting to their hosts as the young ladies themselves were to the American tars. In the mean time, Mr. Lowington and the professors had been invited to dine at the Ulster Club House with Mr. Kennedy and others; and of course their friends, including several officers of the army, were invited to join the excursion.

At nine o'clock, the hour fixed for the return of the students to the boats, most of them had reported, and none of them were far behind the time. Nothing but the excursion and the "splendid time" they had had on shore was talked about among the ship's company. Sunday was rainy, but Monday opened bright and favorable for the guests. At eight o'clock the boats were at Queen's Bridge, and within an hour the entire party, including the archers and their families, many officers of the army, and the band which played at the Botanical Gardens, were on board. When the squadron of boats was within a quarter of a mile of the Young America, the yards were manned, and three times three tremendous cheers were given for the ladies of Belfast.

The ship, always kept with the nicest care, was on this occasion in extra trim. The steerage, in which the larger portion of the company were to dine, had been hung with flags. The decks were as white as sand and holystones would make them, and every rope was hauled taut, and the ends laid in Flemish-coil on the decks. The guests expressed their admiration of the beauty and neatness of the ship as soon as they reached the decks.

When the young gentlemen had had an opportunity to welcome their friends, they were piped to quarters, the capstan was manned, and the anchor hove short. The wind was moderate from the north-west, and the sails were shaken out according to the strict routine of the ship, the first lieutenant giving the orders in detail, which were repeated by the subordinates in their stations. The anchor was tripped, the foretop-mast stay-sail and jib hoisted, and the ship went off, gently careening as the wind filled her sails.

"Isn't it lovely!" exclaimed Grace Arbuckle, a brilliant young lady of fifteen, who had won the first prize at the Botanical Gardens, and had invited Paul Kendall to dine with her family.

"We don't think very much of it now, we are so accustomed to it," replied the second lieutenant.

"But it's magnificent, lovely, to see the ship spread her white wings, and start so steadily. Just look at those sails!" added the enthusiastic young lady.

"I should rather look on deck. I think the loveliest sight is there," replied the young officer, gallantly, as he touched his cap to the maiden.

"I really didn't think the Americans were so smart," said Grace, blushing slightly.

"O, we are!"

"Do you know I think Mr. Haven is the greatest man in the world?"

"The first lieutenant? There is Captain Gordon."

"But he didn't say or do anything."

"He told the first lieutenant what to do."

"And Mr. Lowington didn't have anything to do with it. He was talking to those gentlemen all the time," continued the puzzled miss.

"Why, we know how to handle the ship without him. We could take her across the Atlantic, or round the world."

"Very likely you could. I think the Americans can do anything, if the boys can manage a big ship like this."

"Now, Miss Arbuckle, if you would like to go forward and see more of the ship, I will show her to you."

"Thanks; I should be delighted to go to every part of her."

The band, as the ship gathered headway, had struck up Hail, Columbia, which had been followed by Yankee Doodle, and then by God Save the Queen. As soon as the officers and crew were dismissed from muster, they all hastened to find their Belfast friends, and all of them were soon busy in showing the ship to the guests. Paul conducted Grace to the top-gallant forecastle, where she could look out upon the water, then to the steerage, explaining how the crew ate, slept, studied and recited. The kitchen was shown, and the Irish maiden asked all sorts of queer questions about the galleys and the coppers, which the cook was proud and happy to answer.

"This is the main cabin, or, as the students call it, the professors' cabin," said Paul, as he escorted the lady from the steerage.

"I'm sure it is a good deal better than they have at the college in Belfast," replied Grace. "I should think they might be happy here."

"Probably they are," added Paul, as he proceeded to show his fair companion the state-rooms, the dispensary, and the pantry.

"I should like to live here myself," said Grace.

"Perhaps you would not think so favorably of our ship, if you could be on board in a gale of wind."

"Why, what happens then?"

"She plays queer antics then. We have to fasten everything down. Nothing will stay on the tables, and when we turn in, we can hardly keep in our own berths."

"That would be fun. I should like it above all things. Do you think we shall have a gale before we return?"

"I hope not; it would make you seasick. This is the after-cabin," continued Paul, as he led the way from the main cabin.

"The *after*-cabin? This is the one you go into *after* dinner — isn't it?"

"Not exactly. It is the officers' cabin," replied the lieutenant, laughing at her blunder.

"Why do you call it the *after*-cabin?"

"Because it is farther aft, or back, than the other. That is Captain Gordon's state-room, and the next is Mr. Haven's and mine."

"Then you room with Mr. Haven?" exclaimed she, in childish wonder that he should be permitted to share an apartment with so big a man as the first lieutenant.

"I assure you, Miss Arbuckle, that your friend is quite capable of commanding the ship, and can do all that Mr. Haven does," interposed Dr. Winstock, who happened to be near.

"Could you give all the orders to set the sails, Mr. Kendall?" asked she.

"I think I could," laughed Paul.

"For aught we know, he may be captain or first lieutenant after the first day of July."

"I really didn't think he was such a big man," said Grace, looking at him from head to foot, till Paul blushed beneath her gaze.

"I don't think I shall ever be captain," replied he. "Will you look into my state-room?"

She went into all the rooms, into the pantry, asked questions about the barometers, chronometers, thermometers, "tell-tales," and other instruments she found in various parts of the cabin, and finally seated herself on the divan, where she could look through the ports in the stern of the ship. She wanted Paul to tell her about the United States, where and how he lived, whether there were any Indians in Cincinnati, and whether the " States" were not crowded by so many Irish people going there.

"If you should empty the entire population of the United Kingdom into our country, we should only know by the census that we had any more people than before," replied Paul. "We have at least twenty-five states, each of which is larger than Ireland. Some of them are ten times as large; and two or three of them are each bigger than the whole United Kingdom. Why, Ireland is a little island. I should not dare to walk about much on your island after dark, for fear I might fall overboard."

"If you should, I suppose the water is not deep enough to drown you," pouted Grace.

"Of course we do not pretend to vie with the old world in the magnificence of the cities, palaces, and public buildings; but if you should visit the United States in about five hundred years from this time, you will find they surpass the countries of Europe."

"If I am here, and happen to think of it, I will go there," laughed Grace.

"I hope you will, and if I happen to be there, I will try to be as pleasant to you as you have been to me. Perhaps you would like to go on deck now."

Paul conducted her to the top-gallant forecastle, gave her a chair, and seated himself by her side. As the wind was north-west, and it was advisable to take a course which would give a fair wind for the return trip, the ship was running across the North Channel, headed up the Firth of Clyde. The sea was gentle, and the motion of the ship steady. Though a few of the party were slightly seasick, they recovered as soon as the vessel entered the smooth water beyond the channel. The band played frequently, and the excursion was almost as pleasant to the guests as it was to their entertainers.

At two o'clock the Young America came to anchor off the Isle of Arran, where the party dined on the sumptuous fare provided by the steward for this special occasion. An hour was then spent in the boats, in which those who chose were taken ashore, and the boys for the first time stood upon the soil of Scotland. At four the anchor was weighed, and the ship headed for Belfast Lough. The breeze was fresh in the afternoon, so that the ship made twelve knots during a portion of the trip, and came to anchor in Whitehouse Roads at nine o'clock. In due time the guests were landed, and the crew returned to the ship. It was unanimously voted that this was the most delightful day they had spent since the ship sailed from Brockway Harbor.

Paul Kendall, we fear, was a little sentimental, when he went below after landing Miss Grace Arbuckle; and we are quite sure that for weeks and months he looked back with a kind of rapture upon the hours he spent with the pretty and brilliant Irish maiden. Grace manifested so much interest in the ship and her crew — not particularly in the second lieutenant — that she wished to know what happened on board after her departure from Belfast.

"It is quite possible for you to know, Miss Arbuckle," suggested Paul.

"I hope I shall see you and the other officers again some time," said she. "We are going to Switzerland this summer, and shall pass through London and Paris. Perhaps we shall meet."

"I hope so; but we Americans know how to write. If you don't think I am impudent, I will write to you an account of our cruise."

"That would be delightful, Mr. Kendall! Do write," exclaimed Grace.

"I should be very glad to do so," replied Paul. "Will you, in return, tell me all about the archery clubs?"

Perhaps Paul used a little harmless cunning in making the arrangement; but when we consider how pretty, innocent, and fascinating this young lady was, we shall all be ready to pardon him, especially when we remember that he was only sixteen, and did not know any better! Paul was certainly a shade more thoughtful for a few days, and more than once he amused his friend the doctor by speaking in very enthusiastic terms of the Queen of the Archers at Belfast. But he neglected none of his academic or nautical duties. He studied even harder than before, and some of his brother officers in the after-cabin were almost sure that, at the next distribution of the offices, he would displace the first lieutenant, if not the captain.

On the day following the excursion the Young

America sailed, with a pilot on board, for Port Rush, the nearest safe harbor to the Giant's Causeway. A week was spent in exploring the wonders of this interesting region. A trip was made every afternoon to some point in the vicinity, and the boys explored caves in the boats, climbed rugged steeps, leaped from one column to another of the Causeway, and listened to the echoes in the caverns by the sea shore. There was no end to the legends related of the origin of the Causeway, and of the wells, pools, staircases, caves, chimneys, organs, and even pulpits, to which the natural objects had some real or fancied resemblance. The giants who dwelt there seem to have been supplied with every convenience for amusement, as well as for moral and religious improvement. We can give only a single tradition, which explains the origin of the Causeway: —

"The giant Fin M'Coul was the champion of Ireland, and felt very much aggrieved at the insolent boasting of a certain Caledonian giant, who offered to beat all who came before him, and even dared to tell Fin that if it wer'n't for the wetting of himself, he would swim over and give him a drubbing. Fin at last applied to the king, who, perhaps not daring to question the doings of such a weighty man, gave him leave to construct a causeway right to Scotland, on which the Scot walked over and fought the Irishman. Fin turned out victor, and with an amount of generosity quite becoming his Hibernian descent, kindly allowed his former rival to marry and settle in Ireland; which the Scot was not loath to do, seeing that at that time living in Scotland was none of the best, and everybody knows that Ireland was always the richest country in the world. Since the death of the the giants, the causeway, being no longer wanted, has sunk under the sea, only leaving a portion of itself visible here, a little at the Island of Rathlin, and the portals of the grand gate on Staffa."

After a very pleasant week spent in the midst of these wild scenes, the Young America sailed on the 1st of June for the Clyde, in which she anchored off Greenock, after a prosperous voyage.

The ship had hardly been put in order before Mr. Fluxion came on board, but the runaways were not with him.

"Didn't they go to Liverpool in the Waterford steamer?" asked Mr. Lowington, when they were closeted in his state-room.

"The captain landed them at Holyhead," replied Mr. Fluxion, rather crestfallen. "The rascals told him their ship would leave Dublin before they could join her, if they went on to Liverpool, and he landed them in season to take the night steamer. They did not go to Dublin, I need hardly say. They staid at Holyhead only a few hours, and from there I traced them to Chester. They remained long enough to see the cathedral, and then departed. I have not been able to obtain any information in regard to them. In Liverpool I employed two detectives to continue the search, and I have no doubt they will be found in time."

Mr. Lowington was more anxious than ever; but nothing further could be done, and the professor returned to his duties on board of the ship.

CHAPTER XII.

THE JOURNEY OF THE RUNAWAYS.

"NOW we are all right," said Wilton, when he had delivered the Young America's mail-bag at the post office in Queenstown. "We are just in time for the railroad boat to Cork."

"That's so," replied Pelham, consulting his watch, as they hurried towards the pier. "Where is the money, Wilt?"

"In my pocket; it is all right."

"But how much have you? I want to be sure it is all right before I go a great way from the ship, for I don't think it would be exactly hunky dory to be caught in a foreign land without any change."

"I have all that belongs to you, Pelham. How much was there?"

"Let me see. I had sixteen pounds. Lowington owed me fifteen pounds, two and sixpence."

"All right; I will give you the money when we get to Cork," added Wilton.

"Suppose you give it to me now," suggested Pelham, who was not very willing to trust such a fellow as his companion.

"I don't like to handle the money here in the street, where everybody is looking at us," answered the "keeper of the stamps," fumbling about his pocket. "Here are five sovereigns, and I will give you the rest as soon as we are alone."

He handed the gold to Pelham, who was satisfied with this arrangement. The trio of runaways embarked in the railway steamer, and in due time arrived at Cork. They took supper at the Royal Victoria Hotel, where in one corner they found an opportunity to discuss their plans.

"We must buy some clothes at once," suggested Monroe.

"We can't afford to do that," replied Pelham. "We can't get any more money for a month, at least, and fifteen pounds won't last forever."

"But our clothes will betray us," added Wilton.

"No, they won't; they will help us more than they will hurt us. But where are you going next? This is Saturday."

"To Dublin; and from there to London," answered Wilton.

They called for a newspaper, and found there was no train for Dublin till ten at night.

"That won't do," said Pelham, shaking his head.

"Why not?" asked Wilton.

"Lowington will miss us, and he will be up here looking for us within an . hour or two. We must clear out immediately. It won't do to stay here another hour. Look over the paper, and see what trains leave at once."

"Here's a train that goes at seven to Youghal — where's that?"

"No matter where it is; we will go there," said

Pelham, who, in virtue of his superior judgment and energy, had already taken the lead of the party. "We have no time to spare. Don't say a word as to where we are going. The station is the one we have just come from; I have seen 'Youghal' on a car there."

The others approved of his arrangement, and after paying the bill, they walked by an indirect way to the station at Summer Hill. There were two trains in readiness to start, one of which went to Passage, and the other to Youghal. There was a crowd at the "booking office," and Pelham asked a gentleman to procure their tickets for them, which enabled them to pass without being observed by the seller. After various dodges, they slipped into a compartment of one of the carriages, satisfied that they had not been noticed by any policeman, or other officials. They had first-class tickets, and found a section of a carriage which was unoccupied.

"I don't see the need of all this backing and filling," said Wilton, as they took their seats.

"Don't you? Then it's lucky for you I came with you, for you would be carried back to the ship within twenty-four hours," replied Pelham, sharply. "Can't you see that Lowington will make a tremendous row, when he finds we have gone?"

"Suppose he does."

"He will put the police on our track, and telegraph to Dublin, and everywhere else."

"Then of course he will telegraph to Youghal, and we shall be taken up as soon as we get there."

"He won't think of our going to such an out-of-the-way place as Youghal; but I don't mean to run any risks even there. Do you see what I have here?" added Pelham, as he produced a "Bradshaw," which he had purchased at the station.

The book contained the time tables of all the railways in the United Kingdom, and information in regard to all the lines of steamers. Pelham, who had a very good knowledge of the geography of Ireland, studied this work till it was too dark to read its fine print. As he seemed to be master of the situation, Wilton left the whole matter to him, with only grumbling enough to maintain his dignity and equality.

When the train arrived at Youghal it was quite dark. Pelham was so sure that no one could have gone up to Cork from the ship in season to telegraph to this place, that the party left the station without any especial precautions. There was no way to leave the town by public conveyance that night, and it was not prudent to go to a hotel; but after some difficulty they found a lodging-house, where they spent the night, and obtained breakfast in the morning.

At nine o'clock they took the steamer which goes up the Blackwater, and landed at Cappoquin. From this point they proceeded by jaunting car to Clonmel, from which there was a train to Waterford, where they arrived on Sunday night. Pelham hoped to find that a steamer would sail for Liverpool or Bristol on the following day; but there was none till Wednesday evening. On Monday morning they took the train for Kilkenny, after spending the night in an obscure hotel, and wandered about the country till Wednesday, when they returned to Waterford in season to step on board of the Liverpool steamer just as she was leaving the wharf.

"We are safe now," said Pelham, when the vessel was clear of the shore.

"Don't you suppose we have been safe all the time?" demanded Wilton, with a sneer.

"No; I am certain that Lowington or one of the professors is on our track. He will have to follow us up to Kilkenny, and everywhere else we have been. I hope he will have a good time, and see as much of the country as we have," replied Pelham, chuckling at the skill he had used in defeating the purpose of any supposed pursuer.

It was a fact that Mr. Fluxion had traced the fugitives over their entire route, and reached Waterford on Thursday morning only to find that they had sailed for Liverpool in the steamer of the night before.

"I don't believe any one would have troubled us if we had gone direct to Dublin, and from there to Liverpool," continued Wilton. "We have fooled away three days, when we might have had lots of fun in London."

"We have seen the country — haven't we? The fellows on board of the ship haven't been to Kilkenny, and Youghal, and Waterford, as we have," replied Pelham.

"What do we care for those places? I wouldn't have given sixpence to see them," growled Wilton.

"I have one thing more to say," continued Pelham, "and that is, we shall be taken just as sure as we go to Liverpool. I know, just as well as I know anything, that Lowington, or some one else, is following us."

"If you had minded what I said, we should have no trouble about that. Of course people can tell whether they have seen any fellows in the uniform of the ship."

"I should have been glad enough to put off the uniform, if we had money enough to buy clothes. We couldn't buy anything decent for less than four or five pounds, which would make a big hole in our funds."

"Anyhow, as this steamer goes to Liverpool, I suppose we are in for being caught," said Wilton, gloomily.

"I am going to dodge it, if I can; and I expect my uniform will serve me a good turn then. We shall be off Holyhead some time to-morrow. I am going to make the captain send us ashore, or put us into something that will land us there."

"Yes, and he'll do it, over the left," sneered Wilton.

"Leave it to me; and if I hadn't been with you, you would have been caught before this time."

"I don't see it."

It was true, whether he saw it or not, for Mr. Fluxion's plan would certainly have given them into the hands of the police in Dublin, where Wilton intended to go. Off Holyhead, the next day, Pelham played his part so well, that the captain of the steamer stopped his wheels long enough to put the runaways on board a fishing vessel, which was going into that port. At the table, the night before, the captain had inquired into the significance of the uniform worn by his passengers, and Pelham had described the Young America to him, adding that he and his companions intended to join her at Dublin. He was so fearful that the ship would sail without them, that the captain finally yielded, went out of his course to hail the fisherman, and put them on board of her.

At Holyhead they took the first train for Chester. Pelham was a young gentleman of taste and information, and he could not leave this old city without seeing its cathedral, though both Wilton and Monroe protested against any delay for such a purpose. The lieutenant had the stronger will, and the ancient church was visited.

"Well, where are we going now?" asked Pelham, as they came out of the cathedral.

"To London, of course," replied Wilton.

"Why London?"

"Because that's the best place to go. We can have some fun there."

"We can have just as much fun in Glasgow and Edinburgh. Don't you mean to see those places?"

"After we have seen London, perhaps we will go to them," replied Wilton, whose plans were not very clearly defined.

"That's a stupid idea — to go to London first," added Pelham, decidedly. "I am bound for Glasgow next. I wouldn't miss seeing those lakes in Scotland for anything. I would rather miss London or Paris than Loch Lomond."

"Pooh!" sneered Wilton.

"There isn't the least need of our keeping together any longer if we can't agree," suggested Pelham, quietly. "I don't want to drag you into Scotland, if you don't want to go."

"I had just as lief go to Scotland as not, if you will

go to London afterwards," replied Wilton, who had not so much confidence in himself as he had had before he left the ship.

"Certainly, we will go to London, after we have seen Glasgow, Edinburgh, and the lakes."

"All right."

"I think our uniforms won't help us much now, and we may as well make some change in our personal appearance."

"It is about time we did something of that kind. Everybody is looking at us now, as though we were the monkeys in a caravan," added Wilton. "But you said it would cost too much money."

"We needn't buy new suits in full. I can rip the gold lace and shoulder-straps off my coat, and change my cap. You can each of you buy a cheap sack coat and a felt hat."

"That will change the cut of the jib so that we shall not be recognized. We might have done that before."

"If we had, the captain of that steamer would not have heaved to for us to go ashore at Holyhead."

After it was arranged what each of the party should purchase for additional clothing, at Pelham's suggestion, they separated, and procured the articles at different shops, the better to baffle the efforts of any one who might be in pursuit of them. As they were very much fatigued, they decided to remain at Chester over night, and staid at a small hotel, where they made the changes in their clothing. Pelham not only removed the shoulder-straps and the gold bands from his coat, but sewed on a set of black buttons he had bought, after cutting off the brass ones.

When they went to the train for Scotland the next day, they were sure that no one would recognize them as members of the Young America's ship's company. People had stared at them wherever they went before, but now no particular notice was taken of them. In the afternoon they reached Glasgow. Pelham's economy and caution induced them to take rooms at a small hotel, where the prices were low and the accommodations were very inferior, the total expense being only five shillings a day for each boy. Wilton grumbled, as usual; but the funds of the party were already much reduced, and the fear of an exhausted exchequer was strong enough to induce him to yield to his companion.

"We must look ahead, fellows," said Pelham, as he took from his pocket a daily newspaper he had purchased in the street. "I have less than twelve pounds left."

"I have but ten," added Monroe.

"I have more than either of you," replied Wilton, who had paid to his friends the sums they claimed.

"How much have you, Wilt?" asked Pelham.

"I am willing to make an even thing of it among us, and I will give you five pounds apiece, which will make it square," continued Wilton.

"How is this, Wilt?" demanded the lieutenant, gravely. "Did you take more than belonged to us from the safe?"

"Of course I couldn't stop to count the money when I took it," said Wilton, snappishly.

"I don't believe in that," added Pelham, decidedly.

"Nor I," added Monroe.

"You shall have the money whether you believe in it or not. What's the use of being so notional? We might as well be hung for an old sheep as a lamb. Of course your father will pay back anything you use that don't belong to you. You don't mean to go back to the ship, you said."

"Of course I don't; but I don't mean to have a hand in stealing money," answered Pelham, proudly.

"What's the good of calling it stealing? We'll give back all that don't belong to us. You may have the five pounds; but you needn't spend it, if you don't wish to do so."

"I will not take it," replied Pelham. "I'm going to write to my father this very day to send me twenty-five pounds, so that I can get it when we reach London."

"I will do the same," said Wilton, as the lieutenant glanced at the newspaper.

"The Young America is reported at Belfast. We can date our letters there; but we shall not get the money for three weeks, and ten pounds will hardly keep me going for that time."

"You can use the five pounds I will give you, and pay it back when your remittance comes," suggested Wilton.

Pelham was fully resolved, if compelled to take the five pounds which did not belong to him, to enclose a five pound note to Mr. Lowington when he received his funds from his father. The letters were written immediately, dated on board the ship at Belfast. A shilling stamp was affixed to each; but when they were ready to mail them, a new difficulty presented itself to the cautious lieutenant. The letters would be post-marked "Glasgow," instead of "Belfast," where they were dated; and this circumstance might excite the suspicions of the parents to whom they were addressed.

"Of course our folks will have no idea that we have left the ship," said Monroe.

"Not unless Lowington writes to them," added Wilton.

"He won't do that yet a while, you may depend upon it," replied Pelham. "I know how to do it. We will put the three letters into one envelope, and send them to the postmaster at Belfast, requesting him to mail them."

"But what will the postmaster think?" asked Wilton.

"We don't care a fig what he thinks; he won't know anything at all about the matter," said Pelham, as he thrust the three letters into an envelope, addressed it, and affixed three penny stamps. "It is all right now, and we shall have the money when we get to London. Now we will have some supper."

In the evening the trio went to the theatre. Having arranged their plans, and satisfactorily adjusted the financial question, they were disposed to enjoy themselves. Before this time they had been embarrassed by the fear of discovery, of losing their money, and other calamities; but at supper each of them had taken a glass of strong ale, which produced an effect upon them. They had seats in the pit; and as the beer made them rather "chipper" with their tongues, they soon made the acquaintance of a well-dressed young man, who sat next to them, and who made some advances to them.

"Won't you come out and take something with us?" said Wilton, at the intermission between the plays.

"Take something?" replied the stranger.

"Take a glass of wine, or some ale."

"Thanks; I don't object."

The party drank wine on this occasion; and by the time the young salts reached the theatre again, its fumes had begun to operate upon their brains.

"You are strangers in Glasgow, I think," said the young man, when they had taken their seats.

"Yes; we arrived here to-day," replied Wilton; "and we are bound to have a good time."

"I see you are," laughed the stranger.

"Do you live in Glasgow?"

"I do."

"Well, you are a first-rate fellow, and I want to know you better," said the tipsy Wilton. "I suppose you can put us in the way of having a good time — can't you?"

"Perhaps I can; if I can serve you, I'll be glad to do so. Have you been to the Cathedral?"

"We haven't been anywhere. We arrived this afternoon."

"You can go to church at the Cathedral to-morrow, if you like," suggested the Glasgowite.

"Hang the Cathedral!" exclaimed Wilton. "I want to have some fun. What's your name, my hearty?"

"John Sanderson; my friends call me Jock, and

you may call me so, if you like," answered the good-natured stranger, though he no longer appeared to be such.

"All right, Jock! Keep your weather eye wide open tight, and we'll have some sport — won't we, Mr. Pelham?"

"Don't talk so loud, Wilt," said the lieutenant, who was not so much affected by the wine he had drank.

"All right, Mr. Pelham; I'll take a reef in my tongue gear," replied Wilton, in a whisper.

"You are sailors — arn't you?" asked Jock.

"Yes, sir. We are sailors; we've ploughed the briny deep."

"Where's your ship?" continued Sanderson.

"She's in Liverpool, and we've come here to have a good time, — I want you to understand that."

The curtain rose, and the attention of the party was called to the play. Wilton kept still for a time, and being overcome by fatigue and the influence of the wine, he dropped asleep. His position, however, was not very comfortable for a nap, and Pelham waked him to prevent him from falling upon the floor. When the play was finished, he roused himself, and insisted upon taking another glass of wine with Jock. Pelham attempted to interfere; but the juvenile tippler was so wilful that he refused to listen to reason.

"Now, Jock, take us somewhere, and let's have some sport," said Wilton, as they left the wine shop.

"Where will I take you?"

"Just where you please. We want to see the fun, if there's any in the city. Brace her sharp up, and show us the fun."

"Come with me, lads."

He conducted them to a narrow street, and entered a house which Pelham found was a gambling saloon. There were a bar and many small tables, at a few of which men were seated engaged in various games of chance. In spite of the lieutenant's protest, Wilton treated the company again to sherry wine. Jock introduced them to several persons as "his friends" from America.

"I'm glad to see them," said a rakish-looking fellow, who sat at a table with a pack of cards in his hand. "I suppose they want to make some money to-night; if they don't, they are not Yankees. Sit down, gentlemen, and we'll have a game."

"No, I thank you. I don't understand the games well enough to play," replied Pelham, who was by this time considerably elated by the fumes of the sherry.

"We never take advantage of any gentleman's want of knowledge," said the polite gambler. "We shall be fair."

He shuffled the cards and laid the pack on the table.

"Now," he continued, "if you want to put down a sixpence, or a shilling, on the color of the card I turn up, it's as fair for you as for me."

Pelham made no reply, but he put a shilling upon the table, to which the gambler added another.

"Now what color do you bet on — red or black?" asked the man.

"Red," replied Pelham.

The gambler "cut" the pack.

"Red it is," he added. " The money is yours; you see this is entirely fair. In fact, it's *rouge et noir*, in a simple way."

"Half a crown on the red again," said Pelham, pleased with his success, as he put the coin on the table.

This also he won, and then staked half a sovereign, which he lost; but repeating the stake, won again. In a few moments he was deeply interested in the game, and put down a sovereign.

"A sovereign on the red!" stammered Wilton. "I've got the rocks."

"Come with me," said Jock, "and we'll play a game by ourselves."

"All right, my bonnie laddie. Sheet home and hoist away!" replied Wilton, as he staggered off with his new friend, leaving Pelham to pursue his game unmolested.

"Yours," said the gambler, as he turned up a red card. "You are lucky, my Yankee."

The lieutenant was fascinated by his good fortune, and actually won five sovereigns before his luck turned, as it always does in games of chance.

"Another sovereign on the red," said he, in excited tones.

He lost; but he was so sure the next card would be favorable, that he insisted upon putting down five sovereigns, though the considerate gambler advised him not to do so. The pack was cut, and he lost. Still hopeful, he repeated the stake, and lost again. He was naturally cautious, and appalled at his losses, he returned to single sovereigns again. He lost every time, and in ten minutes all his gold was gone. Then he borrowed two sovereigns of Monroe, who was half asleep in a chair at his side; but they did not restore his "luck." It would have been evident to Pelham, if he had been in his sober senses, that the gambler could cut red or black at his own pleasure. He was trying to wake Monroe enough to borrow another sovereign, when the man behind the bar said he must close the saloon, which he did in consequence of a nod from the gambler who had filched Pelham out of all his money.

"Take a glass of wine before we go," said Wilton, whom Jock had permitted to go to sleep again, as he was too tipsy to play "red and black."

The wine was drank; but Pelham persisted that he ought to have a chance to win back his money. The proprietor did not seem to think this was necessary, and declared that he should receive a visit from the police if he did not close his place at once. The visitors were assisted out of the saloon, and Jock kindly offered to conduct them to their hotel, as they did not know the way. Taking Wilton on one arm, and Monroe on the other, Pelham being better able than his shipmates to take care of himself, the young man led them to their hotel, and assisted the night porter in putting them to bed.

They awoke in the morning with violent headaches, as might have been expected. Pelham was disgusted with himself. He had lost all his money, except a few shillings in silver — had gambled it all away. While he was bitterly reproaching himself for his folly, he saw Wilton excitedly searching his pockets.

"What's the matter, Wilt?" demanded he.

"My money is all gone!" gasped Wilton.

"So is mine," groaned Monroe, clapping his hands upon his trousers' pockets.

"Every shilling gone!" exclaimed Wilton.

"I haven't a penny left," added Monroe.

"We're in a pretty fix!" said Pelham, dropping into a chair, utterly despondent.

"I didn't play any," added Wilton. "I was so sleepy I couldn't."

"Neither did I," said Monroe.

"It's a plain case: I have gambled all my money away, and Jock and the others picked your pockets while you were so tight."

"What shall we do? We can't even pay the hotel bill," continued Wilton.

They were a miserable trio of runaways.

CHAPTER XIII.

SOMETHING ABOUT SCOTLAND.

ON the morning after the arrival of the Young America at Greenock, all hands were piped to the steerage to hear Professor Mapps's lecture on the geography and history of Scotland. Before he commenced, however, Mr. Lowington made "a few remarks."

"Young gentlemen," he began, "I ought to say to you that the purposes of this voyage do not permit a thorough exploration of the several countries we shall visit. We can only observe a few of the prominent objects of interest which each nation or division contains. I think you saw enough of Ireland to give you an idea of the country. Doubtless at some future time many of you will visit Europe again, and you will find enough to occupy your attention for two or three years. I am sure you will enjoy such a tour all the more for the present cruise.

"Scotland is full of beautiful scenery, as well as objects of historic interest; but I find we can remain here only two or three weeks; and we must make a prudent use of our time. The entire season might be pleasantly and profitably spent in the waters of Scotland. It will not be practicable to take the ship to the eastern coast; but, fortunately, a large number of the natural and historical objects of interest lie within seventy miles of our present anchorage.

"Young gentlemen, I am happy to say that sight-seeing agrees with the routine of study and discipline on board of the ship even better than I had anticipated. Since we sailed from Brockway you have not lost more than six or seven days, which has been doing remarkably well. After you have seen Glasgow and the land of Burns, — which can be done without interfering with your studies, — we will take a short vacation, to enable you to visit the lakes, Stirling and Edinburgh."

The announcement was followed by a round of applause.

"I cheerfully bear testimony to your general good conduct, and to your devotion to your studies," continued the principal. "I assure you that, while you continue faithful to your duties, I shall afford you every privilege that is consistent with the object of the voyage."

The students hoped he would say something about the runaways, but he did not allude to them; not even the officers knew anything about them, and all were curious to ascertain whether Mr. Fluxion had found them. Some believed that, as the professor had returned to his duties, the deserters had been captured and sent home in disgrace; but those who had the most confidence in Pelham's skill and strategy were satisfied that he had eluded his pursuer.

"Young gentlemen," said Mr. Mapps, as he took his pointer, "I shall not detain you long over the map of Scotland, though the physical features of the country are worth a careful study. Scotland is, as you are aware, the northern division of the Island of Great Britain," he continued, pointing to the large map which hung on the foremast. "It is a peninsula. The length of the boundary line between Solway Frith and Berwick is about eighty miles. The longest line which can be drawn through the country would be from Dunnet Head to the Mull of Galloway, nearly north and south, two hundred and eighty-five miles. What is the area of Scotland?"

"Thirty-one thousand three hundred and twenty-four square miles," replied the boys in concert.

"About the same as Ireland, which is a little larger," added the professor, "and therefore about the size of the State of Maine. You perceive that on the west and north there are many large islands. Their united area is about forty-two hundred square miles. What is the population?"

"Three millions," replied the boys.

"For fifty years preceding 1851 its average increase was nearly eighty per cent.; but during the last ten years it has been only six per cent. It has about the same population as Pennsylvania, the State of New York containing one million more than Scotland. The surface is irregular and mountainous. Scotland is divided into the Highlands and Lowlands by a very indefinite line, which extends across the country, near its centre. The Highlands are subdivided by the chain of lochs extending from north-east to south-west, now so united that they form the Caledonian Canal.

"There is a list of nearly sixty mountains in Scotland, but none of them would be called high even in the United States. Ben Nevis, one of the Grampians, and the highest in the United Kingdom, is nearly two thousand feet less in height than Mount Washington. Ben Lomond, which is within twenty miles of us, and which perhaps you may ascend, is a little more than three thousand feet high. Ben Ledi, which you will also see, has nearly the same elevation.

"There are no rivers in Scotland of any considerable importance, all of them being less than two hundred miles in length. In Scotland the estuaries of these rivers receive the name of friths or firths. Above them the rivers are seldom navigable for large vessels. The Clyde, on which Glasgow is situated, has been deepened by dredging, so that vessels may go up about twelve miles. But these rivers are exceedingly valuable in a commercial point of view, for they furnish the principal cities of Great Britain with salmon.

"The country is abundantly supplied with lakes, which are very long for their width, and many of them are navigable for small steamers, which greatly facilitate internal communication.

"The climate is extremely variable, but the country is remarkably healthy. The temperature averages $47°$, varying from $10°$ to $70°$. The agriculture is superior to that of Ireland. The ordinary grains are raised, but fruits do not mature so well as in England. The mountainous regions can only be improved as pasturage, and the dairy products are important and valuable. Scotland is rich in minerals, and mines of coals, iron, lead, copper, and marble are extensively worked in various localities.

"The people of Scotland are divided, according to their origin, into the Highlanders and the Lowlanders, the former being more essentially Scotch than the latter, whose distinctive features were modified by the intermixture of the Saxons. In the scale of moral and intellectual being, the inhabitants of Scotland hold the highest rank, and no country has produced a better race of men. They are an honest, industrious, and reflecting people. Education has been widely disseminated among them, and institutions of learning are warmly cherished. Perhaps no nation has produced a greater proportion of distinguished poets, historians, philosophers, and mechanicians than Scotland. Burns, Scott, Campbell, Thomson, Montgomery, and Wilson, the poets, were born in Scotland; so were Hume, Robertson, Alison, and Carlyle, the historians; as well as Adam Smith, Dugald Stewart, and Sir William Hamilton, the philosophers, and Watt, the inventor of the steam engine.

"Scotland was known to the Romans under the name of Caledonia; but the early history of the country is not authentic. The feudal system prevailed during the first century, when the Scottish chieftains ruled their own clans. About the year 450 the Saxons invaded and conquered the Lowlands, where they settled, and Edwin, one of their leaders, founded the city of Edinburgh, or, as it was formerly called, Edwinsburgh. Fifty years later, the Scots, a Celtic tribe from Ireland, appeared in the country, settled on the west coast, and eventually became the dominant race. From them the country received its present name of Scotland. During this period the people were converted to Christianity by missionaries sent over from Ireland.

"The country north of the Clyde was conquered by the Danes; but a combination of chieftains, under the leadership of Malcolm, drove them from the main land to the Orkney and Western Islands, of which they had previously possessed themselves. The victor chief was made king of Scotland, under the title of Malcolm II. He was succeeded by his son, and by his grandson Duncan, who, according to the tragic story of Shakspeare's plays, was murdered by Macbeth; and he in his turn was defeated and slain by Malcolm, Duncan's son, who became undisputed sovereign of all Scotland, except the islands still in possession of the Danes.

"During the reign of Malcolm III. William the Conqueror landed in England, and the Normans obtained possession of the country. Malcolm had married Margaret, a Saxon princess, whose brother, Edgar Atheling, was the rightful successor of the crown of England. In the interest of his brother-in-law, the King of Scotland invaded the northern part of England, plundering and ravaging the country. King William, in revenge, entered Scotland with a force so large that Malcolm submitted to his power, and became his vassal. This claim, on the part of England, to the sovereignty of Scotland was the cause of a succession of wars.

"In the thirteenth century the throne of Scotland, made vacant by the death of Margaret, the infant child of Alexander III., was claimed, among others, by Bruce and Baliol. The ambitious King of England, Edward I., having designs upon the kingdom of Scotland, offered to mediate between the competitors. His offer was accepted: but before he would give his decision, he required the Scottish barons to acknowledge him as their 'lord paramount.' Intimidated by his vast power, they yielded, and thus the former claim of England was reëstablished. Edward gave the crown to Baliol, whom he soon intentionally goaded into a war, in which the country was overrun by the invaders, its strong places reduced, and the king captured and sent to the Tower of London. At this crisis, when Scotland seemed to be fully subjugated, Sir William Wallace appeared as an actor on the stage of events, and to some extent retrieved the fallen fortunes of his country. But this valiant Scottish chief was betrayed into the hands of his enemies, and Edward caused him to be cruelly executed in London.

"The unequal struggle was continued by Robert Bruce, of 'spider' memory. He was the grandson of the Bruce who had been the co-claimant with Baliol of the throne. He was not successful at first; but he persevered, encouraged by the example of the patient spider, and at last, in the great battle of Bannockburn, in 1314, defeated and overwhelmed the English."

"What's the spider story, sir? I never heard of it," said one of the students.

"I supposed every boy in the civilized world had heard it," replied Mr. Mapps, smiling. "Bruce lay one day in his tent or cabin, while nearly discouraged by the ill success of his arms, watching a spider which had made several ineffectual attempts to stretch his thread from one point to another. Regarding this spider as a type of himself, he watched it with interest, and when the insect succeeded in his purpose, Bruce interpreted it as a favorable augury, and continued his efforts, which were at last as successful as those of the spider had been.

"Though the war was continued for fourteen years longer, the independence of Scotland was finally acknowledged. During the next century the crown was worn by three successors of Bruce. Robert II. was the son of the 'Steward of Scotland,' which fact gave a name to the house of Stuart, of which he was the first king. The son of Robert III. became James I. of Scotland, who was succeeded by five more kings of the same name, which brings this history down to James VI., the last of the Scottish kings. Mary Stuart, commonly called 'Mary Queen of Scots,' was the daughter of James V. Of her history we shall have more to say at Stirling and Edinburgh.

"James IV. of Scotland married Margaret Tudor, daughter of Henry VII. of England. Henry VIII. left three children, Edward, Mary, and Elizabeth; and when the last died without children, James VI. of Scotland, directly descended through Mary Queen of Scots from Henry VII., became James I. of England; and here ends the separate history of Scotland. The two countries were united by a common sovereignty; but it was not till one hundred years later that they were joined together by law. The government is essentially the same now as that of England, and the people are represented in the two houses of Parliament.

"This is all I have to say at present, young gentlemen; but I shall have frequent occasion to allude to the history of Scotland as we visit various scenes of historic interest."

"You haven't said a word about Rob Roy," added a student, when the lecture was finished.

"I do not consider Rob Roy a person of sufficient consequence to occupy a place in a brief history of Scotland. The scene of his exploits was the region around Loch Lomond and Loch Katrine. He was simply a freebooter. Rob Roy, in plain English, was Robert the Red. His true name was Robert Macgregor. He was a cattle-dealer before the insurrection of 1715 in Scotland. George I. was the first sovereign of the Brunswick family, and some of the people of Scotland wished to have the succession continued in the line of the Stuarts. James II., who left his throne and went to France, was succeeded by his daughter Mary and her husband William of Orange. James made several attempts to recover his crown, as I told you, on the battle-field by the Boyne in Ireland. He had an only son, whom the people of Scotland wished to call to the throne. He is known in history as the Pretender. He went to Scotland, and the people there rallied under his banner. Among them was Rob Roy, the cattle-dealer. His lands were seized, and he commenced a war of reprisal. His daring exploits and a certain nobility of character made him a hero, and his name is a household word in Scotland."

Rob Roy "stock" was rather at a discount, even with those who had read Sir Walter Scott's novel, after the professor's rather contemptuous allusion to that worthy. The students devoted themselves to the studies of the forenoon, and at two o'clock in the afternoon they heard the welcome pipe of the boatswain which called together the crew for an excursion on shore. The boats were lowered, and all hands embarked.

"What is there here?" asked Paul Kendall of his constant friend the surgeon, when they landed at Greenock.

"Nothing of especial interest; but the place is a thriving commercial town, and noted for its shipbuilding," replied Dr. Winstock. "Did you ever read Burns's poems, Paul?"

"A little, sir."

"Then of course you have heard of Highland Mary. She was buried in this town."

"I never read much of Burns's poetry, for the reason that I could not understand the Scotch it contains," added Paul.

"There are plenty of his poems which contain no Scotch, though I think that is the charm of his works. His native humor and pathos are best expressed in the dialect in which he used to think and speak. You will find many memorials of Burns, and perhaps you will have a deeper interest in him when you have seen them. Certainly he was a wonderful poet; and in spite of his intemperance and the irregularities of his life, the people of Scotland almost worship his memory."

"I have often heard of Greenock, but I can't think what it is noted for," said Paul. "I know it is an important seaport, but it is famous for something else that I have heard about."

"It is the birthplace of a very celebrated man; one who had added more to the wealth of Great Britain than any other man; one who has increased the value of its productive industry more than a hundred fold."

"I know who he is now!" exclaimed Paul. "It is Watt, the man who invented the steam engine."

"You are right. He is generally called the inventor of the steam engine, though he did not discover the principle upon which the machine is constructed. But he made it applicable to the purposes for which the engine is now used, and he is justly entitled to all the honor which is awarded to him."

The party visited the Watt memorial in Union Street, which is a structure erected by the son of the great inventor, and contains a beautiful statue of Watt, by Sir Francis Chantrey, purchased by subscription.

After a walk through the town, the party took seats in the train for Glasgow. On this railroad the boys saw fourth-class cars, in which the passengers, paying less fare than the third class, are huddled in without seats — cheap, but not comfortable.

"Renfrew!" exclaimed Paul, and the train stopped at a village with this name. "I have heard of the place before."

"Probably you have heard of Baron Renfrew, who recently visited the United States. Do you know whom I mean?"

"Yes, sir; it was the Prince of Wales."

"It was; and in every official mention of the prince he was called Baron Renfrew. The barony belonged to the Stuart family, of whose origin Mr. Mapps spoke to you this forenoon, and came by descent to the Prince of Wales."

The train stopped a few moments at Paisley, which is an important manufacturing place. After leaving this town, the view from the window of the carriage was very pleasant. The houses of the poorer people were neat and comfortable, and the thrift of the Scotch was apparent in their dwellings and in their gardens. When the party arrived at the station in Glasgow, a sufficient number of carriages were in readiness for them, Mr. Fluxion having engaged them an hour before. The vehicles were a kind of barouche, drawn by one horse, accommodating four persons. They are let by the hour for three shillings. The ordinary cab fare for any distance within a mile and a half is one shilling, and sixpence for every additional half mile, which are only from a quarter to a half of the rates charged in the principal cities of the United States.

The procession of carriages left the station and crossed the Clyde by the Glasgow Bridge, a granite structure five hundred feet in length by sixty in width. A penny toll is collected on this bridge, which Paul Kendall declared no American city would tolerate in its midst.

"Before you have travelled long in Scotland and England, you will find a great many places where your passage is obstructed by a demand for a penny," said Dr. Winstock, with a smile.

"This is the Broomielaw," he added, pointing to the left of the bridge.

"The what?"

"The Broomielaw."

"I don't see any such thing as that," laughed Paul, looking in the direction indicated.

"It is the harbor or basin of the port. You see the forest of masts and the crowd of steamers, extending for a mile down the river. Fifty years ago the water here was not more than three and a half feet deep, and there are men now living in Glasgow who have often waded across the Clyde. The river had been doubled or tripled in width, and now vessels drawing twenty feet of water can come up at full tide."

"There are plenty of steamers here, and some of the smallest ones I ever saw," said Paul, as they passed from the bridge.

"Clyde-built steamers are celebrated all over the world, and the building of them is one of the most important branches of business in Glasgow, which you know is the third city in size in the United Kingdom."

"London is the first, and Liverpool the second," added Paul.

Glasgow, though its importance as a commercial and manufacturing place is of modern origin, is an ancient city, and is said to have been founded about the year 500. Before the American revolution the trade of the city was almost wholly in tobacco, in which large fortunes were made. The war between England and her colonies interrupted this trade, and the people turned their attention to the manufacturing of cotton goods, which has become one of the most productive sources of wealth to the city.

The iron trade, however, is the most notable branch of industry. About the time the revolution in America suspended the tobacco importation, Watt came upon the stage of action with the steam engine, and Glasgow, where Watt spent so many years of his life in studying the principle and perfecting the mechanism of his invention, derived immense benefit from his genius. The coal and iron mines in the vicinity afford abundant material for the iron works.

In 1812 Henry Bell launched on the Clyde the first steamboat ever seen in the United Kingdom, though some abortive attempts had been made by others to apply the steam engine as a motive power to vessels. This was five years after Fulton, the real inventor of the steamboat, had made his celebrated trip from New York to Albany in the Clermont. The immense improvements made in the port of Glasgow have opened new sources of wealth to the city. The building of iron steamers and their engines is now one of the chief branches of business.

"There is not much to be seen in Glasgow, and the city is of little importance to the tourist," said Dr. Winstock, as the procession of carriages turned into Argyle Street. "This is the principal street, and a ride of half an hour will give you a very good idea of the city, which is just like every other commercial town."

The odd names of the streets which the doctor or the driver mentioned amused the boys, as the Trongate and Gallowsgate, — which are a continuation of Argyle Street, — the Saltmarket, Sauchiehall, and the suburbs of Strathbungo and Crossmyloof.

In George Square there is a monument to Sir Walter Scott, a pedestrian statue of Sir John Moore, the hero of Corunna, another of James Watt, and a fourth of Sir Robert Peel, the famous statesman. There are other commemorative monuments or statues in the city.

The carriages stopped before a gloomy and massive Gothic structure, which proved to be Glasgow Cathedral, described by Sir Walter Scott in Rob Roy. It is a very ancient building, but has been "restored," and eighty-one beautiful stained glass windows added. Adjoining the Cathedral is the Necropolis, which is an immense burial-ground, and the last resting-place of some of the most renowned Scottish worthies. It contains a noble and chaste monument to John Knox, the fiery reformer. From the summit of the hill in this city of the dead, the party obtained a fine panoramic view of the city, the river, and the surrounding country, which proved to be more interesting to the boys than deciphering the epitaphs on the monuments.

A visit to the series of parks on the Clyde in the eastern part of the city completed the round of the excursion, and the ship's company arrived at the railway station just in time to take the train for Greenock. Of course they had not thoroughly explored Glasgow, but they had accomplished all the principal proposed, which was to give them " an idea " of the city.

CHAPTER XIV.

THE DESERTERS IN GLASGOW.

WITH aching heads, and stinging consciences, the three runaways sat on the beds and stared at each other in silence, after the full extent of their misfortune had become apparent. Their united funds would not amount to more than four shillings, which was not enough to pay the hotel bill, to say nothing of going to London and Paris, or even of leaving Glasgow. Each of them was thoroughly ashamed of himself, not so much for his vicious and immoral conduct as for his weakness and stupidity in permitting himself to be filched or robbed of his money.

It was Sunday morning. The clock of a church in the vicinity struck nine while they sat staring in dumb misery at each other, so appalled by the fearful misfortune which had overtaken them that they could not finish dressing themselves. There was no tyranny on board the Young America which bore so heavily upon them as the tyranny of their own misconduct, and all of them wished they had not embarked upon such a desperate venture. They were now fully convicted of inability to manage their own affairs, and perhaps could see the necessity of Mr. Lowington's stringent regulation in regard to the finances of the students.

These three boys, even with the burden of taking care of themselves resting upon them, at the first opportunity after they felt secure from pursuit, had become intoxicated, and lost, by gambling and being robbed, all the money in their possession but a few shillings. These facts were a triumphant vindication of the principal's policy; and though the deserters realized the truth, they did not acknowledge it to each other.

Wilton was the worst boy of the three, if not the worst belonging to the ship's company. His recklessness in the use of the wine had been the initial step to their present disgrace and helplessness. He was the first to speak after the long silence which followed the realization of the miseries of their situation. Each was reproaching himself for his own folly, and trying to devise a plan by which the party could be extricated from the desperate circumstances which surrounded them.

"It's no use to cry about it," said he, after he had made up his mind what could be done.

"Nobody is crying about it," added Monroe. "I'm not."

"I think we had better join the Scottish Temperance League," replied Pelham, with a faint attempt at humor.

"Or an anti-gambling league," suggested Wilton, looking sourly at the lieutenant.

"If we hadn't drank any wine, I don't think we should have lost any money by gambling," retorted Pelham.

"You drank as much wine as I did," said Wilton.

"Not quite; at any rate I didn't keep forcing the drinks upon others. One would have thought, from the way you kept calling for sherry, Wilton, that you had a thousand pounds in your pocket. You treated the whole crowd three or four times, and then you didn't know whether you stood on your head or your heels," continued Pelham, sharply.

"And one would think, from the way you gambled, that you had ten thousand pounds in your pockets," added Wilton, angrily.

"If a glass of wine fuddled me as it does you, I shouldn't take more than one."

"Lords and dukes don't play for more than a sovereign, or so, but you put down five."

"I think the pot needn't call the kettle black," said Pelham. "In my opinion it's six one and half a dozen the other; and we may as well dry up on this line of talk. We have all been stupid and weak, and the less we say about it the better. I gambled away all my money —"

"And some of mine," interposed Monroe, rather viciously.

"If I hadn't lost it, you would; but you are two sovereigns better off than you would have been if I hadn't borrowed them of you, for I shall pay all I owe you," replied Pelham, with dignity. "I gambled away my money, and you lost yours. We are all in the same box, and we had better not quarrel about it. What's to be done? That's the interesting question now."

"I don't see that there is anything we can do," replied Monroe, despondingly.

"We are not going to be hung, or anything of that sort," said Pelham, with an effort to be cheerful. "The case isn't half so desperate as it might be."

"It's bad enough, any how," added Wilton. "We are cornered here, without any money; and of course we can't go to London, or anywhere else. We are beggars in a strange land. I suppose we can write to Lowington, and ask him to get us out of this scrape."

"You may do that, but I never will," replied Pelham," decidedly.

"I don't want to do it; but there is only one other thing we can do."

"What is that?" asked Pelham, eagerly, when the conversation began to take a practical turn.

"We are all sailors, and we can ship on board some vessel bound to the United States."

"Ship! What, go into the forecastle of a merchantman as common sailors!" demanded the aristocratic young lieutenant.

"Why not? We can get home that way, if we can't get anywhere else?"

"We are not reduced to such an extremity as that."

"Arn't we? Well, I thought we were," said Wilton. "It's no use for you to put on airs here, Pelham. We are hard up, in a foreign country. You can't borrow, and you don't want to steal. I should like to know what you intend to do."

"I think you will have to trust me in the future, as you have in the past," replied the lieutenant, with a little pardonable vanity.

"Trust you!" exclaimed Wilton, with a sneer

"That's easy enough when we can't muster a sovereign among the three. I don't know that you are any bigger man than Monroe or I."

"If I hadn't managed this business, you would have been in the brig on board of the ship at this present time."

"I don't know that."

"I do; and if you had taken my advice last night, when I told you not to drink any more, we should not have got into this scrape."

"You drank yourself, and gambled away all your money and some of Ike Monroe's. You needn't say anything!" snapped Wilton.

"I don't complain now. I only say if you had heeded me, we should not have been in trouble."

"I don't know about that."

"Don't quarrel about it, fellows," interposed Monroe, who had proved himself to be a cipher in council.

"I don't care! I don't believe in Gus Pelham's putting on airs."

"All right, Wilt; we won't have any trouble," added the lieutenant, rather haughtily. "I don't care about being snubbed; and since we can't agree, we can disagree. I will go my way, and you may go yours."

Pelham rose from his seat on the bed, and completed his toilet without any further remark.

"What are you going to do to-day, Pelham?" asked Wilton.

"Nothing," replied the lieutenant.

"To-day is Sunday. I suppose we can't do anything; but I should like to get hold of that fellow that took us to the saloon," added Wilton.

"You can if you like; I don't want anything to do with him. You can make your plans now to suit yourself, Wilton. I told you I wasn't going to be snubbed; and what I do, I shall keep to myself."

"Don't be so short, Gus," said Wilton.

"To-morrow you can go your way, and I will go mine."

"What do you mean?"

"I mean that we will part company. I'm not going to have a fellow talk to me about putting on airs. I don't like your way of doing things. In the morning we will part company, and I will sail on my own hook."

"You don't mean that, Pelham," added Wilton, who, though crabbedly unwilling to acknowledge that the lieutenant was the ablest and most skilful manager in the party, was not the less conscious of the fact.

"I mean it."

"That isn't fair."

"Why not? If we can't agree, we had better separate. I don't want to be responsible for your blunders, and I won't ask you to be responsible for mine."

"I don't know what you mean by that kind of talk," replied Wilton, who really felt that the loss of Pelham would be a great misfortune.

"It's no use for us to run about this country as we did last night. You made friends with that Jock, and he has been the ruin of us. I shouldn't have done it. You insisted upon drinking, and I couldn't refuse without being mean. I shouldn't have done that. You wouldn't mind what I said, and here we are head over heels in trouble. Last night I followed your lead, and we are cleaned out. Up to this time you followed my lead, and we were safe. We can't get along with divided counsels."

"I suppose you mean that you must be 'cock of the walk,' or you will leave us," said Wilton, smartly.

"I mean just that," added Pelham, boldly.

"Then you may go when you please. I would as lief have Lowington to tyrannize over me as you."

"All I have to say is, that one of us must lead. I won't follow your lead, and if you won't follow mine, that is the end of the whole matter."

"I won't," replied Wilton, decidedly. "I think it is mean for one fellow to attempt to lord it over another."

"There will be no lording about it. If you had taken my advice last night, we should not have got into this scrape. I think I am better able to take care of the party than you are. If you don't think so, I haven't a word to say. You can go where you like, and I will do the same. Nobody's bones will be broken; I shall not tyrannize over you, and you will not get me into any scrape."

"Come, come, fellows," interposed Monroe, alarmed by this conflict for the leadership; "don't get into any row."

"No row at all," said Pelham. "It's all right now."

"I don't ask to be captain," added Wilton; "and I don't want any ruler over me. If we can't go as equals, we won't go together any longer."

"All right, I'm going down to get some breakfast," continued Pelham, as he put on his cap and moved towards the door.

"Don't go yet, Pelham," pleaded Monroe. "Let us fix this thing up. I am willing to follow Pelham's lead," he added, turning to Wilton, "as we have done from the beginning."

"I'm not," added Wilton, doggedly. "I haven't done it yet, and I don't mean to begin now. Shall we see you again, Pelham?" he asked with a sneering smile.

"I shall not leave you to-day. To-morrow, Monroe, I will pay you the two sovereigns I borrowed.

"Where will you get the money?" demanded Wilton.

"That's my affair," replied the lieutenant, sternly.

"Where are you going to-morrow?"

"Don't trouble yourself any more about me. If I want any help from you, I will call upon you for it."

"And when I want a fellow to boss me, I'll give you an invitation to take the situation," sneered Wilton, as Pelham left the room.

"What was the use of doing that?" said Monroe, with deep disgust at the conduct of his companion.

"Do you think I have come here to have a good time, and mean to submit to Gus Pelham? He'll find he isn't a lieutenant here, if he is on board the ship," replied Wilton, with a proper exhibition of independence.

"Humph! here we are without any money, and you are splitting hairs over a silly question about who shall be the leader."

"I don't want any more tyrants. I didn't sell out one to take another aboard so soon."

"Pelham is a good fellow, and knows how to manage things. You can't deny that you got us into that scrape last night. You made friends with that Jock, and asked him out to drink. You made him take us to that gambling hole."

"Are you going to turn upon me, too?" demanded Wilton, indignantly.

"You can't deny it, and you don't. Pelham told you not to drink any more, two or three times. If you had heeded what he said, we should have been all right."

"You are a flunky, Ike Monroe. If you want to put yourself under *Mr.* Pelham's thumb, you can; I shall not."

"All I've got to say is, if we are going to break up in this way, I am going with Pelham. He is twice as safe a fellow to be with as you are."

"Perhaps he is; but he will borrow your money when he is cleaned out, as he was last night."

"I have no more to lend. He promised to pay me to-morrow."

"And he will — over the left."

"He said he would. I believe he will."

"Don't you believe the moon is made of green cheese? That's Gus Pelham's gas. How can he pay you when he hasn't half a crown left? If you want to toady to him, do it."

"I don't want to toady to any fellow, and Gus Pelham don't want any fellow to toady to him. But he's a safe fellow to be with, and I'm going with him."

"Are you?" demanded Wilton, as his companion and crony moved towards the door.

"I am."

"I'll bet you won't!"

"Why not?"

"Because you won't. You and I have hung together through a good many scrapes, and you are not going to cut me now."

"Yes, I am, if you don't make terms with Pelham."

"I'm not going to make terms with Pelham, and you are not going to cut me," replied Wilton, with a malicious assurance.

"What's the reason I'm not?"

"Because you are not. If you do one mean thing, I'll do another."

"What will you do?"

"If you leave me, I'll look out for myself, and put Lowington on your track and Pelham's within forty-eight hours. He's over at Belfast, and it wouldn't take him long to find you after he was informed that you had been in Glasgow."

Monroe threw his cap down upon the bed. He had not the courage to cut his old crony, partly perhaps from the inherent meanness of the act, and partly from a fear that Wilton would put his threat into execution. Wilton smiled at the triumph he had achieved over his irresolute friend, and for the moment forgot the desperate situation of the party. But his aching head soon swept away his exhilaration, and brought him back to the consciousness of his weak and helpless situation. He did not want any breakfast. He had no appetite yet, and he was afraid the landlord would wish to know where the money to pay the bill was to come from.

"Have you any idea what you are going to do, Wilt?" asked Monroe, after he had gazed out of the window in painful silence for a time.

"If we can't do any better, we can ship for the United States," replied Wilton. "I don't want to do that, but we can if we are obliged to do so. I'm going to try something better first."

"What?"

"I'm going to get my money back."

"When you do, you will."

"Well, I will, then. If I only had my money, I would rather be without Pelham than with him."

"How will you get your money back, I should like to know?"

"Call on the police. I had about twenty-five sovereigns in my pocket, you see. That Jock took it from me. My head was rather muddy; but I know just the time when he put his hand into my pocket. I have an idea that I can find the rascal. He belongs to that gambling house, and is sent out to haul in flats."

"But where is the gambling house? I'm sure I couldn't find it."

"I could; and we will go out and hunt it up by and by," added Wilton, with a long gape, as he threw himself upon the bed.

He had not yet recovered from the effects of his debauch, and presently he dropped asleep. When he began to snore, Monroe also lay down, and soon followed the example of his friend. At twelve o'clock they waked again, feeling much better. They went down to the coffee-room, and took a light breakfast. Pelham was not in the house. The landlord was as polite as he had been the day before, and evidently did not suspect that the exchequer of his guests was exhausted.

When Wilton and Monroe had finished their meal, they left the house, intent upon finding the place to which they had been conducted the night before by Jock Sanderson. Neither of them had any idea of the route by which they had been led from the gambling house to the hotel, and they went first to the Theatre Royal. The dram-shop they had first entered, after the play was over, was readily found. As neither of them had been very tipsy before they entered the gambling saloon, their united observation enabled them at last to find the place. It was closed; but Wilton was much encouraged by his success.

While he stood in front of the house, telling Monroe what he intended to do the next morning, a policeman came along, and Wilton, hoping to enlarge his knowledge of the locality, touched his cap, and politely saluted the guardian of the city's morals.

"Can you tell me what kind of a house that is opposite?" he asked, pointing to the building in which the gambling saloon was located.

"There's a dram-shop in it, and very like some gambling is done there," replied the officer.

"Very likely there is," added Wilton, significantly. "Do you know anything of the people who keep the shop?"

"They are bad people, and very sly. It's not a regular gambling house, but they filch strangers of their money occasionally. I am set to watch them."

"Do you know one Jock Sanderson, who goes there?" asked Wilton, anxiously.

"I never haird the name before," replied the policeman, with a smile. "But the people in yon house have as monny names as there are feathers in a blackbird's tail," added the officer, with more zeal than he had at first manifested; for he probably began to suspect that the young sailors before him had been victimized in the house.

Wilton and Monroe described the personal appearance of Jock so well, that the policeman declared it was very like a person who frequented the place, and who had been once arrested for decoying a stranger into the gambling den.

"Come to this place to-morrow morning, and I will go in with you," added he. "Have you been filched in the house?"

"We lost something there last night," replied Wilton, sheepishly.

"Did you, man?" demanded the policeman, eying the young men from head to foot. "Come to me in the morning, then, for I shall be glad to catch the rogue that plundered you."

"We shall get our money, Ike!" exclaimed Wilton, as the policeman passed on.

"Perhaps we may."

"I feel pretty sure of it. I think we shall have a chance to tell *Mr*. Pelham that it is better to be robbed than it is to gamble your money away. Come, we will return to the hotel, for I suppose we cannot do anything more to-day."

As they walked up the street towards the theatre,

a young man came out of an alley near the house which had been the subject of the conversation, and followed them till they entered the hotel. He paused a few moments at the door, and then followed them in.

"Where are the young larks who are stopping here?" he asked of the landlord.

"Two of them have just gone to their room."

"I wish to see them."

"Show him to No. 19," said the landlord to a servant; and the young man was conducted to the room of the deserters.

Wilton and Monroe had just thrown themselves on the beds, lazy rather than tired, though both were still suffering from their intemperance.

"I feel pretty sure we shall get our money back," said Wilton.

"Don't be too sure."

"The policeman knew Jock, though I suppose that is not his real name. I would like to get my claws upon that precious villain."

"You never will see him again, I fear," replied the desponding Monroe.

But at that instant the door opened, and Jock Sanderson — for he was the young man who had followed them from the alley near the gambling house — entered the room.

"Jock!" exclaimed Wilton, springing from the bed; and his more prudent companion was afraid he would put his claws upon the precious villain.

"I'm glad to see you, young gentlemen," said Jock, with every assurance. "I should have called earlier in the day, but that I always make it a rule to go to the kirk in the forenoon."

"Do you, indeed?" exclaimed Wilton.

"Always," added Jock, taking a chair. "Now don't you think you are a pretty brace of young larks? I'll wager a sixpence you haven't been near the kirk to-day."

"We certainly have not," replied Wilton, taken all aback by the impudence of Jock.

"You are doubtless sober, and I came to let you thank me for the good service I did you last night," continued Jock, taking a plethoric purse from his pocket. "Twenty-five sovereigns from one, and ten from the other," he added, counting out the amounts named, and handing each to its owner. "Now you may thank your good fortune that you fell into the company of an honest young man who goes to the kirk."

"What do you mean?" demanded the amazed Wilton, as he took the twenty-five sovereigns.

"You were drunk last night, — beastly drunk for young boys as you are. I was sure you would be robbed of every shilling you had, if I didn't take care of your money for you. I took it from you when you were tipsy, and now I return it to you when you are sober. Take my advice; don't drink, and go to the kirk every Sunday, at least once in the day."

"You are a good fellow, Jock!" exclaimed Wilton. "Don't go yet; I'll send for a bottle of wine, and drink your health from it."

"No; I never drink wine on Sunday," replied Jock, decidedly. "Where is the other lark that was with you?"

"He's gone out."

"I have nothing to do with the money he lost by gambling."

"Certainly you have not," said Wilton, overjoyed at the recovery of his money, and not caring a straw about Pelham's losses.

"I saw you in the street talking with a policeman," continued Jock. "What was that about?"

"We were looking for the money we had lost."

"Well, you have got that."

"Of course we have no further business with the police."

"You see, young larks, I took your money from you to keep you from losing it. You were polite and civil to me at the theatre, and I wished to do you a good turn."

"You have done it, and we are very grateful to you," answered Wilton, with enthusiasm.

"But the policeman might annoy me."

"We will not say anything more to him. We shall leave Glasgow to-morrow."

The answer seemed to satisfy Jock, and declining again the invitation to drink, he left the room. Wilton and Monroe were too much bewildered at the recovery of their lost funds to ask any questions; but the fact was, that Jock was a regular gambling house runner. From the window of the house he had seen the policeman talking with his victims, and having been once arrested, he was fearful of the consequences of his crime. For stealing thirty-five pounds, detectives would follow him all over the United Kingdom. The officer knew him, and he had purchased the silence of his dupes by restoring their money.

"I wonder where Pelham is," said Wilton, after they had discussed the miraculous recovery of their money.

"Perhaps he is looking for the money he lost," replied Monroe.

"He won't find it."

"Probably not."

"We can afford to ride the high horse now. We can give him one, and beat him then," chuckled Wilton.

"We can help him out now."

"We can; but we won't."

"Do you mean to let him go now we have got our money back?"

"Certainly I do; we can afford to let him go. Ike, don't you say a word to him about what has happened. I want to see what he will do, and whether he is mean enough to leave us. If he is, let him go. Don't you say a word, nor give him a hint. If you do, I'll cut you."

"I won't."

"No fellow shall boss me."

Pelham did not come to the room again till bedtime. He said nothing about the separation, and his shipmates did not reveal the good fortune which had astounded them in the afternoon.

The next morning Pelham got up earlier than his room-mates, and went out. At ten o'clock he returned.

"Monroe, here are the two sovereigns I borrowed of you," said he, handing him the money. "Now, good by, fellows."

He paid his bill at the bar below, and left the house.

"He has raised the wind somehow or other," said Monroe.

"Yes; but I see he no longer wears the gold watch and chain, which he used to say was worth more than any other fellow's in the ship. I'll bet he didn't get twenty pounds for both, though they were worth forty. Let him go."

Pelham took the next train for Balloch Pier and Loch Lomond.

CHAPTER XV.

THE LAND OF BURNS.

AFTER study hours on the day following the excursion to Glasgow, the officers and crew of the Young America embarked in the boats for a visit to Dumbarton, about seven miles up the river. Though the town is a very pretty place, the principal object of interest is the castle, which is located on the point of land between the Clyde and the Leven. It is built on Dumbarton Rock, which rises abruptly from the point of junction between the two rivers to the height of five hundred and sixty feet. It is about a mile in circumference, and is crowned by two pinnacles, the highest of which is called Wallace's Seat, whereon are the ruins of a tower in which Wallace was confined. A two-handed sword is exhibited as his celebrated claymore. .

"Young gentlemen," said Professor Mapps, when the ship's company had seated themselves to rest after the fatigues of the ascent, "this is a place of great historic interest. It was one of the four fortified places required to be kept in repair when England and Scotland were united, and has been a stronghold for more than a thousand years. During the wars between England and Scotland, in the time of Mary Queen of

Scots, when Henry VIII. was endeavoring to conquer this kingdom, it was the scene of several important events. The King of France espoused the cause of Mary, and sent a fleet and army to assist the Scotch. As the young queen, then only six years old, was not safe in her own disturbed kingdom, it was deemed advisable by her friends to convey her to France. She was brought to this place from Stirling, and embarked in a French man-of-war which lay in the river below us.

"This fortress was captured in the reign of Mary, in a very remarkable manner, by Captain Crawford, one of the English king's adherents. On a very dark night, with a small party of picked men, he conveyed his scaling ladders to a point beneath the highest and steepest part of the rock, concluding that it would be less vigilantly guarded than the more exposed positions. He was assisted by a deserter from the castle, who was to act as his guide. The first ladder that was raised broke beneath the weight of the soldier who ascended it; but as no sentinels were within hearing of this part of the rock, the noise did not betray the party, and Crawford renewed the attempt in person. The first precipice was successfully scaled, and the bold little band stood on a shelf of the rock, ready to attempt the second height. The scaling ladder was placed in position for this purpose, and the adventurers commenced the ascent. When half way up, one of the soldiers was seized with an epileptic fit, brought on by terror or over-exertion, and could neither go up nor down. It was cruel to throw him over, and the noise of his fall might alarm the garrison; so Crawford lashed him to the ladder. The party descended, turned the ladder over, and went up with the man tied to the under side. The summit of the rock was gained, a sleepy sentinel killed before he had time to give the alarm, and the garrison effectually surprised."

"But what became of the man in the fit?" asked one of the students, when the professor ended his narrative.

"I don't know; I suppose they hoisted him up or down when they had more time to spare," laughed Mr. Mapps. "I do not vouch for the truth of the story, for such events are very often grossly exaggerated. At a later period, and under more prosperous circumstances, Mary visited the rock again; and Queen Victoria, on her way to the Highlands, in 1847, stopped at the castle."

The boats returned to the ship at an early hour, and as soon as they were hoisted up at the davits, to the astonishment of the crew, all hands were piped to unmoor ship. When the anchor was hove short, and the sail-loosers were at work in the rigging, a party of a dozen ladies and gentlemen came off in a shore-boat with Mr. Fluxion. A pilot was already on board, and in a few moments the Young America was standing down the river. As soon as the ship was under way, the party from the shore were introduced to the officers. Among them were four young ladies and two young gentlemen, with whom the after-cabin officers were soon on very intimate terms.

"This was rather a sudden movement, — was it not?" asked Paul of his friend, the doctor.

"It was decided upon this forenoon; but we are not going far to-night," replied the surgeon.

"How far?"

"We shall anchor in Rothesay Bay, at the Island of Bute. It is not more than fifteen miles distant, and if the breeze holds we shall be there by nine o'clock. You have pleasant company, Paul," added Dr. Winstock.

"Not so pleasant as it was in Belfast," laughed the lieutenant.

"No? Why, Miss Rose McLeish is the prettiest girl I have seen in the United Kingdom."

"That may be; but she don't please me as well as a certain young lady I met in Belfast," added Paul, desperately, and with a blush in spite of his effort to be brave.

"Miss Grace Arbuckle — well, I suppose not. By the way, Paul, have you written to Grace, as you promised?"

"Of course I have."

"How many times?"

"Three; twice while we were in the north of Ireland, and once since we anchored here," replied Paul, who looked just then as though he was counting the seams in the quarter-deck.

"You must keep cool, my young friend. Once a month, I should say, would be often enough for a boy of sixteen to write to a young lady," added the doctor, a little more solemnly. "Of course they were love letters."

"Of course they were not, sir. I never wrote a love-letter in my life, and I don't think I ever shall. Do you think, doctor, I'm such a fool as that?"

"I think you like Miss Grace very well, Paul."

"So I do, as a friend."

"Exactly so," replied Dr. Winstock, with a significant nod. "How long letters did you write?"

"From eight to twelve pages; but I only told her about the ship, and what we saw at the Giant's Causeway. In the last one, which was twelve pages, I described our run from Port Rush, and what we did and saw in Glasgow and Greenock," replied Paul, quite earnest in defending himself from the charge of writing love-letters.

"Is that all?"

"Of course I couldn't help alluding to the pleasant time we had in Belfast, and on the excursion to Arran. I'm sure I never had such a good time in all my life."

"I suppose not. Do you think you would have had just as good a time if Miss Grace had not been on board?"

"Certainly not; but I am entirely willing that Grace should show my letters to her father and mother."

"Then it must be all right, Paul."

"Why, I wrote to her just as I do to my sister; and I will show you her letter, if I get one," added the lieutenant.

"I do not ask that, Paul, and I should not read one of Miss Arbuckle's letters to you. I only wished to say that you are rather young to open a sentimental correspondence with a young lady. If you confine it to writing about your travels and the history of the ship's movements, it will all be very well. Captain Gordon seems to appreciate Miss McLeish, if you don't," added the doctor, as he glanced to the weather side, where the guests were promenading with some of the officers and the faculty.

"Well, lads, you have a jolly time of it," said Arthur McLeish, a young gentleman of sixteen, as he stepped up to the second lieutenant.

"Speaking for myself, I can say we do," replied Paul.

"You must have fine times on board," added the Scotch boy. "I wonder could I get into the ship."

"I'm afraid not. Our number is full, and every berth is taken. But it isn't all fun on board, I can tell you. We have to work hard at our studies, and perhaps you wouldn't like to stand your watch at night in a cold north-east gale," suggested Paul.

"O, I wouldn't mind that. My father is going to try to get me in as a pupil. Are all the berths in the cabin taken?"

"In the cabin!" exclaimed Paul. "Do you expect to begin as an officer?"

"Sairt'nly I do," replied the applicant.

"Perhaps you would like to go as captain."

"That would just suit me as well as anything," replied Arthur, seriously.

"Our fourth lieutenant is away, and perhaps you are willing to take his place," laughed Paul.

"I would even take that."

"Perhaps your father can induce the principal to give you that berth."

"I will ask him at once to try," continued the applicant, as he began to move towards the place where Mr. Lowington was talking with the older of his guests.

"Hold on a minute!" called Paul. "Perhaps you are not aware that the officers have to take charge of the ship during their watch. Can you tell me what orders you would give when the ship is to go in stays."

"Go in what? I don't know what you mean."

"What would you say to the quartermaster, if you wished to put the ship on the other tack."

"I haven't the least idea."

"Then I fear you would not answer for an officer," replied Paul, good naturedly.

"I could soon lairn."

But Paul, without "putting on airs," convinced the young Scotch gentleman that he was not competent to be an officer. Then he took him down into the steerage, and showed him how the crew lived and studied, explained to him the routine of ship's duty, and of study; and Arthur was finally reasonable enough to say he would like to join the ship as an occupant of the steerage, which was certainly very condescending in him.

At nine o'clock, the wind still blowing fresh from the north-west, the ship came to anchor off Rothesay, at the head of the bay. The visitors on board were landed, and went to a hotel, as there were not accommodations on board for them.

After study hours, the next day, the whole ship's company went on shore to visit Rothesay Castle, once the residence of the kings of Scotland, and to take a run upon the island. At five o'clock the crew and the guests were on board again. The ship was unmoored, and, in charge of a pilot, sailed to the southward; but the wind was very light, and it was not till sunrise the next morning that she anchored off Ayr. The officers had given up the after-cabin to the guests, when it was found that the ship could not reach her anchorage that night, sleeping in vacant berths or on the floor in the steerage.

It was Sunday when the ship dropped anchor in the harbor of Ayr; and though Mr. Lowington offered to land the guests in the morning, none of the students were permitted to go on shore. Religious services were held under the awnings on deck, which were attended by all on board. Towards night the party from Greenock were landed.

At the usual hour for recreation, the boats were lowered, and all hands went on shore at Ayr, which is the birthplace of Burns, the national poet of Scotland. The town and its vicinity is generally called The Land of Burns. "The Two Brigs of Ayr" were pointed out to them by the Scotch people in the party; but there was hardly one among them who ever heard of the poem relating to them.

"Never haird of the brigs of Ayr!" exclaimed Arthur McLeish, when Paul Kendall confessed that he was ignorant of the existence of any such poem. "You must be vairy ignorant in Amairica."

"We are; we don't know anything. Of course you have read the poem."

"Indeed I have. It's about two bridges, one of which talked to the other," replied Arthur.

"Do you think it a better poem than Evangeline?"

"I never haird of Evangeline."

"Never heard of it!" exclaimed Paul. "How ignorant you must be here in Scotland?"

"Who wrote it?"

"Mr. Longfellow."

"Who is he? He's no' much of a poet, or I should have haird of him. Sairt'nly you will not think of comparing him with Robert Burns."

"I never read anything written by Burns that I liked half as well as the Launching of the Ship."

"That's all because you are a sailor. I like Burns better than any other poet."

"That's all because you are a Scotchman," laughed Paul.

Carriages were provided for the ladies, and the gentlemen who preferred to ride; but the students elected to walk, for the country in the vicinity of Ayr is beautiful.

"Mayhap you never haird of Tam O'Shanter," said Arthur, as they approached the ruins of Alloway Kirk, the neighborhood of which is the scene of that celebrated poem.

"Yes, I have — read it through, in spite of the uncouth words and phrases it contains," replied Paul, to whom the young Scotchman had attached himself.

"The uncouth words and phrases are the beauty of the poem," added Arthur, with enthusiasm.

"To a Scotchman they may be."

"We think there is no poet in the world like Burns."

After a walk of two miles from the town of Ayr, the party reached the cottage where Burns was born. The original structure remains as it was in the poet's day; but additions have been made in the rear. It originally had but two rooms, the kitchen and the sitting-room. The floor was of rough stones, very unevenly laid; and of the two windows, one was only about a foot square. The house was built by the poet's father.

In the churchyard of Alloway Kirk is the grave of Burns's father, marked by a plain tombstone, which was erected to supply the place of the original one, carried off in fragments by relic-hunters. The church was dilapidated in the poet's time, and had the reputation of being haunted; and this popular superstition is the groundwork of Tam O'Shanter, who, in his ride home from the ale-house in Ayr, where he had drank too much, encountered all the witches and the fiends that lurked about the kirk and the graveyard.

> "Kirk Alloway was drawing nigh,
> Where ghosts and howlets nightly cry."

The ghostly crew give chase to the luckless Tam, who spurs on Meg, the good mare he rides.

> "Now do thy speedy utmost, Meg,
> And win the keystane o' the brig;
> There at them thou thy tail may toss;
> A running stream they darena cross!"

But when Tam reached the "brig" poor Meg had no tail to toss, for the foremost of the pursuing host of demons had caught the beast by the tail, and pulled it off! It is fortunate that there is always some way to get rid of witches and fiends; that horse-shoes have wonderful virtues; that certain words have wonderful potency; and Tam O'Shanter's salvation rested in the "well-known fact" that the diabolical band could not pursue their victim beyond the middle of the nearest running stream.

The visitors walked to the river, and Mr. McLeish pointed out the "auld brig o' Doon," whose "keystane" had been the objective point of the hero of the poem. Crossing this bridge, the party reached the Burns monument. It is a memorial structure, for Burns died and was buried at Dumfries. The monument is an open temple, on a high base of granite, having nine pillars to represent the nine Muses, and surmounted by a dome. The grounds, which are tastefully laid out, contain an acre and a quarter of land. In a circular room on the ground floor, various mementos of the poet are exhibited, including copies of the various editions of his works, copies of the several original portraits, a snuff-box made of wood from the timbers of Alloway Kirk, and — more valuable than all the rest — the Bible given by Burns to his Highland Mary, which was purchased in Canada, and presented to the trustees. In a grotto near the enclosure are exhibited the statues of Tam O'Shanter, and Souter Johnnie, his boon companion.

The excursionists spent another hour in wandering on the banks of the Doon, which still "bloom sae fresh and fair." The country was very beautiful, and the boys, without knowing much of what the poet had done to immortalize it, were delighted with the scenery. Mr. McLeish, who had the history of Burns at his tongue's end, was full of enthusiasm on the subject. He told those who cared to hear him, that the poet lived at Mauchline and Mossgeil, carrying on a farm with his brother Gilbert; and at these places he wrote some of his best poems. He was unsuccessful in his farming scheme, and published an edition of his poetry at Kilmarnock, to raise the money to enable him to emigrate to Jamaica. He had paid his passage; but the friends of Jane Armour, afterwards his wife, prevented him from leaving. He went to Edinburgh, where he remained a year, and published an edition of his works. He returned home with five hundred pounds, half of which he paid his brother for the farm at Mossgeil, and used the balance in stocking a farm for himself in Dumfriesshire. He was made an officer of excise, which yielded him from fifty to seventy pounds a year. His dissolute habits and the cares of his office caused him to neglect his farm; and as it paid him nothing, he was obliged to give it up. His life in Dumfries, as it had been before, was a continued struggle with poverty, as it must be with all tipplers. His constitution was delicate, and his bad habits made such inroads upon it, that it was completely broken down, and he died at the early age of thirty-seven.

Burns was a remarkable man. His genius was of the highest order, and he was admired and petted in private by those who, on account of his dissipated habits, would not acknowledge him in the street. His popularity was immense in all classes of society, and his funeral was attended by vast multitudes from all parts of the country. His poetry came from the deepest depths of his heart, which was attuned to the most delicate emotions. While there is much to condemn, both in the poet's life and in his works, there is so much to admire, that one can hardly think of his faults while moved by the brilliancy and pathos of his works.

Though it was nearly dark when the ship's company arrived on board, the Young America was got under way immediately. As only a quarter watch was required on deck in ordinary weather, it was not considered any great hardship to make the run back to Greenock by night, and before daylight she was at her former anchorage in the Clyde, the visitors returning from Ayr by railroad.

Early in the morning, Mr. McLeish and his son came on board, and after some conversation with the principal, Arthur was provided with a uniform, and the berth belonging to Wilton was assigned to him. It appeared that he had teased his father, who had, with much persuasion, induced Mr. Lowington to receive him.

"Here I am, Paul," said the young Scotchman, walking up to the second lieutenant on the quarter-deck, as soon as he had dressed himself in his sea-rig. "Don't I look like a sailor?"

"Not on the quarter-deck," said Paul, with a smile. "Seamen are not allowed abaft the mizzen-mast."

"The mizzen-mast?" added Arthur, inquiringly.

"That one," replied Paul, pointing to it.

"Mr. Lowington is a friend of my father, and he won't mind it. I was going down into the cabin to have a talk with you."

"Into the cabin!" exclaimed Paul, laughing.

"Yes, into the cabin: that's what I said."

"But you mustn't go into the cabin."

"What's to hinder?"

"There are more than fifty of the students forward who never set a foot in the after-cabin. They are not allowed to do so."

"I'll no stand that," said Arthur. "What's the hairm of my going into the cabin?"

"It is contrary to the rules of the ship."

"Don't you see that Mr. Lowington is a friend of my father?"

"That will make no difference. Mr. Lowington serves all alike. If you work your way into the cabin, it will be all right. Yesterday you were a guest; to-day you are a sailor. You must leave the quarter-deck, or there will be trouble."

"Can't a seaman speak to an officer?"

"He may; but he must not go on the quarter-deck to do it, nor anywhere when the officer is on duty, unless he speaks about the business 'of the ship.'"

"Hoot, man! This is all nonsense!" exclaimed Arthur, in disgust.

"While you were on board the ship as a guest, did you see any of the seamen in the cabin or on the quarter-deck?"

"I didn't obsairve — yes, indeed, I did! I saw twenty of them pulling yon ropes."

"Of course; to set the spanker, or trim the sails, they must go on the quarter-deck; but never, unless they have something to do, or when ordered there. You saw none of them in the cabin," continued Paul, walking forward himself in order to get the new hand out of trouble. "The ship's rules are hung up in the steerage, where you can read them."

"I was going to ask you what I should do; but I'll no stand it to have a parcel of Yankee boys lording it over me."

"The officers will treat you well; but you must obey orders, and keep in your place."

"My place will be where I choose to go," replied Arthur, with spirit.

Paul attempted to reason with him; but while he was engaged in this up-hill work, the ship's company were piped to muster, and a small steamer was approaching the ship from Greenock. Breakfast had been served at an early hour, and it was plain that something was about to happen. Mr. Lowington took his stand, and presented Arthur McLeish as a new scholar. He then announced that the steamer approaching the ship would convey the party to Dumbarton, where they would take the train for Loch Lomond, the Trosachs, and Edinburgh, not to return till Saturday.

This information was received with three hearty cheers; and the students, who had been before required to put on their best uniforms, were sent below to bring up their little bags and blankets for the trip.

"I suppose I'm to go with you," said Arthur; "though I would rather stay on board of the ship."

"Of course you will," answered Paul.

"What a piping!" exclaimed the new scholar, as the boatswain's whistle sounded, a few moments later.

"All hands aboard the steamer!" shouted the boatswain; and in a short time the ship's company were landed at Dumbarton, where they took the train for Balloch Pier, at the foot of Loch Lomond, where in fifteen minutes more they arrived.

CHAPTER XVI.

PELHAM'S ADVENTURE.

WHATEVER else may be said of Pelham's conduct in leaving his companions, he was certainly straightforward. He spoke his mind and acted his convictions. Though he was not opposed on principle to taking a glass of wine, or even to gambling, he was unwilling to follow the reckless leadings of Wilton. He did not desire to direct the movements of the trio because he simply wished to exercise the power this position would confer upon him, but to save the expedition from any further disaster.

He had ability and discretion, in which his fellow-deserters were sadly lacking. He was a bold and determined fellow, and only needed the firm foundation of a high principle to make him an entirely reliable one. He possessed a high sense of honor, as he understood the meaning of this word, and there were many noble traits in his character. He fully believed that Wilton was the author of the misfortunes which had befallen them, and with the ideas of discipline he had obtained on board of the ship, he foresaw nothing but trouble and disaster if Wilton was permitted to have his own way.

He paid Monroe the two sovereigns he had borrowed of him from the proceeds of the sale of his watch and chain, which had brought only fifteen pounds; and when he had done this, he felt that "honor" required nothing more of him. On the thirteen pounds in his pocket after he had discharged this "debt of honor," he intended to travel as economically as possible to London, by the way of Loch Lomond and Edinburgh.

Taking the eleven o'clock train from Glasgow, with an excursion ticket which was good for one month, he reached Inversnaid about two o'clock. He had come from Balloch Pier by the steamer; but a tremendous shower commenced just as the boat left the wharf, and he was unable to see the scenery of the lake, for the saloon on deck was crowded, and he was forced to seek shelter from the drenching storm in the lower cabin. Being a young man, with a taste for the sublime and beautiful in nature and art, he was greatly disappointed. Through the round ports, by which the cabin was lighted, he obtained a partial view of the beauties of the locality; but Ben Lomond was obscured in mists, and the fair islands were reeking with moisture.

As the steamer approached Tarbet, the storm ceased, and he was in a measure compensated for what he had lost by a scene which can only be observed after a heavy fall of rain. The summit of Ben Lomond was buried in the black clouds; but as the sun came out, its glittering sheen was reflected in ten thousand miniature cascades upon the mountain sides, presenting a magnificent spectacle, which enchained the attention of all who had the soul to appreciate it. Myriad streams of water were coursing down the steep sides of the lofty height, which leaped over obstructions, or were scattered in flaky masses.

In the rapture of the hour, Pelham quite forgot that he was a deserter from the ship; and when the steamer was approaching the pier at Inversnaid, he decided to stop at this place, and make a trip down the lake and back on the following day. From the boat he obtained a view of the little bay and waterfall, where Arklet Water discharges itself into the lake, and this pleasant sight strengthened his determination.

> "This fall of water, that doth make
> A murmur near the silent lake,
> This little bay,"

were appreciated by the runaway officer as well as by Wordsworth, when he wrote the lines, at this place, "To a Highland Girl."

The hotel was beautifully situated, and he found he could live there for eight and sixpence a day. After dinner he carefully ciphered up his probable expenses. He had twelve pounds: he could go from Edinburgh to London, third class, for thirty-three shillings; and reserving this sum, he could afford to spend ten shillings a day. He could find a cheap hotel in Edinburgh, where he could subsist for seven shillings a day; and he could therefore ventur to exceed the ten shillings in such an interesting locality as Loch Lomond.

Pelham was satisfied with the result of his calculations, being sure that he should hear from his father, and receive the twenty pounds for which he had written while in Glasgow.

The sun was shining pleasantly now, though no reliance can be placed upon the weather among the mountains of Scotland. Pelham walked over to the waterfall, crossed on the foot-bridge, and gazed at the cascade till he was satisfied for the present. Though he had not listened to the lecture of Professor Mapps, on the Clyde, he was familiar with Rob Roy's exploits, and had ascertained the locality of a cave bearing his name, situated on the lake about three quarters of a mile above the landing. At the pier he obtained a small row-boat, and preferring to be his own boatman, he turned a deaf ear to the guides and rowers who beset him, and pushed off alone. The lake at this point is about a mile in width, and he pulled across to obtain a nearer view of Wallace Island and Inveruglas Island, on which is an old stronghold that belonged to the Macfarlanes. The scenery on this side of the lake is grand; several high mountains, including Ben Voirlick, which is nearly as high as Ben Lomond, are within two or three miles of the shore.

Determining the position of Rob Roy's cave by the number of boats in the vicinity, he pulled towards it; but before he had gone half the distance across the lake, the tourists around were all hurrying away. It became dark, and Pelham realized that they had been driven away by one of those sudden storms which make sight-seeing in Scotland so uncomfortable. But Pelham was a sailor, and he was bound for Rob Roy's cave. He did not wish to be drenched in a cold rain, but the cavern would shelter him, and he continued on his course.

"Pull for the pier, mon!" shouted a boatman, rowing with all his might.

"Where is the cave?" asked Pelham.

"There, by the side of the rock wi' twa e's in it; but dinna go there now. There'll be a rain, and a blaw. Ye ha' time to reach the hotel; but keep close to the shore."

Pelham was too much of a sailor to fear a "blaw" on a fresh-water lake, and he pulled for the rock "wi' twa e's." Fastening the boat to a stone, he climbed up the steep rock, and, through a fissure, entered a deep and extensive cavern, just as the rain began to fall in torrents. The visitor explored the place, and tried to be sentimental enough to fancy the reappearance of the tartaned chieftain, surrounded by his horde of wild Highlanders, emerging from this den to lay waste and destroy the possessions of his enemies; but it was a damp and dingy hole, and it was impossible for the imagination to be very airy under such circumstances. Pelham went to the mouth of the cave to look upon the lake, now enveloped in mists and rain. The wind was blowing very fresh, and came at times in heavy gusts.

Thrusting his head out at the narrow aperture, he glanced up the lake, and his attention was immediately attracted by a handsome sail-boat, which seemed to be veering wildly about in the fury of the storm. The skipper had let go the peak-halyard, but the sheet was fast at the stern. She was coming down the lake, and when opposite the cave, Pelham discovered that the only occupant was a small boy, not more than ten or eleven years old.

"Let go your throat-halyard!" shouted Pelham.

"I can't — help me!" cried the boy, in terror.

The occupant of Rob Roy's Cave descended the rock with the intention of going to the assistance of the bewildered navigator, when a gust of wind more fierce than any which had yet come, struck the sail in such a position that it received the full force of the blast. The boat careened, the water poured in over the side; then she righted and swung round, which brought the boom over to the other side. In swinging it struck the boy, and knocked him overboard.

Pelham pushed off from the shore, appalled by the accident he had witnessed. A few strokes of the oars brought him to the scene of the disaster; but the boy was not in sight. He had doubtless been stunned or stupefied by the blow from the boom, and had sunk. The lieutenant gazed down into the water, and discovered him on the bottom, apparently tangled in the grass or weeds that grew there. His impulses, generally noble, prompted him to do his duty; and throwing off his coat and shoes, he dived after the luckless boatman. The water was not very deep, and he seized the boy, tearing him with some difficulty from his hold on the weeds and grass. With the little fellow enclosed in one arm he rose to the surface. The wind had driven the boat from the place, and he could only swim for the land. He struggled hard with his burden, and reached the shore, though, if it had been ten feet farther off, he could not have done so, for he was completely exhausted by the violence of his efforts.

But a moment of rest from such a desperate struggle gave him strength to attend to the needs of the poor boy. He turned him with his face down, rolled him, rubbed him, and carried out, as far as he could, the surgeon's instructions which had been given to the whole ship's company for such an emergency as this. While he was thus employed, he heard voices on the lake. A boat, pulled by two men, with a gentleman seated in the stern sheets, was rapidly approaching the rocks. Pelham did not intermit his labor, and before the approaching boat touched the shore, he had the satisfaction of seeing some signs of life in his patient.

"Merciful Heaven! Is that Rob?" exclaimed the gentleman, leaping from his seat in the stern of the boat.

"I don't know who it is, sir; but it has been a narrow chance for him," replied Pelham, speaking with great difficulty, so exhausting had been his exertions for the boy.

"Is he dead?" gasped the gentleman.

"No; he's doing very well. There! he opens his eyes. He will be all right in half an hour."

And for half an hour the gentleman and his two men worked over the young patient, guided by the directions of Pelham. The sufferer could speak now, and was in condition to be conveyed to a better place for treatment. The gentleman, who appeared to be the father of Rob, was so painfully anxious, that he hardly spoke to Pelham, except in regard to the boy's recovery; but the case was now entirely hopeful.

"You will come with us, my friend — won't you?"

said the gentleman, as he bore the boy in his arms to the boat.

"I will, sir, if you desire it," replied Pelham. "The sail-boat has drifted ashore, I see. I will get her off and bring her down."

"Don't mind the sail-boat; it is of no consequence," added the father of the boy, as he ordered his men to pull with all their might for home.

Pelham recovered his row-boat, and pulled to the sail-boat. Finding there was not much water in her, he hoisted her peak, and taking his own boat in tow, stood down the lake. The wind had abated considerably, though it was still fresh; but the boat, when properly handled, behaved very well. Again the rain had ceased, and the sun came out, and its warm rays were welcome to the boatman, shivering with cold, after the bath he had taken. In a short time he overtook the row-boat, — just as it was making a landing at the mouth of a small creek above the hotel. Seeing the moorings of his craft, he skilfully ran them down, and made her fast. Lowering the sail, he jumped into the row-boat, and pulled her to the pier just as the gentleman stepped on shore with the boy in his arms.

"Let me get down. I'm well enough now, father," said Rob, struggling to release himself when he saw Pelham.

The father complied.

"What was it you said to me, when you shouted from Rob Roy's Cave?" demanded the little fellow of his deliverer, who, though he recognized him as the person he had seen on the rock, had no idea of what he had done for him.

" I told you to let go your throat-halyard," replied Pelham.

" Poor fellow ! I suppose he didn't know what you meant," added his father.

" I did not, indeed. I tried to get the sail down, but it would not come down for me," replied Rob, rather languidly, for he had not recovered from the effects of the accident. " I was so frightened I didn't know what I did."

" How came you in the boat, Rob? Who was with you? " asked his father.

" No one was with me, father. I didn't mind what you said, and you must punish me for it," added the lad, with childish simplicity.

" Come to the Lodge, now, and have dry clothes upon you," said his father.

" Isn't he coming, too, father? " continued Rob, pointing to Pelham.

" Yes, you will certainly come to the Lodge with us."

" Thank you. I think I will return to the hotel in the boat I took from there," replied Pelham, who could not help thinking that the gentleman whose son he had saved at the peril of his own life was taking the matter very coolly, for he had not even thanked him yet.

" I will send your boat back. Do me the favor to come to the Lodge with me. It is about our dinner hour, and I should be pleased to have you dine with us."

"I thank you, sir; but you see I am in no condition to dine."

"Oblige me by coming. I have been so distressed about poor Rob, I haven't had an opportunity to speak a word to you. You shall be furnished with dry clothing, and Donald will return your boat to the hotel."

The gentleman was so earnest that Pelham was induced to accept the invitation, especially as Rob, who had taken his hand, would not release him.

"May I ask you for your name, my young friend?" said the father, as they walked towards the Lodge.

"Augustus Pelham, sir."

"Thank you; and I am Mr. Robert McLaurin, well known in this part of Scotland. Mr. Pelham, I need not attempt to express my obligations to you for the service you have rendered. Rob seems to be quite well now, and I feel as though I had been lifted out of my own grave. I hope I may be able to serve you in some small way, though it would of course be impossible for me to do anything in proportion to what you have done for me and mine — God bless you for it!" And the tears ran down the father's cheek, as he thought of the fearful scene he had witnessed off Rob Roy's Cave.

Pelham realized that Mr. McLaurin was not so insensible as he had feared he was, and he expressed his gratification that it had been in his power to serve him.

"I am very nervous now, and we will say nothing more of the circumstances at present, if you please," added the grateful father, as they entered the Lodge, which was a beautiful country house.

The party were welcomed by Mrs. McLaurin, who, without knowing what had happened to him, grasped the dripping Rob in her arms, and pressed him to her bosom. A young lady of sixteen, very pretty and very graceful in her movements, was hardly less zealous in her devotion to the boy, and Pelham, before he was introduced, understood that she was Rob's sister.

"The poor boy has been overboard, and this young gentleman pulled him out," said Mr. McLaurin.

Nothing more was needed to insure Pelham's hearty welcome, and he was taken to the hearts of the whole family, not excepting the servants, who loved little Rob most enthusiastically. Dry clothing and big fires were immediately in demand. Mr. McLaurin was not a large man, and a suit of his clothes was furnished to the lieutenant, while his own could be dried. It was not a very good fit, and the gallant young gentleman, who had already cast "sheep's eyes" at Miss Maggie McLaurin, did not deem himself in presentable shape for such company. But there was no alternative, and he soon found that his new-made friends did not look at his dress, only at his face.

Though Pelham had dined at the Inversnaid Hotel, his exertions had sharpened his appetite, so that at six o'clock he was in condition to take his place at the hospitable board of his host. The roast lamb and the boiled mutton were superior, and the guest did ample justice to them, as well as to the other viands.

Thus far, nothing had been said about the exciting event of the day, Mr. McLaurin begging that it might not be discussed until after dinner; but when he had taken his glass of wine, in which Pelham did not scruple to join him, his nerves were in condition to permit a reference to it.

"Now, if you please, Mr. Pelham, we will discuss poor Rob's affair; for even yet I do not fully comprehend the extent of my indebtedness to you," the host began. "My nerves are in bad condition, and they have been terribly shaken to-day."

"I do not desire to talk about the matter, sir," said Pelham. "I will return to the hotel, and if you please I will call to-morrow."

"O, no! I am anxious to know how it all was; but I have feared to say anything about it. We will let Rob tell his story first."

Thus called up, Rob narrated the incidents of his voyage. He had walked down to the lake, and finding the sail-boat at the landing-place, he had got into it, — not with the intention of sailing, but only to sit there. He had often sailed with his father and the boatman, and had steered the boat under the direction of the skipper. The sail was hoisted, and he was at last tempted — though he had been told never to get into the boat when alone — to push off from the shore. The wind was light, and, coming from the southward, had carried him up the lake. He could steer pretty well as long as there were no difficulties. The shower and squalls came from the northward, and had driven him back down the lake.

"I unfastened the rope and tried to get the sail down; but I was frightened when the wind blew so hard, and didn't know what to do," continued Rob. "When I was going by Rob Roy's Cave, Mr. Pelham shouted something I couldn't understand. Then the wind struck the sail harder than ever, and something struck me in the head, and I'm sure I don't remember anything more till I found Mr. Pelham rubbing my head, on the rocks by the cave."

"The boat came about, and it was the boom that hit you in the head, Rob," added Pelham.

"Go on, Mr. Pelham; your story comes next," said Mr. McLaurin, nervously.

"I saw Rob go overboard, and I pushed off my boat; but when I reached the spot, I didn't see anything of him," continued Pelham. "I looked down in the clear water, and there I saw him at the bottom among the weeds. I dived after him; but he was holding on to the weeds so hard that it was all I could do to pull him away from them."

"Merciful Heaven!" exclaimed Mr. McLaurin, unable to control his feelings, while Rob's mother clasped him to her heart and wept like a child.

"I came to the top of the water with him, but the wind had driven both boats out of my reach, and I had to swim for the shore," continued Pelham. "Though the distance was not more than twenty yards, it was the hardest swim I ever had in my life."

"Bearing poor Rob in your arms," gasped the boy's mother, as she embraced him again.

"I had one arm around him, and swam with the other; but I got ashore with him at last. I thought then the last drop of breath had gone out of my body. I breathed a moment, and then went to work upon the boy."

"I know the rest, my fine fellow; and if I cannot

reward you, the good God in heaven will," exclaimed the fond father, fervently. "My story is a very short one. I missed Rob when the storm came up. He wasn't to be found in the vicinity. I was told the boat was gone, and I feared he had taken it. I called two men; they pulled till we came to the sail-boat, half full of water. O, you don't know what agony I suffered then! but I bade the men pull with all their might, and we came to the cave, where I saw you at work over poor Rob. I thought he was dead; and you can't tell what I suffered. He's my only boy, and my youngest born. Thank God, he is safe now! We shall always think you are a greater man than Bruce or Wallace. Clinging to the weeds at the bottom was he! O, merciful Heaven! But for you, we should never have seen him again. Rob, why don't you get down on your knees to your preserver!"

"Don't do it, Rob," laughed Pelham.

"I'm almost crazy, my noble fellow, and you must pardon me if I'm wild. I can't help it;" and Mr. McLaurin grasped the two hands of Pelham, and wept, and behaved in so extravagant a manner that it was quite embarrassing to the lieutenant.

The mother and the sister of "poor Rob" were hardly less profuse in their demonstrations; and as he was a mere youth, both of them kissed him in the exuberance of their gratitude. After a while they were more reasonable; but Bruce, Wallace, and the heroes of Scotland, "were nowhere," compared with the young stranger, in the estimation of the family.

"My young friend, you haven't told us who or what you are," said Mr. McLaurin. "Very likely you are a Southron."

"No, sir; I'm an American," replied Pelham, now for the first time feeling the awkwardness of his position.

The thought of lying to this host was intolerable to Pelham, whose sensibilities had been quickened by the demonstrations of gratitude made by his new friends. It would be mortifying to acknowledge that he was not the noble-minded young man he was supposed to be; that he was a deserter and a runaway from his ship.

"An American! I am glad to know that, and I shall love you all the more for it," replied the host. "You are a tourist, then?"

"Yes, sir."

"And you seem to be a sailor."

"I am, sir. I belong to the Academy Ship 'Young America.' I came up here for a run through Scotland. I am delighted with this beautiful country."

"And I hope you have a long furlough from your ship. I read about her in a Dublin paper. It's a fine institution. She's at Belfast, I think."

"Yes, sir. I suppose she will be in the Clyde soon."

"I am glad to hear it; and for your sake, I shall invite the whole ship's company to the Lodge."

Pelham thought that Mr. Lowington would not be willing to accept any hospitalities for his sake; but at present he was not prepared to tell his considerate host the whole truth. He felt mean and little, more so than he had ever felt before in his life. He only needed a clean conscience to make him the happiest young man in the world, and he envied Paul Kendall and others who had been noble and manly without swerving from the path of rectitude.

"I have taken a room at the hotel, sir; and I think I will return there now," said he; and he wished to be alone, that he might consider his position.

"Not while I have a guest-chamber in my house, Mr. Pelham — if you will permit me," interposed Mr. McLaurin. "I will send Donald down for your luggage."

"We sailors don't carry much luggage, sir," replied Pelham. "I have none at all. I am not prepared, sir, to mingle with good society."

"Don't mind the preparation. A clear head and a noble heart are the best preparation for any society. Let my house be your home. Myself, my family, my servants, my horses, my boats, are all at your service."

The runaway officer would gladly have escaped this aválanche of kindness; but Mr. McLaurin and his family were in earnest, and were so hurt when he gently insisted upon going back to the hotel, that he could not help yielding. The guest-chamber was opened for his use.

In the solitude of his room, after he had severely reproached himself for his unworthiness, he decided to tell his kind host the whole truth, and to be governed by his advice; but day after day passed by, and he had not the courage to do it. He rode with Maggie, he sailed all over the lake with Rob, and was not only *fêted*, but lionized, by the family and their friends — all of which only increased his sense of unworthiness. Several times he proposed to continue his journey to the Trosachs and Stirling, but his obliged friends always contrived a way to defeat him. Finally, when he was more resolute, — after hearing that the ship was at Greenock, — the whole family spent a week with him in the mountains and the city, and he could offer no good excuse for not returning to Inversnaid with them.

And still, though he intended each day to do it, he neglected to confess his misconduct to his kind friend, and ask his advice.

CHAPTER XVII.

LOCH LOMOND.

LOCH LOMOND, the pride of the Scottish lakes, is the largest sheet of fresh water in Great Britain. It is about twenty-three miles in length, the lower part being about five miles wide, and diminishing in breadth till it has the appearance, in the northern half, of a river from half a mile to a mile in width. But the chief interest of the lake is in its beautiful scenery. While the country which borders its lower banks is moderately uneven, that on its northern shores is rough and mountainous. The lake is studded with islands, about thirty in number, which add a rare charm to the prospect as seen from the deck of the steamer.

> "Yon emerald isles, how calm they sleep
> On the blue bosom of the deep!
> How bright they throw, with waking eye,
> Their love-charms on the passers-by!"

On several of these islands are the ruins of ancient castles and fortresses, and every foot of ground in the vicinity has its historic interest.

In the lower part Loch Lomond is not more than sixty feet deep, while in the upper section it varies in the middle from three hundred to six hundred feet.

It is navigable for steamers in its entire length and breadth, and forms an important channel of communication between Glasgow and the Highlands. In the vicinity of the lake may be found some of the most picturesque scenery in Scotland, and excursion tickets are issued by the railway companies which include a round trip from Glasgow or Edinburgh through this beautiful section. Mr. Lowington had provided tickets of this description for the entire ship's company.

On the arrival of the train at Balloch Pier, the students tumbled out of the carriages, eager to obtain their first view of the lake. In their enthusiasm they exceeded the bounds of good order, and the boatswain's whistle piped them back to the pier, for they were crowding ladies and gentlemen, and upsetting little children, in their mad flight.

Usually the boys were required to march in column, but the principal was not disposed to subject them to any unnecessary restraint. He was in favor of military order, of which he had often seen the need since the arrival of the ship, and he hoped at no distant day to have his arrangements completed so that martial movements would become a pastime to the students. For more than a year, Professor Badois, who was an accomplished musician, had been training twenty of the boys to play on the various instruments necessary to constitute a band. They had made considerable progress; but the professor would not yet permit them to play in public.

"Young gentlemen, you will remember who and what you are," said Mr. Lowington, sternly, as the line was formed on the pier.

"Come you up here, Paul Kendall!" shouted Arthur McLeish, who had perched himself on the hurricane deck with his legs hanging over the side.

The new scholar had not heeded the pipe of the boatswain, and was making himself as comfortable as possible, without regard to discipline.

"Mr. Kendall, you will direct McLeish to take his place in the line," said Mr. Lowington, as the boys smiled at the coolness of Arthur.

Paul touched his cap, and obeyed the order; but Arthur declined to heed the summons.

"I've got a nice place here to show you the scenery, and I'm not going down again for nothing."

The second lieutenant tried to persuade him; but Arthur was as contrary as a mule, and he was obliged to report his refusal to the principal.

"Mr. Fluxion, may I trouble you to bring that boy into the line?" added Mr. Lowington, quietly.

The professor leaped up to the hurricane deck, and politely invited Arthur to take his place. He was surprised to receive a flat refusal.

"What's the use of my going down when you are all coming up here?" demanded the refractory pupil.

"We don't argue the matter," replied Mr. Fluxion.

"I don't think the question admits of any argument," answered McLeish, coolly.

"Neither do I," added Mr. Fluxion, as he took the rebel by the collar, and dragged him from his position.

"Hoot, man! What are you doing?" sputtered Arthur.

"No argument," replied Mr. Fluxion, as he led the new scholar down the steps, and then to the pier, to the great amusement of the passengers and of the ship's company.

"You will obey when you are spoken to," said Mr. Lowington, when the rebel was put into the line.

"I will report to my father how you treat me," growled Arthur.

"Silence; not a word!" added the principal, in such a tone that the rebel did not deem it prudent to disobey. "You have a great deal to learn yet."

Mr. Lowington then informed the boys that they were not sheep, but young gentlemen; and that they must go on board the steamer like gentlemen, and not like sheep. They went on the deck in good order this time, and the passengers, who had been annoyed by their rudeness before, were so far pacified by the change in their manner, that they smiled pleasantly upon them. The students were dismissed from the line on the deck, after being admonished that crowding and rudeness were not to be tolerated, and permitted to find such places as they chose to observe the scenery.

"There'll be a muckle row here, soon," said the Scotch boy, as he walked up to Paul on the deck, as the steamer was starting.

"Don't be foolish, McLeish," replied the lieutenant, rather coldly. "You must obey orders always."

"What difference could it make about my going down upon that pier?" snarled Arthur.

"When the boatswain pipes all hands, you must mind the call."

"A fig for the boatswain and his pipe! Now, Paul —"

"You must not call me Paul."

"What shall I call you?" sneered the new scholar.

"Mr. Kendall."

"And will you call me Mr. McLeish?"

"No; but when you are an officer and I am a seaman, I shall call you Mr. McLeish, and you will call me Kendall."

"That will never be. When I went to school last, I taught the master to respect me, and I'll do the same here."

"Why did you leave that school?" asked Paul, suspiciously.

"There couldn't be two masters, and the governors turned me out," laughed Arthur. "I'll have my revenge on them for the way they treated me here."

"I shall be obliged to report any such language as that, if you use it to me."

"Report it! I was mistaken in you," said McLeish, angrily, as he turned on his heel and left the lieutenant.

"Bully for you, McLeish!" exclaimed a student by the name of Templeton, who was one of "our fellows." "Fluxion brought you up all standing, but you have the pluck."

"You talk like a man. That snivelling Paul Kendall threatened to report what I said to the principal," said Arthur, who was fast proving himself to be a turbulent fellow; and the reason why his father had been so anxious to have him admitted to the ship as a pupil was by this time apparent to all.

"A chap like you must give the flunkies a wide berth," added Templeton.

"I'll no go in the same berth with them at all."

"That's right."

"The principal and that professor insulted me. I never had a man lay his hand on me before; and I'll be revenged upon them for it if it costs me my life. I've the blood of the MacGregors in my veins, and I'll no submit to an insult from any man. They may expal me as soon as they just like."

"You have the real grit," replied Templeton; "but don't get yourself into trouble for nothing."

"It'll no be for nothing."

"What are you going to do?"

"I don't just know yet; but I'll do something that will make the nobs respact me," added McLeish, shaking his head. "You'll *halp* me — won't you?"

"That depends on what you intend to do. We don't put our fingers into the fire for the mere sake of burning them," replied the prudent Templeton. "We came pretty near taking the ship, and sailing her on our own account, on the voyage over We should have done it, if our leaders hadn't quarrelled among themselves."

Perhaps Templeton believed they came "pretty near" doing all this; and as McLeish wanted to know about it, he told the whole story of the "Chain League," occasionally pausing to ask a question about the scenery or the lake, which his Scotch auditor, who was familiar with the locality, answered, giving full particulars without losing the run of his companion's story.

"Yonder is Inch Murrin," said he, in reply to Templeton's question, as he pointed to a long, narrow island on the port hand of the steamer. "It is a deer-park now, belonging to his grace the Duke of Montrose. It was once the residence of the Earls of Lennox, and at the end there is the ruin of a part of the castle. You elected the captain of the ship, you said?"

"Yes; we elected Shuffles — that fellow sitting on the rail there; he looks as meek as Moses now, and the fun has all gone out of him. It lay between him and Pelham, the lieutenant that ran away. There was some trick about it," continued Templeton; and he proceeded with the narrative of the intended mutiny, in which McLeish was intensely interested.

"What's this land on the port bow?" asked the speaker, suspending his story, as the steamer approached a group of islands.

"On the what?"

"On the port bow."

"Dinna talk that gibberish to me," said McLeish impatiently; and when he was vexed, he generally introduced a Scotch word or two, or spoke with a broad Scotch accent. "I don't understand it."

"It's time you did, if you mean to be a sailor. The port side is on the left — over here," added Templeton, pointing to an island. "That's Inch Cailliach, or The Island of Women, because there used to be a nunnery there."

Templeton continued the recital of the mutiny which did not take place, after the steamer had touched at Balmaha Pier, and while she was crossing the lake to Luss.

"Our leaders quarrelled, and that spoiled the whole

thing," he added, in conclusion. "Either Pelham or Shuffles was competent to handle the ship."

"Can't we try it over again?" asked McLeish, nervously, for the daring scheme was quite to his taste.

"Perhaps we might; but Pelham has run away, and Shuffles has joined the "chaplain's lambs," replied Templeton.

"And you have no leader?" added the Scotch boy.

"We have twenty of them; but the thing is to get the right one."

"I will be the leader, for I would like to run a rig with the men who insulted me."

"You!" laughed Templeton.

"I am descended from the MacGregors, and I have the blood in me for anything."

"You would make a pretty captain, when you don't know port from starboard. Confound your descent! We don't care a fig for that."

"I'll show the fellows what I am before we get back to the ship; and my word for it, the nobs will respact and fear me, and you Yankees will learn what a Scot can do."

"See here, Sawney —"

"Don't you call me Sawney," interposed McLeish.

"Didn't you call me a Yankee just now?" retorted Templeton.

"I'm a MacGregor."

"I don't care what you are! If you think you are a bigger man than any of us, you will find yourself mistaken."

"I'll teach you what a MacGregor is made of."

"And I'll teach you what an American is made of."

There was a very offensive assumption in the tone and manner of McLeish, which Templeton could not endure, and being a fighting character, he was quite ready to rebuke the arrogance of his companion at the first favorable opportunity. It was not likely that a mutiny would be undertaken at once, and not until it had been determined which was "the better man." This cross-fire of sharp words was continued until the steamer touched at Rowardennan Pier. At this point the boatswain's whistle sounded on the hurricane deck, and all the ship's company hastened to obey the summons, anxious to learn the next step in the programme.

"Young gentlemen," said Mr. Lowington, "it was my intention to proceed immediately to Loch Katrine, and spend a day there; but this is a remarkably clear day, such as we might not have again for a fortnight, and I have changed my plans. I have decided to ascend Ben Lomond, and spend the night at Inversnaid."

Most of the boys applauded; for the ascent of a mountain so celebrated as the one before them would be a rare treat.

"This change will subject you to much fatigue and discomfort, for we must take our chances for accommodations at Inversnaid. You will have to sleep as you can to-night."

"The soft side of a pine board is good enough," added one of the boys.

"Form the line," said Captain Gordon; and the students, each of whom was provided with a blanket strapped to his little bag, formed in procession.

"Lead on," added Mr. Lowington. "The steamer stops but a moment."

Captain Gordon led the way down the steps, and over the plank, to the shore.

"Pier dues, if you please," said a man with a bag slung from his shoulder, as he placed himself in front of the captain.

"I will attend to that," interposed the principal, taking the porter aside to pay for the whole party.

"What does that mean?" asked Paul Kendall of the doctor.

"Every person who lands at any of the piers on the lake must pay a penny for pier dues. It used to be two pence," laughed the doctor.

"Good! They have become half civilized in this respect. I shouldn't think the people would submit to these small-potato annoyances," added Paul.

"Of course the people here must get as much as they can out of tourists who travel this way."

It was about ten o'clock in the forenoon when the ship's company landed; and after Mr. Lowington had made arrangements for dinner at the hotel, on the return of the party, the ascent of the mountain was commenced. It was four miles by the path to the summit; but the boys had, in a measure, become familiar with the feeling of the ground under their feet, and reached the top without much fatigue, though Mr. Lowington was careful to make frequent halts to rest them.

The view from the summit was grand, even to sublimity. The country beneath them was spread out in an immense panorama, as lovely as it was extensive.

At the north were the Grampian Mountains, extending peak on peak from east to west. The hills of Argyleshire looked like mounds in the distance. The students followed with the eye the windings of the Forth, and measured the broad expanses of the Firth of Clyde, while to the eastward could be distinctly seen the Castles of Stirling and Edinburgh.

A couple of hours was spent on the mountain, and a lunch, brought up by the hotel porters, was served out to the party, so that all were in excellent condition for the down-hill tramp. While the company were eating, a Scottish piper made his appearance, and regaled them with a variety of native melodies. The boys were especially delighted with one inspiring air, and when they were informed that its name was "Ben Lomond," they called for several repetitions. A bagpipe, to any other person than a Scotchman, is not a remarkably sweet-sounding instrument; but played by a Highlander on the summit of Ben Lomond, and discoursing the melodies of Scotland, it becomes a minstrel's lyre of wondrous power and sweetness.

It was easier to go down the mountain side than to go up; and the excursion was finished without accident or incident, though Arthur McLeish rendered himself rather offensive by a ridiculous assumption of superiority. Happening to meet Templeton in a by-path, out of sight of any of the faculty, he insisted upon settling the "little difference" they had l ad in the forenoon; but Templeton, though willing enough, was too prudent to risk discovery. His refusal was misconstrued by McLeish into cowardice, and he became more overbearing than before. The young bully accidentally dropped his cap over a crag where he was seated, rallying Templeton for his refusal to fight.

"Go you down and bring up my cap," said he.

"Go yourself," replied Templeton, sharply.

"If you won't fight me, you shall bring my cap."

"When I do, you tell me of it," answered Templeton, getting up and walking off.

"The next time we meet alone, I shall whip you," called McLeish.

"When you do it, I shall be there."

When the boatswain's whistle sounded for the descent, McLeish appeared with his cap on his head; but it was plain enough to a few of "our fellows" who had witnessed the scene, that a fight was not far distant. At four o'clock the party dined at the hotel, but it was six before they reëmbarked on the steamer.

Three miles above Rowardennan, the boat ran in near the shore, to enable the tourists on board to see an arched cavern, which is called Rob Roy's Prison.

"Was Rob Roy imprisoned there?" asked Paul Kendall of Mr. Mapps, who was talking with Dr. Winstock.

"No; I suppose there is some tradition of his keeping his prisoners there," replied the professor. "I know of nothing authentic in regard to this cavern, or of what is called Rob Roy's Cave, a mile above Inversnaid. The chieftain was outlawed for his crimes, and he revenged himself by levying black mail upon his enemies, the principal of whom was the Duke of Montrose. On one occasion, as related in the introduction to Scott's Rob Roy, the tenants of his grace were paying their rents to the steward, when the outlaw, at the head of an armed party, entered the room, and seized about three hundred pounds in cash. Rob Roy seated himself at the table, coolly examined the accounts of the tenants, and gave them receipts in the duke's name, saying that he would settle with his grace. He then compelled the steward to go with him, and kept him in custody for five or six days on an island in Loch Katrine, which, Sir Walter says, ' is still called Rob Roy's Prison.'"

"Then this cave is a humbug," added Paul.

"I don't know; I have not been able to find anything in regard to it. It is possible that the outlaw used it as a prison in levying black mail."

In about forty minutes from Rowardennan, including a short stay at Tarbet, the steamer arrived at Inversnaid. The boys seemed to have a passion for caverns, and when it was known that Rob Roy's Cave was only a mile distant, they petitioned the principal for permission to visit it. Mr. Lowington consented, though he thought the boys were tired enough for one day; but word was given out that those who did not wish to go might remain at the hotel. A cave, however, was irresistible, or, at least, those who were too much fatigued to walk a couple of miles were ashamed to own it. Only one decided not to visit the cave, and that one was McLeish, who said he had been there a dozen times, and did not care to go again.

As soon as the ship's company had departed, McLeish went down to the landing, and engaged a small row-boat, in which he pulled up to the cave, reaching his destination just as the party had completed their exploration of the rocks. By this time the boys were pretty well fagged out, and the mile to the hotel seemed longer than the ascent of Ben Lomond in the forenoon; and when the order was given to return, they promptly obeyed. When McLeish, who was not a skilful oarsman, arrived, they were all out of sight in the bushes and trees above the cliff.

McLeish did not care to be seen by any one, for he had been ordered to stay at the hotel till the party returned. He had disobeyed, and hired a boat; not that he wanted the sail, but only because he thought it would be pretty to do just what he was told not to do. He rowed up to the cave, hoping he might find a straggler to keep him company on his return. He did find a straggler; but it was just the one he did not wish to see. It was Mr. Lowington, who, with his usual care and prudence, was examining the locality, to see that no one remained behind, either by accident or design.

McLeish happened to see him as he stepped down from the cliff, and realized that he was caught. Instead of running away, however, he pulled with all his might towards the cave.

"What are you doing here, McLeish?" demanded the principal, sternly.

"If you please, sir, one of the fellows has tumbled over the cliff, and I don't know but he is dead!" shouted the rogue, apparently beside himself with excitement.

"Where?" demanded Mr. Lowington, appalled at the intelligence, and not suspecting a trick.

"Just above here, sir. You can't get to him without a boat," added McLeish, as he ran up to the shore.

The principal leaped into the boat, and McLeish pulled vigorously till he came to a kind of shelf in the rock, beneath a perpendicular cliff.

" Right there, sir!" exclaimed the young rascal, as the boat touched the rock. " Step ashore, Mr. Lowington, and keep to the right."

The principal, trembling with anxiety for the injured pupil, leaped on the shelving rock, with hardly a glance at its surroundings.

" Now, pull back and get the surgeon, as quick as you can. Where is the boy?" demanded Mr. Lowington, as McLeish pushed off, and he found his progress in the direction indicated by his guide cut off by a perpendicular rock.

" He's all in your eye!" replied McLeish, with a kind of a whooping laugh.

It needed nothing more to convince the principal that he had been deceived by the new pupil. He looked around him, and found that he was on the shelf of a rock, not more than two feet wide, with the perpendicular cliff on one side and the lake on the other. He could not climb up on the one hand, and could only escape without a boat on the other, for the deep water extended up to the verge of the precipice.

" Then no boy has been injured," said he, after he had measured his situation.

" Not one of them; they are half a mile from here by this time," chuckled the young reprobate.

Without regarding his own situation, Mr. Lowington experienced a feeling of relief to be assured that none of the boys were injured. If they were safe, it mattered little to him whether he spent the night on that narrow shelf or in his bed at the hotel. He had sacrificed his personal comfort too long to be much disturbed by the position in which he now found himself placed.

"Young man, what do you intend to do?" he asked, quite mildly, certainly not in the storm of passion which the young villain expected.

"Well, dominie, I have you in a safe place," replied McLeish, coolly poising his oars so as to keep the boat about ten feet from the rock. "It is almost dark, and the boats are all in by this time, and there is no chance for you to get off to-night, unless I take you off."

McLeish paused when he had thus delivered himself, expecting a reply; but Mr. Lowington said nothing.

"You insulted me this morning, dominie. You ordered one of your blackguards of professors to take me by the collar; and that was an insult no Mac-Gregor can bear."

Again he paused and stared at the Young America's fountain of authority, now isolated by the rock and the deep from his power. He expected a thunder-sweep of invective and reproach, and he was disappointed because it did not come, for the principal stood in silent yet noble dignity.

"You have lost your tongue — have you, dominie? If you'll go down on your knees, beg my pardon for the insult put upon me, and promise to treat me well, I will let you off the rock. Can't you speak, dominie?"

"I have nothing to say, except that for this breach of discipline you will be punished on your return to the ship," replied Mr. Lowington, calmly.

"That's where ye are — is it, dominie? You may be very sure, then, I'll no return to the ship. Ye can't treat a MacGregor like a dog."

"I never argue with students," added the principal.

"You don't! Then I'll leave you where ye are. In the morning, I'll come and see ye again. If you feel like apologizing for the insult put upon a MacGregor, I'll take you off then. But let me *tal* ye, dominie, the night is long and cold, and if the waters rise, they'll drown you. Can ye speak yet, dominie?"

Mr. Lowington made no reply.

"You'll think better of it before ye see the light of the morning. Good night to ye, dominie," continued McLeish, as he pulled away from the spot.

He expected to be recalled; that the principal would apologize rather than remain all night on the narrow rock. He ceased rowing when he had gone some distance down the lake; but no sound disturbed him, and he returned to the Inversnaid Hotel.

CHAPTER XVIII.

THE MISFORTUNE OF THE RUNAWAYS.

UNDOUBTEDLY Jock Sanderson was an honest young man, as proved by the return of the gold he had taken from Wilton and Monroe, when it was morally certain that the police would be on his track by the following morning, if not sooner. Wilton, who was quite sure he could see entirely through a millstone if the hole went through, and who did know the way from the frying-pan into the fire, thought it was very kind of Jock to interest himself so much in the affairs of a couple of strangers as to take charge of their money and restore it at the right time. Jock was disinterested, and even magnanimous, when he had the coin in his own hands, to take so much trouble and such a long walk for the mere sake of returning it. Wilton thought so, though he prudently resolved not to get so drunk again as to require the services of such a disinterested friend.

It is more than probable that Jock had other views himself. It is possible that he regarded the restoring of the gold to the " young larks " as an act of personal self-denial indulged in from prudential motives, but not the less a sacrifice on that account. It may be that he performed the noble deed under the impulse of generous emotion, as a man may give a hundred dollars to charity, and regret it to the end of his life. At any rate, Jock felt that he had overdone the "generous impulses," and had sacrificed five and thirty pounds to his own pusillanimous terror.

On Monday forenoon, as it was not then imperative upon him to go to the kirk, he called at the small hotel where the runaways lodged, possibly with the hope of reclaiming some portion of the filthy lucre which the nobility of his nature had prompted him to sacrifice. Pelham had just departed on his separate course, and the other two runaways were considering what they should do, and where they should go. Wilton did not intend to waste any of his time in observing the beauties of the Scottish lakes. He was in favor of London and Paris before the gold was exhausted. But Edinburgh was a great city, not much out of their course in the journey to the metropolis, and it was decided to go there at once.

"There is a train at quarter of twelve, and we shall be there in a couple of hours," added Wilton, consulting a railway programme he had obtained in the street.

"We shall not see the lakes, then," said Monroe.

"Hang the lakes! What do we care for them!" replied Wilton, impatiently. "I came off for a good time, and I'm going to have it. In London we can go to the theatre every night, and see the palaces in the daytime."

The door opened, and Jock Sanderson entered without the formality of a knock.

"Well, my larkies, how is it with ye to-day?" said

the self-sacrificing young man. "I warrant ye did not go to the kirk after I left you yesterday."

"How are you, Jock? I'm glad to see you," replied Wilton, heartily.

"You may well be glad to see me. How is it ye are not gone?"

"We are just going."

"Where are you going?"

"To Edinburgh."

"You are in luck, then, for I'm going there myself to-day. You'll lose all your money again before night, if I don't look out for you."

"No, we are going to be careful now," added Wilton, sheepishly.

But Jock kindly offered to take charge of the "larkies," and at the appointed time they took the train for Edinburgh, with which their devoted friend was as familiar as with Glasgow. A double-bedded room was obtained in a cheap hotel, and of course they went to the theatre in the evening; for such amusements suited Wilton better than examining the wonders of the "Modern Athens" in which he sojourned.

"Jock, I'm going to have a good time to-night, but I'm going to be careful. How much money do I need to spend?" asked Wilton, after supper.

"At the Princess's Theatre the tickets will be two shillings," replied Jock.

"I'm going to leave my money at the hotel. How much shall I take with me!"

"Not more than five shillings," answered the prudent Scotchman.

"But I want to pay for your ticket, of course," said the liberal Wilton.

"Sairtainly; take six or seven shillings — not more. But where are you going to put your money?'

"I have a nice place for it, where no rogue would find it," added the cunning contriver, as he lifted the bed-clothes and thrust his purse into an opening in the mattress.

"Don't do it, larkie. It's no safe there. How do you know but some one in the passage or in the next rooms haird what ye said?"

"I'll risk it."

"I'll do the same," added Monroe, as he put his gold into the other bed.

"You are mad," protested Jock. "The beds may be changed, you may have been overhaird, or the house may burn down."

"There is no danger," said Wilton, who had so often used his bed as a hiding-place for interdicted wares that he had full confidence in the security of the mattress.

Jock was eloquent in his denunciation of the policy of the "larks," but Wilton was as headstrong as usual. He even offered to take charge of the gold himself; but, though Wilton had perfect faith in the immaculate honesty of Jock, he wished to prove that the bed was a safe place. He was determined to have his own way, and he had it. The party went to the Princess's, saw Mr. Phelps as Sir Pertinax McSycophant, — in which he brawled in broad Scotch, — drank all the wine and beer they could stand under, and returned to the hotel at midnight.

On their arrival Wilton insisted on having a Welsh rarebit and a glass of beer before he turned in. But the moral Jock declared that his digestion would be deranged if he ate any more, and it was not proper to drink another drop. He went to his chamber, which was on the floor below that of his companions; but he did not go there till he had visited the room of the "larkies," having procured the keys of both rooms for this purpose. Lifting up the beds, he emptied the purses of his jolly friends into his pockets, and restored them to their hiding-places, having first filled them with copper coins.

In his own room there was a grate, in the flue of which he placed the ill-gotten gold, after he had rolled it up in a piece of newspaper. He then locked his door, and went down stairs to the coffee-room, where his companions were waiting for the rarebit. They had drank part of their ale, and both of them were so fuddled that they hardly knew where they were, or what they were doing.

"Come, larkies, go to your bed," said Jock, as he took Wilton by the shoulder with one hand, while he dropped the key of his room in his jacket pocket with the other.

"Top up your boom, old fellow," stammered Wilton, who was disposed to use nautical slang when he was tipsy. "I don't go to bed till I've had my toast' cheese."

The rarebit came then; a portion of it was eaten, and the rest of the ale drank.

"Come, now, lads! I have to go back to Glasgow in the morning," said Jock, lifting Wilton from his chair, while the waiter did the same service for Monroe.

"I'm ready now. Where's my key?" said Wilton, in muddled tones.

"In your pocket, where you put it," answered Jock.

"All right," added the young tippler, as he took the key from his side pocket. "See here, you Scotch humbug; take a reef in your toplights! Do you want to bet five shillings I find my money where I put it?"

"Perhaps you will."

"Will you bet?"

"Yes, anything to get you to bed!"

"Waiter!" roared Wilton.

"Sir?"

"Witness, he bets five shillings."

"Yes, sir," replied the waiter.

The tipsy young gentlemen were led to their room. The servant was not disposed to leave till he had been paid for his trouble. Wilton tore open the bed, and after fumbling about some time, produced his purse.

"There, you Scotch humbug, you owe me five shillings," stuttered he, as he held out the purse, apparently the same as he had left it. "You've lost the bet."

"So I have. I will pay it in the morning. Get into bed now, and go to sleep."

Jock gave the waiter half a crown, when the young inebriates were ready to get into bed. Asking Monroe, who was the more sober of the two, to lock the door, he left the room and retired to his own apartment.

At eight o'clock in the morning he knocked at the door of the revellers, and was admitted. He told them he must leave for Glasgow at once, and had come to bid them good by.

"Is your money all right?" he asked.

"All right," replied Wilton, putting his hand on the purse which he had placed under his pillow.

"Then I will pay my bet."

"Never mind that," protested Wilton.

But Jock, with his usual magnanimity, insisted upon paying the five shillings, and, shaking hands with both of the runaways, bade them an affectionate adieu. On his way down stairs he took the roll of sovereigns from the flue in his room, and in half an hour was on his way to London by the east coast, instead of Glasgow.

Wilton and Monroe went to sleep again, and slept till the middle of the forenoon. When they waked and dressed themselves, very likely they thought that such debauchery as that in which they had indulged was unprofitable in a physical point of view; for their heavy, aching heads must have brought this truth home to them. But before they left the chamber, they made the amazing discovery that their golden sovereigns had been mysteriously transformed into base copper coins. Neither of them could account for the change, and neither of them suspected Jock Sanderson.

The runaways were confounded by this repetition of their former misfortune; but they promptly sent for the landlord, and informed him of the loss. An investigation was commenced, and the police sent for. Wilton, anxious to recover his money, told the whole truth in regard to his intoxication. The detective, who had been sent to work up the case, examined the servant and the runaways. Jock Sanderson was wanted, but of course he could not be found. Wilton and the servant — to whom Jock had given half a crown — were quite sure the absentee had not stolen the money. He had eloquently protested against the plan of hiding the money in the bed, and had taken the pains to assure himself that the money was all right before he parted with them. A man who had occupied the adjoining chamber had left for London at quarter of ten the night before.

The officer, after visiting Glasgow with Wilton, and looking into the gambling saloon where the runaways had suffered before, was satisfied that Jock was the thief; but Jock was not to be found. He had left Scotland, and it was doubtful if he was ever found. He was a professional swindler, and Wilton wilted when he realized the fact. He had been dull and stupid, as well as vicious and intemperate. He began to think that he was not capable of taking care of himself, especially when Monroe reproached him for permitting Pelham to part company with them.

A week was used up in vain efforts to recover the money lost, and then the landlord manifested an anxiety to know whether his bill was to be paid or not. Wilton had a gold watch worth a hundred and twenty-five dollars in New York. The landlord took him to a respectable jeweller, and telling the story of the robbery, induced him to purchase the watch for twelve pounds. Monroe had a silver one, which brought three pounds. Both of the runaways were thus enabled to pay their bills at the hotel.

They had not yet lost all hope of recovering their money, for it was expected the detectives in London, whither Jock had been traced, would arrest the rogue. Every day they went to the police office to ascertain if there was any news of the swindler; but Jock took good care of himself, and nothing was heard of him. Another week passed away in vain waiting, and the funds of Wilton were wasting away, Monroe's exchequer being already exhausted. The landlord, in consideration of their misfortunes, boarded them for thirty shillings a week. In another week or two they expected to find remittances from home in London, and when, on the 1st of June, they read in the newspaper that the Young America had arrived, two days before, at Greenock, it was not deemed prudent to remain in Scotland any longer. Wilton paid the bill at the hotel, and they were on the point of starting for the railroad station, when a man whom they had frequently seen about the hotel spoke to them.

"Where now, my lads?" said he.

"To London," answered Wilton.

"No, I think not," added the stranger, with an unnecessarily broad grin on his fat face.

"I don't know that it makes any difference what you think," retorted Wilton, smartly, and offended by the manner of the man.

"Ah, but it does," laughed the man. "I've had my eye on you for a fortnight."

"Who are you?"

"Perhaps you know one Mr. Fluxion. You needn't answer. I think you know him well. He followed you till he was tired of the job, and then he employed me to continue the search. I am a detective, at your service."

Wilton and Monroe looked blank.

"Perhaps, if you had not gone to the police to find your money, I might not have come across you so soon. I traced you from Chester to Glasgow, and there I heard that two young men had been robbed. I see your ship is at Greenock."

"What do you intend to do with us?" demanded Wilton, appalled at the man's position.

"I shall merely return you to your ship, if you are willing to go."

"Suppose we are not willing to go."

"Then I must get out a warrant and arrest you for stealing," added the detective, grinning at the chagrin of his victims.

"For stealing!" exclaimed Monroe.

"For taking sixty pounds from the ship's safe. Will you go with me quietly, or not?"

"We will go with you," replied Wilton; for the idea of being arrested for stealing was terrible, even to him.

"That's sensible, and I won't trouble you as long as you behave well. I should have introduced myself before, but I was waiting for your ship to arrive. I suppose you haven't heard from the young blood who left you at Glasgow?"

"Pelham?"

"Ay, that's his name."

"We have not."

"Then I can give you news of him," chuckled the detective. "He is at Inversnaid — living upon the fat of the land."

"Where's Inversnaid?" asked Wilton.

"On Loch Lomond. There were two of us on your track, — Bulden and me, — and when you separated, Bulden went after Pelham, and I followed you to Edinburgh. Bulden wrote me a letter the other day, and he says his young gentleman is a perfect Julius Cæsar, and he don't want to disturb him. Mr. Fluxion and I travelled together one day, round about Holyhead and Chester. He told me the ship's company would visit Edinburgh; but as you think of going to London, I can't just wait for them to come here."

It was surprising that one who could talk so fast had kept quiet for more than a week while watching the runaways. But Mr. John Gearing, the fat detective, was a Napoleon in his business. He laughed, kept fat, and followed out a thread so fine that no one else could see it. He graciously related to the two rogues, upon whom he had kept his eye so long, the whole story of Pelham's adventure.

Gearing and Bulden seemed to be making a good job of the business intrusted to them by Mr. Fluxion, and to be in no hurry to restore the runaways to their employers. The Young America was in the north of Ireland when they first discovered their victims; and, fearing the ship might leave before they could reach her, they preferred to wait for her arrival in Scotland, knowing she would first anchor at Greenock.

"Now, young gentlemen, we will start for Glasgow, instead of London," said John Gearing.

"We are all ready," replied Wilton, who had no more idea of being returned to the ship than he had of being made a Knight of the Bath.

He believed it would be an easy matter to escape

from such a fat, lazy, good-natured fellow as John Gearing. On their arrival in Glasgow, it was necessary for the party to cross the city to reach the Greenock and Paisley Railway, for the ship was still at her anchorage at the mouth of the Clyde. In passing through Buchanan Street, Wilton invited Gearing to take a mug of beer, an invitation which John Gearing never refused. They sat down at one of the tables in the public house. The jolly detective enjoyed his ale, and was disposed to prolong the pleasure it afforded. Wilton asked to be excused for a moment, and slipped out at the back door, followed by Monroe.

They forgot to return; for, seeing a gate open in the yard, they accepted the suggestion which it seemed to offer, passed out into a lane, and thence into a back street. On Sundays, when every dram-shop must be closed, this back-yard entrance was used to admit the regular customers. Wilton and Monroe travelled rapidly, and in a few moments reached the railway station from which they had come. A train was just starting for Edinburgh, and taking third-class tickets, they were out of the city before John Gearing had finished his mug of ale.

John Gearing was shrewd and sharp; but, while imbibing his favorite beverage at the expense of his prisoners, — though he did not regard them as such, — it seemed unkind to suspect them of a trick. He finished his ale, and began to wonder that the young gentlemen did not return. He went to the back door, and saw the open gate. Their prolonged absence was explained; but John Gearing was not disconcerted. Perhaps, as the detective business was quite dull, he rather enjoyed the prospect of following the runaways for another week or two, at the expense of his employer.

Having entire confidence in John Gearing's professional skill and perseverance, as long as he is paid ten shillings a day, we will leave him to find the two runaways, and return to Mr. Lowington, who was left in a very uncomfortable and cheerless position on the rock at Loch Lomond. He was too dignified and independent to exchange any argument or use any persuasion with such a reprobate as Arthur McLeish. It involved less sacrifice to remain all night on the rock than to make degrading terms with a rebel.

The sun had gone down; the twilight had faded into the gloom of night, and the waters rippled at his feet in the darkness as they had in the light. No friendly sail was to be seen on the lake, and no sound of footsteps echoed from the rocks above. The principal was not too dignified to be fatigued by the care and labor of a faithful supervision of the students under his charge, and he was well nigh exhausted. He sat down upon the cold, damp rock, but turned up his coat-collar, and prepared to spend the night in this gloomy situation.

But when he had given up all hope of succor, it came. Above the gentle ripple of the little waves at his feet, he heard, in the gloom of the evening, the "lapping" sound which a boat makes in going with a gentle breeze through the water. A white sail was immediately descried in the darkness.

"Boat ahoy!" called the principal, in tones so dignified that no one would have suspected the unpleasantness of his position.

"On shore!" replied a voice from the boat, which was only a short distance from the rock.

"This way, if you please," added Mr. Lowington. "I need assistance."

"Ay, ay, sir," replied the person at the helm, as he ran the boat up to the rock.

There were in the boat, besides the helmsman, a gentleman, two ladies, and a lad of ten or eleven. The gentleman courteously extended his hand to Mr. Lowington, and invited him to come on board, which the principal was very willing to do.

"Indeed, sir, this is quite an adventure," said the polite gentleman, as he handed Mr. Lowington to a seat. "The shelf is a very uncomfortable place to spend a night. Did your boat break adrift?"

"No, sir; I was left there by a person who wished to play a trick upon me," replied the principal.

"Let the boom over, if you please, Mr. McLaurin," said the skipper of the boat.

"Pelham!" exclaimed Mr. Lowington, as he identified the voice of the fourth lieutenant of the ship.

"Mr. Lowington!" added the runaway, feeling as though he should sink through the bottom of the boat.

"Ah, is it possible!" ejaculated Mr. McLaurin. "This is a very unexpected pleasure; but we are not the less glad to see you, sir, for through our young friend Mr. Pelham we know all about you. Indeed, sir, you will permit me to congratulate you upon having such a noble young gentleman in your nautical school as Mr. Pelham."

Mr. Lowington did not exactly "see" it; but the Scotch gentleman introduced his wife, daughter, and son. They had been up to Glen Falloch, at the head of the loch, and having dined late at the Inverarnan Hotel, the light wind had prevented them from reaching home before dark. When the boat arrived at the landing, Mr. McLaurin had told all about the "glorious" conduct of Pelham in saving the life of poor Rob. The principal's heart glowed with generous emotions while he listened to the recital of his pupil's noble deed; but he could not forget that Pelham was a runaway, if not a thief.

When the party landed, Mr. Lowington accepted an invitation to visit the lodge, and on his arrival at the house, sent a note to Mr. Fluxion. The absence of the principal was not discovered till the party reached the hotel; for no one kept the run of his movements. He was not present at tea; but no one supposed that he was not about his business, wherever it happened to be. McLeish had returned, and it was not discovered that he had been away from the hotel.

Most of the boys had retired when the note came for Mr. Fluxion, but McLeish was not of this number. He was too nervous, after what he had done, to go to sleep. He had made up his mind to leave the ship's company in the morning, in season to avoid the consequences which would follow the return of the principal. He was well satisfied with his own conduct; he had obtained a revenge worthy of a MacGregor in his own estimation, and he could not resist the inclination to whisper his daring deed to one or two congenial spirits. Though he was not now on the best terms with Templeton, he was the most hopeful confidant within his reach.

"Do ye mind what I told you in the morning, Templeton?" said he, with more Scotch twang than usual.

"About what — licking me?" replied "our fellow," gruffly.

"No, not that; about the dominie that insulted me."

"What of it?"

"Can ye keep a secret?"

"Of course I can."

"Will ye keep it?"

"Certainly I will."

"I'm even with the dominie now."

"What do you mean?" asked Templeton, curiously.

"Ye don't see the dominie anywhere — do ye?"

"No, I haven't seen him since we were at the cave."

"I made him a prisoner up there, and he'll stay where I put him to-night," chuckled McLeish, who proceeded to describe what he had done more particularly.

"You'll catch it in the morning," said Templeton.

"I'll no be here when he comes back. I'll take the steamer down the lake before saven in the morning, and he'll no be back as soon as that. Will ye go with me?"

"I haven't any money."

"I have a matter of five pounds about me."

If it had been any other person, Templeton would have considered the proposition, but he did not think favorably of the bully in a runaway excursion; yet he promised to give his answer early in the morning.

"I'll think the dominie will respact me in the morning, and feel that a MacGregor is not to be insulted," added McLeish.

"Are you sure the principal can't get off the rock?" asked his companion.

"Quite sure."

At that moment Mr. Fluxion walked up to McLeish, who was seated in front of the hotel, and taking him very unceremoniously by the collar, dragged him into the house, and up stairs to a chamber.

"What are you doing, man?" sputtered McLeish, as the professor of mathematics pitched him into a chair.

An instant later Mr. Lowington, who had instructed Mr. Fluxion to secure the reprobate before his return should give him the alarm, entered the room, and McLeish needed no further explanation. The principal detailed the trick which had been played upon him to the professor.

"I shall have to trouble you to return to the ship in the morning with this McLeish, and hand him over to Mr. Peaks, who will keep him in the brig till we return," added Mr. Lowington, mildly.

"In the brig — is it?" exclaimed McLeish, who had heard of that institution. "You'll no do it!"

"I think we will. If you don't behave yourself, I'll put you in irons at once," replied Mr. Fluxion.

"Why don't you expal me? That's all you have a right to do," protested the rebel.

"We don't expel boys; we make them obey orders," added the principal.

"I'll no stand this," roared McLeish, becoming very violent.

Mr. Fluxion had a pair of irons with him, which he had carried in his bag with special reference to Wilton, when he expected to arrest him. He took them out, and in spite of an energetic resistance on the part of the culprit, put them on his wrists. He roared like a bull then, and it was not till Mr. Fluxion threatened him with a gag that he consented to hold his peace. He was locked up for the night, and finding he made nothing by resistance, he submitted for the present to his captor.

Agreeably to his promise, Mr. Lowington returned to the lodge to spend the night with Mr. McLaurin; and he spent the greater part of it in the parlor with Pelham and his host. While the principal was at the hotel attending to the case of McLeish, the runaway, of his own accord, had made a " clean breast" of his desertion to his kind friend, who was amazed that one so " gloriously noble " should be an offender.

When Mr. Lowington returned, they held a conference on the subject. Mr. McLaurin begged that Pelham might be pardoned and restored to favor, without detriment to his position as an officer. After a great deal of argument, the principal yielded the point.

" But," added he, " his lost time will certainly deprive him of his office on the first of July; and his rank then will be very low."

" Can nothing be done?" pleaded the grateful host. " Surely he ought not to suffer for his noble conduct."

" He will not suffer for that, but for running away and losing his marks."

" I do not complain," interposed the culprit. " My conduct makes me feel mean, and I think the steerage will be the best place for me."

" I certainly cannot give him any marks which he

did not earn, though he may make them up if he can. He shall take his place as an officer, with free pardon, to-morrow morning. I can do no more for him," added Mr. Lowington, firmly.

Mr. McLaurin wanted to do something more for him — wished to make him a present; but the principal said his father was a very wealthy man, and a gift in money would be offensive. While the party were in Edinburgh, a few days later, he gave him an elegant gold watch and chain, to take the place of the one he had been obliged to sell.

CHAPTER XIX.

STIRLING CASTLE.

"I HAVE a letter from John Gearing," said Bulden, the detective, addressing Mr. Fluxion when he went on board the steamer in the morning with his prisoner.

"What does he say? Has he found the other two runaways?" demanded the professor.

"He has; but the rogues gave him the slip in Glasgow. He will certainly catch them again. I suppose my work is finished," added Bulden.

"Not quite," replied Mr. Fluxion, glancing at McLeish, who had sullenly taken a seat in the saloon of the steamer. "You saw the lad I brought on board?"

"I did, sir."

"Before I reach the ship, he will attempt to run away. He does not know you, and you will prevent his escape."

The steamer went on her way. Bulden had before reported to Mr. Fluxion in regard to Pelham, though not till after the return of the party from Rob Roy's Cave. When the boat touched at Luss, McLeish jumped through one of the open windows of the saloon, and made his way to the shore; but great was his astonishment when Bulden, who had gone upon the pier for the purpose of watching him, took him by the collar and dragged him on board again. The attempt to escape was repeated at Balloch Pier, but with no better success; and before noon he was consigned to the care of Peaks, and locked up in the brig. Bulden was sent to the assistance of John Gearing in the search for Wilton and Monroe. and Mr. Fluxion returned to the party in Stirling.

After breakfast at the Inversnaid Hotel, the boatswain's whistle piped the ship's company together. Mr. Lowington appeared with Pelham. The fourth lieutenant had put on his cap, and sewed the shoulder-straps and gold lace upon his coat; or rather it had been done by the fair hands of Maggie McLaurin, under his superintendence, and he looked as much like an officer as ever. The principal explained his position, narrating in detail the noble conduct of Pelham at Rob Roy's Cave. The story was thrilling, and the boys cheered when it was finished.

Mr. Lowington could not justify the act of running away, but he was willing to let the good deed balance the bad one. Pelham then made a speech himself, expressing his gratitude for the kindness and consideration which had been bestowed upon him. He confessed his error, and told how mean he felt, when the inspiration of the good deed he had done raised him above the low plane of a rebel and a runaway. He was willing now to acknowledge that a free use of their own funds would be a great injury to the students, fostering vice and promoting insubordination.

"Pelham is one of the lambs now." sneered Templeton. "I'll bet Wilton don't come back with any such whimpering as that."

Then Mr. McLaurin wished to speak to the boys, and Pelham did not lose anything by the enthusiasm of this gentleman. Most of the students thought more of Pelham than ever before, though his boldness, skill, and address had always made him a favorite. It is probable that even now he only regarded his past conduct as dishonorable, rather than morally wrong; and it is doubtful whether he had any higher principle now than before. He was hardly reformed, as Shuffles had been. His brave deed had elevated his standard, and he was simply ashamed of his misconduct.

It had been arranged that the students should walk to Loch Katrine, a distance of five miles, not only because they preferred to do so, but because it would afford them a better opportunity to examine the country. Mr. McLaurin and his family were present in his carriage, intending to accompany the party through to Edinburgh. A good road was built through a desolate valley, passing near Loch Arklet. An occasional smoky-looking hut was seen, one of which was said to be the birthplace of Helen MacGregor, Rob Roy's wife. This was the country of the chieftain, and the party turned aside from the new road to visit the ruins of Inversnaid Fort, built to check the operations of the MacGregors, and at one time commanded by the celebrated General Wolfe, who fell at Quebec.

Paul Kendall gratified his curiosity by entering the hut of a Highlander. It was rather better than an Irish hovel, but not much. The scenery in the distance was grand and sublime.

"We are coming to Stronachlachar Pier now," said Pelham to Paul, as they obtained their first view of Loch Katrine.

"What a name!" laughed Paul.

"Stronachlacher is quite mild, compared with some names they have here in the Highlands," replied Pelham. "It would break your jaw to speak them. Here is one," he added, giving Paul a paper on which he had written an unpronounceable name.

"Ard-ceen-a-chno-cain," said Paul, spelling it out. "It makes my teeth crack to think of it;" and he handed back the paper.

The party descended the hill to the pier, at which lay a very small steamer, called the Rob Roy. She was a propeller, with clean lines, and was handsomely fitted up. She had just arrived from the Trosachs, and made her return trip without delay. The students hastened on board, delighted with the boat and with the magnificent scenery of this wild region. The water was pure and clear, and the mountains only terminated at the brink of the lake.

"This is the finest sheet of water in Scotland, many people say," observed Pelham to Paul. "The city of Glasgow is supplied with water from it."

"They have good water then, I should judge from the looks of it," replied Paul. "But this is the scene of Scott's poem, The Lady of the Lake."

"Yes; have you read it?"

"I have; I read it on board of the ship since we arrived at Greenock."

"The localities mentioned in the poem are at the other end of the lake; at least most of them are."

The students were divided into little parties on various parts of the deck, viewing the shores and the distant mountains. Mr. McLaurin, and others who were familiar with the locality, were busy pointing out the various objects of interest.

"There's the Goblin's Cave," said the enthusiastic Scotchman, as he pointed to a deep and romantic hollow under the crest of Ben Venue. "You should visit it, lads; but I dare say you haven't the time. On the other side is Ellen's Isle. You see it's a steep hill rising out of the lake, and covered with dense foliage. The poem says, —

> 'For Douglas, to his promise true,
> That morning from the isle withdrew,
> And in a deep, sequestered dell
> He sought a low and lonely cell.
> By many a bard, in Celtic tongue,
> Has Coir-nan-Uriskin been sung;
> A softer name the Saxon gave,
> And called the grot the Goblin Cave.'

Beyond the island you see Ben A'an, and off in the distance is Ben Ledi."

The lake was now quite narrow, and completely shut in by the lofty steeps on either side. After a run of about twelve miles, the little steamer entered a small inlet, with lofty crags overhanging it, and made fast to a rude pier.

"This is what they call the Trosachs," said Pelham, who made good use of the information he had obtained by imparting it to others.

"It is a very wild place," replied Paul; "but I suppose we have plenty of such in our own country."

"Yes, there are enough of them among the Catskill and the White Mountains. Between you and me, Paul, there is a good deal of humbug about these places. We shouldn't think half so much of them if they were at home. I suppose you can find as wild and picturesque scenery along the Baltimore and Ohio Railroad."

"But this is very fine, for all that. Rob Roy, Roderick Dhu, the fair Ellen, Douglas, and others, lend a charm to these scenes. Where do we go next?"

"I suppose we are to run about here for an hour or two," answered Pelham.

This proved to be the programme, and for a time the students explored the mountain recesses, climbed the steep crags, and viewed the lofty peaks, but working their way all the time towards the Trosachs Hotel — a fine building erected in imitation of a castle. At this point they found a procession of stages, or rather wagons, on which they were to be conveyed ten miles to Callender. These vehicles, like those which ran from Inversnaid to Stronachlacher, were huge boxes placed between the wheels, with a door at the rear to receive the luggage. On the top of this box were seats, placed crosswise, and extending out over the wheels, for the passengers.

The students were loaded into these stages, each of which was drawn by four horses. On the front seat, with the driver, were Dr. Winstock, Paul, and Pelham. Mr. McLaurin and his family had the seat behind them.

"On your right is Loch Achray," said Mr. McLaurin. "It's a beautiful sheet of water."

"It isn't much of a lake," replied Paul, with his usual bluntness.

"It is not as large as Loch Lomond," added the Scotch gentleman.

"Loch Lomond is a very small lake."

"We in Scotland think it is large."

"We have lakes in the United States where a steamer goes out of sight of land," added Paul, who could not help occasionally putting in a word in favor of his own country.

"But I dare say Lake Superior and Lake Erie are not so fine as this little piece of a loch; at least you can't see all their beauties at a glance. A small diamond may be very brilliant."

"Very true, sir; but we have some beautiful lakes in our country. Lake George and Lake Winnepiseogee are hardly excelled in beauty, I am told, by any lakes in Europe," persisted Paul. "We should call that Loch Achray only a pond. But I think Scotland is a beautiful country; and if I couldn't live in the United States, I think it would be my next choice."

"Thank you; that is very handsome," laughed Mr. McLaurin, as the stage drove over a stone bridge near the eastern extremity of Loch Achray. "This is the Brigg of Turk."

"What does it mean, sir? Who was killed on the bridge?" asked Paul.

"No one; but the couplet from the Lady of the Lake is quite familiar here in Scotland:

'And when the Brigg of Turk was won,
The headmost horseman rode alone.'

That's all; and the horseman was a mere hunter, who

had outstripped his companions in the chase. Here is Duncraggan," added the gentleman, pointing to a few low cottages. "You remember the fiery cross, in the Lady of the Lake, with which the clans were called to the service of their leader. The messenger galloped along this road.

> 'Speed, Malise, speed! the lake is past,
> Duncraggan's huts appear at last,
> And peep, like moss-grown rocks, half seen,
> Half hidden, in the copse so green.'

Indeed, lads, the region is all poetry and romance, as well as history. On your left you have a fine view of Ben Ledi."

"What does that mean, Mr. McLaurin?" asked the curious Paul. "Why do you call your mountains Bens? Is it short for Benjamin?"

"No, my lad. Ben means a hill. Ben Ledi is a contraction of Ben-le-dia, which means the hill of God. It is reputed that heathen rites were performed on the summit of the mountain. On your right now is Loch Venachar. As it is only five miles long and a mile wide, I dare say our friend the lieutenant will not consider it much of a lake."

"A mere puddle," laughed Paul. "But I must say the country is very pleasant."

"On the other side of Ben Ledi is Loch Lubnaig, which we call a fine sheet of water; and to the north of that is Loch Voil, on the shore of which is Balquhidder, where Rob Roy was buried."

Mr. McLaurin continued to describe the country, and to mention its historical and romantic features, until the procession of stages drew up in front of the

Dreadnought Hotel in Callander. The stages stopped but a moment, apparently from the force of habit, and then proceeded to the railway station, at which the ship's company took the train for Stirling, where they arrived after a ride of an hour. The party went to the Royal Hotel, and after a hasty lunch, they started for the castle, which is the chief object of interest in the city. Dinner was ordered for five o'clock, and it was the intention of Mr. Lowington to reach Edinburgh that evening, as accommodations for the night had been engaged there.

In its physical features, Stirling, like Edinburgh, is a very remarkable place. It is located in the midst of a level region, upon which most of the town is built. The castle is situated on a long and narrow hill, approached by a gradual ascent on one side, while the other three are precipitous steeps. The castle is at the northern extremity of the hill, and its walls are on the verge of the steep cliff.

The party followed the street up the ascent of the hill, and as this is the oldest portion of the town, the buildings were quaint and odd compared with modern structures. In front of the principal entrance of the castle there is a smoothly-gravelled space, used as a drilling and parade ground for the troops. Most of the soldiers were dressed in the ordinary uniform or fatigue dress of the British army; but a portion of them were Highlanders, and were clothed in the costume of the country, consisting of "bare legs" with tunic, Scotch cap and feathers, with a profusion of plaids. The dress is very imposing, and the boys of the Young America forgot the castle for a time in observing these men.

The soldiers not on duty were very civil to the visitors, and several of them offered their services as guides. They were engaged in sufficient numbers to give all the information the party required. Professor Mapps had quite as much to say as the guides, beginning as far back as the reign of Alexander I., who died in the castle. In 1304, it held out for three months against the besieging forces of Edward I., but was finally captured. To prevent it from falling into the hands of Robert Bruce, the English having held it for ten years, Edward II. entered Scotland with a vast army, and was defeated on the eventful field of Bannockburn, which can be viewed from the walls of the fortress. The Stuarts of Scotland used it as a royal residence. James II. was born there; James V. was born and crowned there. The latter was the father of Mary Queen of Scots, and when he died, his daughter, though only a few days old, was crowned queen in Stirling Castle; but she resided in the palace but a short time before she was sent to France to prevent her capture by the English.

From the esplanade, the party crossed the drawbridge over the outer ditch, into a space walled in by storehouses and batteries, and passing the inner ditch, entered the lower square, which is flanked by the palace and the Parliament House. The walls of the former, built by James V., are covered with a profusion of ornamental sculpture, exceedingly grotesque, and, to a modern taste, tawdry and inappropriate. The upper square is flanked by the palace, the Parliament House, and the Chapel Royal on three sides, and by the ramparts on the fourth. On the left of a narrow passage-way is a low building, which contains the Douglas Room, the chapel being on the opposite side. This apartment is one of the greatest celebrities of the castle, for in it was perpetrated a deed which is full of historic interest, and which Mr. Mapps described in detail.

The Earl of Douglas was a powerful noble, who set at defiance the authority of law and the king, and was guilty of the most oppressive acts. He had entered into a private agreement with the Earls of Ross and Crawford to support one another in all feuds, even against their sovereign. The king, James II., invited him to a conference in Stirling Castle, giving him a safe-conduct as security for his personal protection. James endeavored to persuade him to renounce his compact with Ross and Crawford; but the proud noble positively refused. The king, out of patience and roused to the highest pitch of anger, stabbed him with his dagger, exclaiming, "If thou wilt not break the bond, this shall!" The nobles in attendance hated Douglas as heartily as did the king, and completed the work he had begun. The body of the murdered earl was thrown out of the window, which was pointed out to the students by the Highland soldier, into the garden below. The body was supposed to have been buried near the spot where it fell. Three hundred and fifty years afterwards a human skeleton was found a few yards from the window, which was believed to be the remains of Douglas.

The Highlanders who acted as guides had the history of the castle and its occupants at their tongues' ends, and rehearsed it with great glibness, though some of the boys occasionally interrupted the current of the chronicles by asking the speakers if their legs were not cold in the winter, or what the emblems and ornaments upon their persons meant. On the cap of each of these men was a metallic thistle, which brought the national emblem of Scotland under discussion.

"The order of the Thistle," said Professor Mapps, when a soldier had told all he knew about it, "is said to have been instituted by Achaius, King of Scots. On the night before he gained a great victory over the King of England, he pretended to have seen a bright cross in the heavens. It was oblique in form, like that on which the apostle St. Andrew suffered martyrdom. The emblems of the Knights of the Thistle are the thistle and the St. Andrew's cross. I do not know the original significance of the thistle, but the flower and the motto are singularly appropriate and harmonious, — 'NEMO ME IMPUNE LACESSET' — *Nobody shall provoke me with impunity*. The character of the Scotch people could not be better described in a whole volume."

Leaving this interesting historical spot, the ship's company went out upon the ramparts, which commanded a magnificent view of the surrounding country, including the lofty peaks of Ben Venue, Ben A'an, Ben Ledi, and other noted mountains in the Highlands. Following the wall, they came to "Queen Victoria's Lookout," where her majesty, on a recent visit, sat down to observe the fine prospect. Near it was Queen Mary's Lookout; and in the rear of the palace, the Ladies' Lookout, where the court in ancient days looked out upon the country around the castle. The soldier also pointed out the battle-grounds of Stirling and Bannockburn.

The castle was more interesting to the students than any similar structure they had yet visited. It was still a garrisoned stronghold, and the batteries in various parts of the works bristled with cannon. Leaving the castle, the party visited the cemetery, the Ladies' Rock, from which the ladies of the court surveyed the knightly feats of arms performed by their admirers on the broad plain below. A glance at Grayfriar's Church, built by James IV., was enough to satisfy them. In the cemetery were statues of Henderson, Erskine, Knox, and other religious reformers, the latter of whom used to lecture Queen Mary for her French follies, and especially for her dancing and music, which he declared were the works of the devil.

The visitors were conducted to the plain where the tournaments were held in the days of the Jameses. The rock on which the castle is situated rises abruptly from the plain to a height of more than two hundred feet. While the students were gazing up at the lofty heights and the frowning battlements, a carriage stopped in the road near them, and a couple of gentlemen, alighting from it, approached the spot. One of them greeted Mr. McLaurin and his family, and was immediately introduced to Mr. Lowington as the Mayor of Stirling.

"I regret very much that I did not find you before, sir," said his worship. "I have been laboring to be civil to our welcome visitors, and I beg to extend to you the hospitalities of our town."

"In behalf of the students of our ship I thank you, Mr. Mayor," replied Mr. Lowington. "I had no intention of intruding upon the notice of the municipal authorities of Stirling."

"We are happy to see you and your ship's company, and to extend to you all a cordial Scottish welcome. I went to the hotel when I heard of your arrival, communicated to me in a note from my friend Mr. McLaurin. I beg the privilege of extending to you an invitation to dine with me."

Mr. Lowington explained that he had ordered dinner for his party; but the hospitable mayor informed him that he had taken the liberty to usurp the charge of the dinner at the hotel, and to countermand the principal's order. Then mounting a rock, he addressed the professors and the students, welcoming them to the town, and extending to them the hospitalities of the place.

"Mr. Mayor, allow me to introduce Captain Gordon, commander of the ship Young America," added the principal.

The mayor took his hand; Captain Gordon mounted the rock, and removing his cap, proceeded to indulge in the American luxury of speech-making. He addressed his worship in the most eloquent terms, and his speech would have done credit to a member of Congress. He thanked him for his courtesy, and expressed the pleasure the company had derived from visiting Scotland, alluded to the Scotchmen in the United States as earnest, industrious men, and useful citizens, and assured him that the party would long hold in pleasant remembrance their visit to the an-

THREE CHEERS FOR THE MAYOR OF STIRLING.

cient city of Stirling. "In conclusion, shipmates," he added, "I propose three cheers for the Mayor of Stirling."

The captain called one, two, and three, swinging his cap, as each cheer was poured out with a force that seemed to shake the castle on its firm foundation. His worship gracefully acknowledged the compliment, and dismissing the carriage, walked with the party to the field of Bannockburn, on which there was nothing particular to be seen, except the "bore-stone," whereon the standard of Scotland is said to have been elevated, though the mayor explained the positions of the opposing armies.

When the ship's company reached the hotel, Mr. Fluxion, who had come direct from Glasgow by railway, was awaiting them. He reported to Mr. Lowington that his prisoner had been safely committed to the brig, and left in charge of the boatswain. On his return, the professor had called on the father of the young reprobate. The young man had given his father a great deal of trouble by his wayward conduct, and he was entirely willing that the discipline of the ship should be enforced so far as his son was concerned.

Mr. Fluxion delivered several letters to the principal, which had been sent to the ship. One of them seemed to afford him a great deal of satisfaction, and it was soon evident to those around him that he had something he wished to say.

"Young gentlemen," said he, "I have the pleasure of informing you that the Josephine has arrived at Liverpool."

"The Josephine!" exclaimed Paul Kendall, who had never heard of any such vessel.

"What's the Josephine, sir?" asked Captain Gordon.

"She is the neatest little topsail schooner that ever was built," replied Mr. Lowington, unbending from his dignity more than he was in the habit of doing.

"I never heard of her," added Paul.

"Nor I," said the captain.

"She is to be the consort of the Young America. I saw her hull before we sailed from Brockway, and a more beautiful model never floated on salt water."

"I don't understand what she is for," continued Paul. "I supposed she was named after Josey Martyn, your niece."

"She was named after my niece. Many of you are aware that there have been more applications for berths on board the ship than I could accept. There were over twenty young men waiting for vacancies when I left the United States. To accommodate them, as well as to carry out certain other plans of my own, I had the Josephine built. She is a vessel of one hundred and sixty tons, and Captain Bean, who came out in her, informs me in this letter that he made the passage from Boston to Liverpool in eighteen days, and that she frequently logged thirteen knots. When we arrive at Liverpool, where the Josephine will wait for us, I shall put her in commission."

"Have the new scholars come over?" asked Captain Gordon.

"No; but they will arrive by steamer early in July," replied the principal.

"Will the new hands go into the Josephine?" inquired Paul.

"They will not; she will be handled by old sailors. Her officers will be appointed by the merit roll of the ship from our present students. But we will let this matter rest till we reach Liverpool."

Here was a new sensation, and those who had heard Mr. Lowington's statements immediately communicated them to the rest of the crew. The excitement for a time was intense, and the boys did not cease to wonder to what uses the Josephine would be applied. They talked about independent cruises in her; they canvassed the merits of the various officers, indulged in many speculations in regard to her future commander; and some declared they would rather be captain of the Josephine than of the Young America.

The extra preparations required to make the dinner worthy the hospitality of the Mayor of Stirling involved a delay of an hour; but at six o'clock the ship's company sat down at the tables, with the principal officers of the city. The dinner was as elaborate as mine host of the Royal Hotel could make it in the short time given him, and the hungry young tars did ample justice to the viands. The mayor, the principal, the professors, and the eminent citizens, made pleasant speeches, and half a dozen of the juvenile members of the party declaimed in "spread-eagle" style.

His worship expressed his regret that the company could not remain another day, and the students formed in column to march to the station at eight o'clock. They were attended by the municipal officers, to whom they gave three cheers as the parting words were spoken. At half past eight the train departed, and in an hour and three quarters they were in the capital of Scotland, where they lodged at a hotel on Princes Street.

CHAPTER XX.

PAUL KENDALL IN EDINBURGH.

THE students were up at an early hour in the morning, exploring the streets in the vicinity of the hotel, for they were in a hurry to know what Edinburgh looked like. Paul Kendall was one of the first to leave his bed, moved by a laudable curiosity to see the lions of this noted city. When the ship's company returned to Greenock, the second lieutenant employed all his leisure time for several days in writing a letter to Miss Grace Arbuckle, which contained a full account of his experience in Edinburgh. As this young gentleman had excellent taste and judgment, his letter shall take the place in this chapter of a more formal description of the city.

"Dear Miss Grace Arbuckle:

"I remember that you told me you had never been in Edinburgh, and for this reason I am going to tell you all about the city, just as I wrote it down in my diary. I don't pretend to be a philosopher, or anything of that sort, though I have some Yankee notions of my own.

"The ship's company arrived with Mr. McLaurin and family at ten o'clock last evening — that was

Thursday; and we marched up, two by two, to the Edinburgh Hotel, in Princes Street. It was pitch dark when we got in, and I couldn't see a thing; but this morning I turned out — that's the sailor lingo for getting out of bed — and rushed down into the street. I took my stand on the sidewalk in front of the hotel, and stared around me like 'one from the country'; and as you were never in Edinburgh yourself, you must take my word for it, that it is the oddest, strangest, queerest, funniest made up place that ever was invented.

"Directly in front of me, on the other side of the street, was a magnificent monument to Sir Walter Scott, and beyond this were the Princes Street Gardens; and beyond them was the castle, on a high hill which is just like that on which Stirling Castle stands; that is, it is a steep precipice on three sides. Between the castle and the street, where the gardens are now, there used to be a 'loch,' — they call every puddle a loch here in Scotland, — which has been filled up, and the town very much improved. The railroad runs through this hollow now.

"This was the first sight I had of the town. On the side of the hill from the castle the buildings were very high; if I counted right, one of them was thirteen stories high, though I found, when I went up the hill, that they were only four or five on the other side. The old town is built on the hill, and the new one all around it. I should think the Edinburghers would be in danger of tumbling off some of the high places, for parts of the city, it seemed to me, were built right over other parts. I think the attic of some houses must be the down-cellar of others, for I am confident many of the buildings rest on the tops of others. It wouldn't be a good place to have earthquakes in, and I hope they won't have any.

"As you must be, like all young ladies, passionately fond of statistics, I ought to tell you that the city is about two miles long and two miles wide, and contains about one hundred and seventy-five thousand inhabitants. You would not forgive me if I forgot to mention these important facts.

"I stood in the street for ten minutes — I never stand still longer than that, except at recitation — looking at the place. I can't give you any idea of it, and I have a great mind to tear out the pictures in my guide-book and send them to you; but I hope to see you again some time, — I really hope so, — and then I will show them to you. Just as soon as I got an idea, as Major Rogers would say, of the place, I rushed across the street to the Scott monument, which is two hundred feet high, and the *tallest* thing of the kind I ever saw. It is a splendid Gothic tower, containing a statue of Sir Walter in a sitting posture, with gingerbread work enough on it to make it cost heaps of money — nearly sixteen thousand pounds — I call it eighty thousand dollars in my journal which is for my mother to read, and I am not sure she knows that a pound, at 4.44\frac{4}{9}$, with exchange added, makes it worth about five dollars. A staircase, consisting of two hundred and eighty steps, leads to the top of it, from which they say there is a fine view; but I was too lazy to climb up.

"I walked about the streets till breakfast time, and made up my mind that Edinburgh was the finest city

I had seen on this side of the ocean. It is full of monuments and statues to all the kings and great men. I believe when a royal individual visits a city, the people straightway set up a statue of him; and a fellow can hardly turn round in Edinburgh without being in danger of knocking one of them over. *I* didn't knock any over.

"After breakfast I heard Mr. Lowington — I always take my cap off when I mention that name, if I happen to have it on, for he is as much bigger man than George III. as the Scott monument is higher than Rob Roy's gravestone — I heard Mr. Lowington begging Mr. McLaurin not to write any notes, or say anything to any mayors, lords, or dukes, for public dinners and receptions are an awful bore to him. The landlord of the hotel then drummed together a quarter of a hundred one-horse barouches, into which the ship's company loaded themselves; and of course all the Scotchmen stared at us as we strung through the streets.

"We went first to Holyrood. Of course you know that this was the royal palace of the Scottish kings, and that Mary Queen of Scots lived here. Professor Mapps gave us a jolly long lecture about the palace and the abbey, and about Mary. I used to think she was a very nice woman, handsome, affectionate, and everything a lady ought to be; and I used to pity her for the troubles and misfortunes that came to her; but I have altered my mind. I think she was a wicked woman, and I am glad she wasn't my grandmother. I couldn't help thinking once that her son James, who became king of England, was an unnatural monster, because he didn't make a bigger row when his mother was beheaded by Queen Elizabeth's order; but I have since concluded that he acted the wisest part, for the least said was soonest mended. You will excuse me if you think I am an image-breaker, but I shouldn't want such a woman as Mary Queen of Scots to sew the buttons on my shirts.

"We went into the palace, and Mr. Lowington paid the everlasting sixpence without grumbling. I suppose a lawyer here would charge you sixpence for the privilege of reading his sign. The building is in the form of a quadrangle, with towers at the corners, whose tops look like inverted *tops*, though I suppose they are right side up. We went in, and up stairs to a long, narrow room, which looked as musty as the attic of a country tavern. It was the picture gallery, and its walls were covered with portraits of the kings of Scotland, real and imaginary, some of whom reigned four hundred years before the Christian era — the latter, I suppose, painted from photographs taken by Edinburgh artists.

"I did not feel much interest in the old gentlemen whose faces looked down upon me from the walls, though I did glance at a few of them, whose biographies I had read. We went through a lot of state apartments, and into Lord Darnley's rooms. In some of them there were pieces of ancient tapestry, upon which a great deal of needlework had been done. I suppose a lady could appreciate them, but I could not. When I went into Darnley's rooms, I could not help wondering how Mary happened to marry such a ninny, for he was as wicked as he was vain and stupid, and I am not surprised that she wanted to get rid of him, horrid as were the means to which she probably consented.

"When we came to the apartments of Queen Mary, I was really interested. The first was her audience chamber. The roof is panelled, and the walls are hung with tapestry. There is a bed in it in which Charles I. slept while he resided at Holyrood. In this chamber John Knox used to scold Mary for being so vain. I don't think much of J. Knox, and I am not surprised that he didn't make a better woman of Mary.

"The next apartment was Queen Mary's room, and contains the bed in which she used to sleep; at least they say it is, but I doubt whether the people of Edinburgh, who keep their eyes open, believe it. The hangings of the bed were of crimson damask once, with green fringes and tassels, but they are faded and half decayed now. Leading out of this room were the queen's dressing and supping rooms, and half hidden under the tapestry is the door opening to the private stairs by which Darnley and his companions came up to murder Rizzio, the secretary of her majesty.

"The room in which Mary was taking her supper with two or three friends when the assassins entered, is very small, and is contained within one of the turrets. In this room Darnley's party stabbed the secretary, who crouched behind Mary for protection. She was quite spunky, and forcibly resisted Darnley, who dragged Rizzio from behind her. They upset the table, and had an awful time; but the poor secretary was pulled out of the room through the bed-room, the rascals stabbing him all the way into the audience chamber, where he fell dead on the floor. The exact spot where he dropped was identified by marks of blood, which they say are still visible, but I 'couldn't see it.'

"So far as Darnley was concerned, he was paid back in his own coin. He was blown up with powder in a house where he lay sick, and if his wife was not a party to his murder, she was just as bad as that, or she wouldn't have married the man that *did* kill him. Bothwell was a bad man, and died in a dungeon, and then Mary was beheaded herself, so that justice seems to have been done to all of them.

"From the palace we went into the ruins of Holyrood Abbey, and read the tablets on the ground which marked the last resting-place of some of the kings, queens, and nobility of Scotland. Darnley was buried in the royal vault, and Rizzio in a passage leading from the quadrangle.

"When we had seen the palace and the abbey, we took seats in the carriages again, and by the fine road called The Queen's Drive, went to the top of Arthur's Seat, which is a hill about eight hundred feet high, where we obtained a good view of the city and the surrounding country. We drove along at the foot of Salisbury Crags, where Sir Walter Scott used to take his walks when he was thinking up a subject for a book.

"Coming down from Arthur's Seat, we went to Calton Hill, where we saw the beginning of the national monument to the Scottish heroes of Waterloo, unfinished because the funds fell short; Nelson's monument (admission 3d.!), from which a ball is dropped every day at one o'clock, Greenwich time; and a monument to Dugald Stewart, and another to Playfair, — which seemed more familiar to me than anything else, because I have studied Playfair's Euclid.

"We drove through the Canongate and the High Street, stopping on the way at the John Knox house, visiting his sitting-room, bed-room, and study. It was quite interesting to me as a specimen of an old house, rather than from its association with the savage. reformer. We passed the Canongate Tolbooth, or court house, with a spire, little turrets, and a clock projecting out into the street, supported by brackets. It is a very odd-looking building, and showed us what Edinburgh was in 1591.

"At the head of the street we came to the esplanade in front of the castle, where there is a monument to the Highlanders who fell in India, and a statue to the Duke of York and Albany. Crossing the moat on a drawbridge, we were shown the state prison where the adherents of the Stuarts were confined before their trial and execution. Passing into the palace-yard, we entered the crown-room, Mr. McLaurin having obtained an order for our admission. The crown, sceptre, and sword were in an iron cage, in a dark room lighted with gas.

"After the murder of Rizzio at Holyrood, Queen Mary went to Edinburgh Castle for safety; and here her son, James VI. of Scotland, or James I. of England, was born. We were admitted to the room where his majesty first saw the light, though it was a very small and mean apartment for a queen. There are initials and inscriptions on the wall to commemorate the event. When the young king was only eight days old, he was let down in a basket, two hundred and fifty feet, to some friends below, who took him to Stirling to receive Catholic baptism. Of course the baby lay still, or there would have been no King James to follow Elizabeth.

"We went to Queen Margaret's Chapel, which is said to be the oldest in Scotland, and roamed round among batteries, magazines, and prisons, till we could not tell north from south. On the Bomb Battery is an immense gun, called Mons Meg. The bore is twenty inches, and it is hooped like a barrel. An inscription on the carriage says it was used at the siege of Norham Castle in 1513. It was kept in the Tower of London for a time, and finally restored to this castle.

"From the battlements of the castle we look down hundreds of feet into the streets below, and the rock in some places is perpendicular. The guns point in every direction, and it seems to me it would not be convenient for the city of Edinburgh to rebel against the government. The place is garrisoned by Highlanders, and we saw a parade of them on the esplanade as we went out.

"Our procession of teams next went down into the Grassmarket, which is a wide street or square. Our driver pointed out the spot where public executions used to take place, and where the Covenanters were burned, which is marked in the pavement. From this point we drove through the Cowgate, which is inhabited by the lowest and dirtiest class of people in the city; but right above you there is another city, for the Cowgate passes under a bridge fifty feet high, across which extends one of the principal streets. There are several of these bridges, and the passenger actually looks down upon the 'low life' of the city.

"After we had taken a lunch, we visited several cemeteries, — The Grange, Grayfriars, Dean, — and saw the graves of Dr. Chalmers, Hugh Miller, Lord Jeffrey, Christopher North, and others.

"After dinner I walked up Princes Street, with Pelham, — he was not with us in Belfast, — to St. John's Chapel, connected with which is an old cemetery. We found the grave of De Quincey, the opium-eater. I observed the same peculiarity in the epitaphs which I had noticed at The Grange and other burial-places. They are very particular to put the occupation of the deceased upon his tombstone; as, 'Here lie the mortal remains of John McDougal, Plumber in Edinburgh;' and 'Nineteen feet south-east of this stone repose the remains of Mrs. Jennie McFarland, wife of Alexander McFarland, Bookbinder in Edinburgh.'

"On the whole, I like Edinburgh very much indeed; but one ought to stay here a week in order to see and understand the place. The next day we took a train and went to Melrose, visiting Abbotsford, the residence of Sir Walter Scott. I was really thrilled by the thought that I stood in the house of the author of Ivanhoe. In one of the readers I used at school there was an account of Scott's last days, and the localities were very familiar to me by name. We walked through the rooms where he ate, slept, studied, and wrote. His library is a large room, sixty by fifty; has a carved oak ceiling, and contains twenty thousand volumes. A door leads from it into the study, where most of his books were written. The writing tables at which he worked, and the arm-chair, covered with black leather, in which he sat, are still there. In a little room there is a glass case, under which are seen the clothing Sir Walter wore just before he died. The hall and the armory are hung with stags' horns and all kinds of weapons.

"After we had visited Melrose Abbey and Dryburgh Abbey, we returned to Greenock direct by the way of Peebles and Glasgow. We have had a splendid time, and have seen a great deal of Scotland. I like the country very much indeed, better than I do Ireland, — or at least better than any part except Belfast, — for I don't think I ever enjoyed myself anywhere so much as I did while in your city. I hear that we sail for Oban on Monday, and that from there, after we have had a run through the Caledonian Canal, we go to Staffa and the Island of Skye. If we do, I will tell you all about it.

"I almost forgot to say that the Young America is to have a consort after we arrive at Liverpool, for the topsail schooner Josephine, built for a branch of our Academy, is waiting for us there. Mr. Lowington says she is a splendid little vessel, fitted up something like the ship. We are to have twenty or thirty new scholars; but the old sailors, like me, are to go in the Josephine. Just now we are all wondering who will be her commander, and some of us in the after-cabin would rather be captain of her than of the ship.

"I hope I shall not fail to see you when you are in England this summer, for I want to show you the Josephine. She is small, and easily handled, compared with the ship; and if we should meet you and your parents, I hope we shall have another excursion somewhere. If there has been another shooting match in the Botanical Gardens, I shall depend upon hearing all about it from you. Please to give my kindest regards to your father and mother, and believe me still,

"Very truly yours,

"PAUL KENDALL."

It was Saturday night when the ship's company went on board of the Young America. After the excursion to Stirling and Edinburgh, Arthur McLeish was still in the brig, where he had been carefully guarded by the boatswain, and where he had had an opportunity to consider the error of his ways. On Sunday morning, when the steward carried him his breakfast, he expressed a desire to see the principal, and was conducted to the main cabin; but he only wished to inform Mr. Lowington that he preferred expulsion to such an imprisonment as he was undergoing. He was told again that boys were not expelled from the Academy, but were compelled to obey the rules. He was remanded to the brig again for further consideration of the matter.

On Monday morning, the ship sailed for Oban, and as she went outside of all the islands, McLeish was terribly seasick. He was taken on deck, and permitted to lie on a blanket by the side of the skylight; but he suffered severely, and apparently repented of his misconduct. He made humble apologies and fair promises, so that when he recovered he was permitted to go to his duty. What his penitence amounted to, and how well he kept his promises, the sequel will show.

The ship came to anchor in the harbor of Oban after a run of thirty-six hours. The trip through the wild scenery of the Caledonian Canal to Inverness was made in the steamers, and the ship's company saw Ben Nevis, visited various castles, and enjoyed the picturesque views with which the Highlands abound. From Oban the ship went to Staffa, and after exploring Fingal's Cave, sailed for Stornoway, a town in the most northern of the Hebrides. On her return she made a harbor at Portree, in the Island of Skye. In these northern regions the students studied Nature in its wildest phases, visited caves, peaks, and mountain lochs; but the routine of school duty was hardly intermitted for a single day.

From Portree, on the 25th of June, the ship departed for Liverpool, and after a pleasant passage of three days, anchored in the Mersey, the first port in England which the Young America had visited. The pilot moored her a short distance from the Josephine, and officers and crew immediately sprang into the rigging to obtain a fair view of the graceful little craft.

" Isn't she a beauty! " exclaimed Paul Kendall, as he gazed with a sailor's interest at her graceful lines, her raking masts, and her tapering spars.

" She is all of that," replied Pelham, rather gloomily. " I suppose I have no chance of going in her."

"Perhaps you will; your chance is as good as any one's."

"I think not; I fooled away all my chances. I was gone about three weeks; I have tried to make up my back lessons; but of course I can't expect to accomplish much."

Pelham, since his return to the ship, had behaved in the most exemplary manner. His daring deed in Loch Lomond had won for him the sympathies of the faculty and the officers; but Mr. Lowington had already decided that the rules of the ship could not be varied, any further than to remit the punishment for his misconduct. There was a standing regulation that any scholar might make up lost lessons and receive his marks; but Pelham had missed too many recitations to expect to make them all good; though, as he was a good scholar, it was hoped that he would save his position in the after-cabin, especially as nine new officers would be required for the Josephine.

When the ship swung round to her anchor, everything was put in order as usual. Captain Bean came on board from the Josephine, and reported the details of his voyage to Mr. Lowington. Towards night, after the arrival of the ship had been duly reported in the city, a boat, with two men and two boys in the stern sheets, was announced as approaching the accommodation ladder.

CHAPTER XXI.

CONCLUSION.

"HOW are you, Wilton?" shouted Templeton, as he recognized the runaways in the boat.

"How are you, Monroe?" added another of "our fellows," who was standing in the main rigging.

When it was certain that the runaways were actually alongside, a tremendous sensation pervaded the ship, and all seemed to feel that authority had been vindicated; that though the deserters had been absent over a month, the hand of justice had overtaken them at last.

Bulden and Gearing, the two detectives who had arrested the runaways, marched them up the ladder to the deck of the ship. They were cowed and crestfallen, though they looked upon their shipmates with a smile, and tried to seem unconcerned. When Mr. Lowington and Mr. Fluxion came forward, the deserters touched their caps from the force of habit.

"Well, young gentlemen, you have returned," said the principal.

"We have been brought back," replied Wilton, sullenly.

"Then you did not come back willingly?"

"No, sir; we would not have come back if we

could have helped it," answered Wilton, who thought these replies were smart and plucky.

"Where have you been since you left Glasgow?" asked Mr. Lowington.

"To London."

"Mr. Peaks," called the principal.

"Here, sir," replied the boatswain, stepping forward and touching his cap.

"Commit these two young gentlemen to the brig, and allow no one to communicate with them."

Of course the deserters expected this, and they did not attempt to resist the order. Following Peaks to the steerage, they were locked up in the ship's prison, and left to think of their experience in running away, which, as our readers know, had not been altogether pleasant. But Wilton was not yet subdued. A certain weak and wicked pride prevented him from acknowledging the error of his ways. Surly and spiteful he went into confinement, with a determination to escape if he could, and to do all in his power to subvert the discipline of the ship.

John Gearing related the incidents of his pursuit of the runaways, magnifying the difficulties he had overcome in order to enhance the value of his own services. Wilton and Monroe had gone to Edinburgh when they escaped from their captor. Fearing an immediate pursuit, they hastened to Leith, the seaport of Edinburgh; and finding a steamer about to sail for London, they embarked in her, taking a second cabin passage, for which they paid fifteen shillings apiece.

On their arrival in London, they engaged a bedroom for five shillings a week, and proceeded to view the city, intending to remain there until remittances came from home. The steamer by which the money was expected to come would be due within two weeks, and Wilton proposed, as soon as their funds were in condition, to put a greater distance between himself and the ship.

John Gearing was shrewd, as we have before intimated, and having been joined by Bulden, their united wisdom was a heavy odds against the deserters. They knew very well what the boys would desire to see first. Gearing had tracked them to Leith, and reached London almost as soon as they did. He went to all the notable places in the city, from St. Paul's to the Thames Tunnel, taking such information as the door-keepers and porters could give him; but being in no hurry to find them, he contrived to miss them for a week, for London is a large city, and the addition of two boys made but a slight impression upon it.

When Bulden joined him, they made the round of the music halls in a single evening without success. But as it was certain that the runaways would visit these places, and drinking ale and listening to comic songs were entirely to John Gearing's taste, the pleasantest way to find the boys would be to spend all their evenings in these resorts, especially as the ship paid for the beer and the admission fees.

Wilton and Monroe had been in London a week before they discovered what music halls were. They entered one in Oxford Street, drank ale, and listened to the music. It was a cheap recreation for persons of low taste, and they went to another the next evening in Holborn.

"Our money will certainly be here to-morrow," said Wilton. "There's a telegraph in the evening papers from Crookhaven."

"I hope so," replied Monroe, moodily, for he was about tired of the life of anxiety he was leading.

"We will be off for Paris as soon as we get it. We shall have a high-o time there."

"Twenty pounds apiece will not last us long. What shall we do when it is gone?" asked Monroe.

"Write for more, as soon as we get the first remittance."

"Suppose the money should come payable to Mr. Lowington's order, or something of that kind," suggested Monroe.

"O, it won't! Don't croak, Ike. Have some ale?"

"Thank you; I don't care if I do," said John Gearing, suddenly dropping into a chair by Wilton's side.

"Where did you come from?" demanded Wilton, startled by the sound of that familiar voice, and thrown into confusion by his presence.

"I came from Glasgow since I saw you last. I hope you've been well. Are you ready to go to Liverpool with me?"

"No, I am not!" answered Wilton, angrily.

"Well, I'm sorry you are not; for you must go there with me," laughed John Gearing. "Shall I ask one of the London police to arrest you, or will you go quietly?"

Wilton was appalled at the idea of being arrested, and Monroe actually trembled with fear. The detective went with them to their lodgings, spent the night with them, and the next morning, after paying their bill, — for their own funds were exhausted, — and sending for Bulden, started for Liverpool with them. They had been there a week when the Young America arrived, living with their captors in a small hotel, closely watched, day and night, by one or the other of them. Wilton did not cease to look for a chance to run away again until the boat which conveyed him off was alongside the ship. He made one attempt, which failed; and now, when he found himself in the brig, he set about studying up some method of getting away.

After the detectives had told their story, Mr. Lowington paid their bill, and they departed, apparently well pleased with the profitable employment they had received.

McLeish had heard the story of the deserters, and as soon as he had an opportunity he took a look at them in their prison. He sympathized with them; and not being allowed to go on shore, he considered how he might serve them and himself at the same time. There would be an opportunity, when the ship's company were on shore, for him to do something for them. But everybody was so busy on board that the boats only went ashore for supplies for three days.

There were only two days more in the month when the ship anchored in the Mersey. The boys talked of nothing but the Josephine and the offices, which were to be distributed on Thursday. Many of them were exceedingly anxious about the result. Some in the after-cabin feared they should be sent to the steerage, and some in the steerage feared they should not be sent into the after-cabin. .The eventful day came;

and after the recitations had been completed, and the results added for the month, all hands were piped to muster. There were beating hearts in the ship then, for a brief period would decide who were to be officers and who were to be disappointed. Mr. Lowington mounted his rostrum, and there was nothing to be heard but the waves beating against the side of the ship.

"Young gentlemen, before announcing the results of your last quarter's work, I wish briefly to review the events of that period," the principal began; and he proceeded to state the chief incidents of the cruise, commenting upon them as he went along.

He gave the history of the deserters to the ship's company, including their misfortunes and their final arrest, which seemed to make an impression on the crew. He commended officers and seamen for their general good conduct, and assured them that he was disposed to trust them as far as they would permit him to do so.

"One of the principal elements of good seamanship," he continued, "is self-reliance — confidence in one's own ability. Although the officers of the ship have handled her with very little dictation from me, they have always felt that there was some one near upon whom they could cast the responsibility when it became too heavy for their own shoulders. I purpose to establish a school in which there shall be no evading the responsibility of your positions. Alongside of us lies our future consort, the Josephine. To-morrow she will be put in commission. With the exception of two professors, who are not seamen, a boatswain and carpenter, and the cook and stewards, there will be none but students on board of her. The officers will be absolute there."

This announcement caused a great sensation, for the captain of the Josephine would be a great man.

"Of course the Josephine will be generally near the ship, and the two vessels will sail in company so far as practicable. By the next steamer thirty students, perhaps more, will arrive, all of whom will be quartered on board of the ship, and the crew of the Josephine will be selected from those now on board.

"Young gentlemen, Captain Gordon is so faithful and devoted, both as a scholar and a seaman," added the principal, with a smile, "that I think none of you will be able to displace him from his present position. I find that he stands nine merits ahead of the next below him, and is still entitled to the highest place in the ship. I wish to open the way for the ambition of others who have done remarkably well, and therefore I have concluded to create a new office — that of past captain. Hereafter, during the present year, no student will serve more than one term as captain. Of course this rule will increase all your chances of promotion; and I have learned that, in the service, promotion is one of the chief incentives to fidelity. Having two vessels, we are now a squadron, and I shall appoint Captain Gordon to the honorable position of flag officer."

Mr. Lowington smiled, as Captain Gordon touched his cap in acknowledgment of the compliment..

"Three cheers for Flag Officer Gordon!" shouted Paul Kendall; and they were given.

"I shall have a cabin built for the new officer at once. It will occupy the space abaft the state-rooms in the after-cabin. And now, young gentlemen," continued the principal, taking a paper from his pocket, which made the hearts of some of the students leap up into their throats, " I will announce the names of the officers for the next term. The highest in rank will command the Young America; the second, the Josephine; the third will be first lieutenant of the ship; the fourth, first lieutenant of the consort; and so on; but there will be but nine cabin officers attached to the Josephine.

" Captain Gordon has the highest number of merits. Between the next two there is a difference of only one mark; and Joseph Haven, being the highest, will be captain of the ship for the ensuing three months."

The announcement was greeted with a cheer; but so intense was the anxiety to know who the next in order was, that the cheer was rather faint.

" Only one merit below him stands the commander of the Josephine," added Mr. Lowington, with a pause and a smile; " and he is Paul Kendall."

The cheer given when the name was called was very emphatic and decided, and the professors, led off by Dr. Winstock, clapped their hands vigorously. Mr. Lowington shook hands with Captain Haven and with Captain Kendall, congratulating them upon the distinction they had won. Paul blushed; but he was the happiest student on board the ship, and thankful that Haven had beaten him by one mark, for he had obtained the position he desired above all others.

There were other beating hearts on the deck of the

ship, and the principal continued to read the merit roll. Most of the cabin officers went up to higher places than before, and ten passed from the steerage to the quarter deck. Pelham, who had struggled so hard since his return to keep his rank, came in as second master of the Josephine. He declared that he was satisfied with the result, especially as his place was in the cabin of the schooner.

The list was read through, and there was the usual amount of grumbling, " our fellows " doing the greater part of it. Twenty-four petty officers and seamen were detailed for the Josephine. As it was understood that nearly all the crew desired to be in her, because there was a novelty about the new vessel, Mr. Lowington, wishing to be fair about the detail, required every third name to be entered on the Josephine's books as the list was called. If any did not behave well, they were to be exchanged into the ship. It so happened that McLeish was one of the twenty-four; but as he had behaved well since the ship sailed for Oban, he was not set aside, though he was still deprived of certain privileges.

The next morning, the first day of the new term, the officers and crew of the Josephine were ordered to their vessel, and in a short time the star-spangled banner was floating at her peak as a signal that she had " gone into commission." On ship and shore around them was displayed another flag — that of England; and what adventures the students had, what famous places they visited, and what voyages the ship and her consort made, shall be narrated in " RED CROSS, OR YOUNG AMERICA IN ENGLAND AND WALES."

www.ingramcontent.com/pod-product-compliance
Lightning Source LLC
Chambersburg PA
CBHW031848220426
43663CB00006B/538